Fashioning the Body Politic

Fashioning the Body Politic

Dress, Gender, Citizenship

Edited by
Wendy Parkins

Oxford • New York

First published in 2002 by
Berg
Editorial offices:
150 Cowley Road, Oxford, OX4 1JJ, UK
838 Broadway, Third Floor, New York, NY 10003–4812, USA

Berg is an imprint of Oxford International Publishers Ltd.

Library of Congress Cataloging-in-Publication Data
A catalogue record for this book is available from the Library of Congress.

British Library Cataloguing-in-Publication Data
A catalogue record for this book is available from the British Library.

ISBN 1 85973 582 7 (Cloth)
       1 85973 587 8 (Paper)

Typeset by JS Typesetting, Wellingborough, Northants.
Printed in the United Kingdom by Biddles Ltd, Guildford and King's Lynn.

Contents

Contents

Acknowledgements

I am very grateful to all my contributors for their commitment and enthusiasm for this project. The quality of their work and their friendly emails have encouraged and sustained my work as editor.

I would also like to thank everyone at Berg for their assistance throughout this project. Maike Bohn (formerly of Berg) was invaluable in getting this volume off the ground and Kathryn Earle has been tremendously helpful and supportive from start to finish.

Finally, I want to acknowledge the love and support of my family. Geoff (as ever) has been a great source of encouragement and inspiration; Madeleine has been very patient while mum finished her book; and Gabriel (who appeared halfway through this project!) was a wonderful sleeper.

Notes on Contributors

Simonetta Falasca-Zamponi is Associate Professor of Sociology at the University of California, Santa Barbara. Her work focuses on the relationship between politics and culture. Her publications include *Fascist Spectacle: The Aesthetics of Power in Mussolini's Italy* (1997).

Roger Griffin is Professor of Modern History at Oxford Brookes University, where he specializes in the theory and evolution of generic fascism. Since the publication of *The Nature of Fascism* (Pinter, London, 1991) he has continued to have a impact on fascist studies with documentary readers, encyclopedia and periodical articles, and chapters which explore the implications for specific aspects of fascism of the centrality of the myth of national rebirth. His latest project is an investigation of the relationship between modernity and fascist projects for the renewal of Western civilization.

Stephanie Hemelryk Donald is Senior Lecturer in Media and Communications at the University of Melbourne. She is the author of *Public Secrets, Public Spaces: Cinema and Civility in China*, *The Global Media Atlas* and *The State of China Atlas*. She is co-editor of *Media in China: Content, Consumption and Change*; and *Picturing Power in the People's Republic of China: Posters of the Cultural Revolution*.

Margaret Maynard studied dress history at the Courtauld Institute in London. She is a Senior Lecturer in Art History in the School of English, Media Studies and Art History, The University of Queensland. She has published extensively on dress, design, cultural studies and Australian colonial art and photography. Her second book, entitled *Out of Line. Australian Women and Style* was published by UNSW Press in 2001.

Wendy Parkins is a Lecturer in the School of Media, Communication and Culture at Murdoch University, Western Australia. She has published articles on suffragette bodies in *Feminist Theory* and *Continuum: Journal of Media and Cultural Studies*, and on women's modernity in *Women: A Cultural Review* and *Tulsa Studies in Women's Literature*.

Tammy M. Proctor is an Associate Professor of History and Director of the University Honors Program at Wittenberg University in Springfield, Ohio. She is the author of articles on Guiding and Scouting in Interwar Britain and South Africa as well as a forthcoming book, *On Their Honor: Guiding and Scouting in Interwar Britain*. Currently, she is working on a history of women and intelligence during World War I.

Regina A. Root, an Assistant Professor of Spanish at Old Dominion University, Norfolk, Virginia, writes on the interrelationship between fashion and literature in Latin America. She has conducted extensive archival research of nineteenth-century fashion magazines in Argentina, Chile and Uruguay. Most recently, her work has appeared in *Folios*, *Fashion Theory* and *Designis*. She is currently at work on *The Latin American Fashion Reader*.

Christine Ruane is Associate Professor and Director of Graduate Studies in History at the University of Tulsa. She is the author of *Gender, Class, and the Professionalization of Russian City Teachers, 1861–1914* and is currently working on a history of the Russian fashion industry from 1700 to 1917.

Mary Vincent is Senior Lecturer in History at the University of Sheffield, UK. Her *Catholicism in the Second Spanish Republic* was published by OUP in 1996 while articles on religion and gender in 1930s Spain have recently appeared in *History Workshop Journal* and *Gender and History*. She also edits the journal *Contemporary European History* and is currently working on a study of Franco's 'Crusade'.

Richard Wrigley is Principal Lecturer in the History of Art at Oxford Brookes University, and the author of *The Politics of Dress in Revolutionary France* (forthcoming Berg 2002).

List of Illustrations

Introduction: (Ad)dressing Citizens
Wendy Parkins

On 11 February 1999, female legislators from both the left and right of the political spectrum wore jeans to the Italian parliament. A couple of days later, women in the Californian State Assembly also wore jeans in support of their Italian counterparts. Both groups of women were staging a protest against a ruling in Italy's Supreme Court of Appeals that it is impossible to rape a woman wearing jeans. The Italian court, overturning the conviction of a 45-year-old driving instructor earlier found guilty of raping his 18-year-old student, had ruled that jeans cannot be removed 'even partially, without the active cooperation of the person wearing them' (Nadotti 1999: 18; see also Tagliabue). In these protests, jeans, possibly the most ubiquitous item of clothing in the Western world, became a site of semiotic contestation as the female legislators disputed the court's interpretation that the removal of a woman's jeans signified compliance rather than violent assault. This item of clothing was also given a political significance, however, as women, who in their elected capacity as legislators represented the body politic, wore an item of everyday, casual clothing in a domain where such dress would usually be considered inappropriate, signifying a casual or disrespectful attitude to the sober business of law-making.[1] Such violation of the dress code was intended to signify the women's outrage at the Appeals Court's failure to recognize the physical violation at the centre of the case before them and gestured towards the implications for all women when an item of clothing alone is construed to signify consent. As Anna Yeatman has argued, modern political subjecthood depends on the concept of an individual who is not subject to the authority of any other except by their consent and who is also free to withdraw this consent (2001: 141). The capacity for consent, then, lies at the heart of modern citizenship. The 'denim defense' protests drew attention to the fact that, despite the presence of women in state and national parliaments, the status of women's citizenship remains problematic in the modern body politic where, as Nancy Fraser (1989: 126) has argued, 'the capacities for consent and speech, the ability to participate on a par with others in dialogue . . . are connected with masculinity' in modern democracies. In showing the body politic to be a gendered construction, the women protestors also demonstrated the way notions of citizenship may be bound up with and understood through notions and practices of dress. These protests can be read as attempts to refashion the body politic through drawing attention to the significance – and the signification – of dress in political contexts. The incidents in Italy and California provide a contemporary example of the central concerns of this book: how forms or items of dress – from the ceremonial to the everyday – can themselves become sites of political struggle, how they can be used variously to contest or legitimate the power of the state and the meanings of citizenship.

It is a grounding assumption of *Fashioning the Body Politic* that, as Rita Felski (1995: 150) has put it, symbolic political practices, 'rather than simply expressing an already constituted sphere of "real politics" grounded in the economy or the state, may themselves operate as instruments of transformation, ways of reconstituting the social and political world'. Practices of dress and fashion will be viewed not simply as reflecting social and political change but rather, as Joanne Entwistle (2000b: 80) has put it, understood as practices that are 'always and everywhere *situated* within a society and a culture' (emphasis added). Beginning, then, with a consideration of the concept of the body politic as an enabling myth of modern nation states, this introduction will consider the means by which the body politic may be fashioned. The corporeal metaphor of the 'body politic' is a deliberately chosen one in this context, as it offers a different emphasis from understanding the political domain in the modern nation state as, say, a public sphere. By insisting that practices of bodily display and performance associated with dress may be understood as political (although not always contestatory), a critique of a Habermasian model of a sphere of 'legitimate' politics as only that based on rationality and deliberation will also be offered.

In medieval and early modern Europe, as Nicholas Mirzoeff (1995: 59) states, 'the quasi-divine Body politic was symbolized by the ritual anointing of the monarch during the coronation ceremony, which separated the king from all other lay persons'. In the medieval doctrine of the king's two bodies – which posited that the sovereign had both a 'body natural' (the physical, mortal body) and a 'body politic' (the state as a metaphysical, immortal corporation) – 'the natural body of the king thus *represented* the body politic' (Peters 1993: 545, emphasis in original). Through portraiture and sculpture as well as through the vestiture of the king's material body, the body politic 'became entirely dependent on visual representation' (Mirzoeff 1995: 60). As Andrew and Catherine Belsey have argued in their analysis of the portraiture of Elizabeth I, for example, portraits of the monarch sought to symbolize the legitimate authority she embodied. Elizabeth's portraits, at times verging on the anatomically impossible, represented a 'dis-embodied, extra-human Queen' (Belsey and Belsey 1990: 18) and through the morphology of the queen's body and its extravagant dress proclaimed her sovereignty and right to rule (Belsey and Belsey 1990: 14–15).

The significance of visual representation in the political domain, a significance obvious in the splendour and conspicuous display of the monarchical states of Louis XIV or Elizabeth I, is shown in *Fashioning the Body Politic* to be an ongoing if problematic one in the modern era of disembodied authority. 'If the state is figured organically', argues Mirzoeff (1995: 61) in his examination of the body politic, 'its corporeal representation is central to maintaining the central illusion of modern state fetishism, that the state is a really existing and palpable body. How can this body be imagined without using the medium of the king's body?' This problem of representing the state after the king's body was revealed as human, as in fact only one body and that expendable, was a problem not only for France during and after the Revolution but more generally in modern nation states and, as several contributors to this book argue, practices of dress could be deployed by states to resolve this problem of representation.

There is, however, a strong tradition of modern political thought (from Rousseau to the Frankfurt School), suspicious of or opposed to any kind of spectacularization or theatricalization of the political, summed up by Walter Benjamin's critique of the 'aestheticization of politics'.[2] In this view, any kind of visual representation of the state or symbolic politics encodes illegitimate, anti-democratic and oppressive forms of power. For Jurgen Habermas, for instance, the transition from absolute monarchy to modern nation state is a transition from 'representative publicity' – an illegitimate form of politics based on the display of the king's body as well as enacted in the costume, speech, and bodily comportment of the monarch and court (Habermas 1989: 206; Peters 1993: 545) – to a legitimate form based on critical dialogue and rational deliberation (see Fraser 1989: 126; Landes 1995: 93–4). 'Representative publicity' which made visible the king's social power or his embodiment of the state, can, for Habermas (1989: 8), only be understood as 'completely unlike a sphere of political communication'; it is fundamentally opposed to dialogue or debate and signals a lack of public participation (Peters 1993: 545–6). 'The source of legitimacy', for Habermas, 'is deliberation itself' (Habermas 1992: 446, quoting Manin): 'like Rousseau and Kant, [Habermas] assumes that a formal or procedural conception of public life alone is enough' (Peters 1993: 564). As John Durham Peters (1993: 565) has succinctly put it, 'Beyond all symbolic politics, for Habermas, lurks the king's body, which must not be resurrected'.

While the chapters by Simonetta Falasca-Zamponi and Mary Vincent are devoted to examining the deployment of symbolic dress by fascist states in the 1930s, a Habermasian dismissal of practices of display as always 'bad politics' overlooks the multi-accentuality of dress in political contexts, the capacity of dress to be articulated to a variety of causes and contexts. As the chapters by Regina Root and myself argue, practices of display or adornment could be deployed within a sphere of political communication by those unenfranchised by or opposed to existing political formations as a means of contestation or critique. The narrative trajectory from 'bad' display to 'good' speech, which Habermas posits, moreover, has been disputed by historians, especially those examining the political context in France both prior to and during the French Revolution (see, for example, Hunt 1984; Landes 1988 and 1995; Huet 1982; Harris 1981). The work of these historians insists on the importance of performance and display in the political – what Joan Landes (1995: 101) has identified as an 'always already theatricalized public sphere' – and shows the semiotic capacity of practices of dress to either contest or reinforce existing arrangements of power and 'flesh out' the meanings of citizenship. This emphasis makes this an important reference point for any consideration of dress, gender and citizenship: not only did the political culture of the French Revolution generate many of the ideas and practices of politics that persist today, but it also illustrated the imbrication of politics with culture (Hunt 1984: 2, 15). During the French revolutionary period, as Hunt (1984: 53) has argued:

> Different costumes indicated different politics, and a colour, the wearing of a certain length of trousers, certain shoe styles, or the wrong hat might touch off a quarrel, a fistfight, or a general street brawl. During the Revolution, even the most ordinary objects and customs became political emblems and potential sources of political and social conflict. Colours, adornments, clothing, plateware, money, calendars, and playing cards became 'signs of rallying' to one side or another . . . By making a political position manifest, they made adherence, opposition, and indifference possible. In this way they constituted a field of political struggle.

Clothing became invested with political significance during the revolutionary period, from the wearing of the national cockade to proposing a national civil uniform.[3] As Richard Wrigley discusses in his chapter and elsewhere (Wrigley 1997), items of clothing such as those associated with the *sans-culottes* formed part of a complex visual economy in which political meanings and values were contested, reconfigured and restated. The fluidity and contestation of meanings associated with revolutionary dress may perhaps account for a growing movement from late 1792 to regulate and prescribe certain forms of dress (Harris 1981: 296–9). While the Convention decreed in 1793 that freedom of dress was the right of all citizens (Harris 1981: 311), dress and its regulation recurred as points of contention.[4] As Hunt has outlined, debates around dress at this time were focused on three main concerns: eliminating class distinctions; distinguishing public officials; and shaping a national identity (1984: 75–86). Implicit in all of these concerns was a paradox informed by a Rousseauian dream of social and personal transparency (Jay 1993: 90–3): through culturally prescribed forms of self-presentation and dress, not only could a citizen-subject's 'true' political character be made manifest (Hunt 1984: 81) but the unique character of the new body politic could be signified. As Wrigley expresses it in this volume, 'the visibility of popular political activity was legitimized through a vocabulary in which the vestimentary became emblematic, in a way which was polemically construed as signalling a form of political authenticity.'

As the French example made clear, however, not just any*body*'s dress could be deployed to refashion the body politic. The body is never simply a neutral clothes horse on which items of clothing are placed to signal political affiliation, like sandwich-board advertising or the wearing of team colours. As Entwistle (2000b: 77) has argued, dress is always about bodies; dress is a situated bodily practice (Entwistle 2000a: 325). And, of course, there are no bodies in a general sense but rather specific bodies, marked by gender, sexuality, class and ethnicity, for instance. As Falasca-Zamponi's chapter in this volume stresses, only *certain* bodies can corporealize the state. Just as, historically, fashion and dress have been distinguished by gender, so too fashioning the body politic has also involved a *gendering* of the body politic. Hunt's discussion of dress during the French Revolution, for instance, is concerned with male dress: the public officials donning classical robes and cloaks to signify the dignity and legitimacy of their social authority – and hence of the state – were men (Hunt 1984: 78–80), as were the *sans-culottes* (see Wrigley). Women, from the beginning of the revolution, had also adopted items of clothing, badges and symbols which signified their political loyalties, for instance adopting a distinctive style of dress for the national festivals of the revolution in the form of white dresses decorated only by the tricolour (Harris 1981: 292–3). Despite such practices, women's capacity to embody the new regime or revolutionary ideals through dress or symbolism was always more problematic than men's. When the most radical of the women's political groups, the Societie des Republicaines-Revolutionnaires, tried to impose the wearing of the *bonnet rouge*, they were derided for their efforts (Harris 1981: 296).[5] The revolutionary political imaginary was deeply conflicted about issues of gender and citizenship, as debates about the relative merits of Marianne and (David's proposed statue of) Hercules as symbols of revolutionary ideals illustrated. As Hunt (1984: 104) has argued:

> In the eyes of the Jacobin leadership, women were threatening to take Marianne as a metaphor for their own active participation; in this situation, no female figure, however fierce and radical, could possibly appeal to them. Hercules put the women back into perspective, in the place and relationship of dependency. The monumental male was now the only active figure.[6]

The banning of all women's clubs by the Convention at the end of October 1793 marked a more formal exclusion of women from full participation in the new body politic (Hunt 1984: 104).

Men's grand or official dress has a long history of signifying women's exclusion from, or problematic relation to, citizenship, even prior to the interest in the dressing of public officials during the French revolutionary period. In *Three Guineas*, Virginia Woolf (1992: 177) reflected on the ostentation of men's public costumes, using the metaphor of a procession to represent citizenship: women were figured as onlookers, bemused at the excessive regalia worn by men rather than full participants in the passing parade. In a more specific historical instance, Elizabeth Currie (2000: 168) has argued that in sixteenth-century Italian cities, 'Women possessed no direct equivalent of men's civic dress, which was applauded as a means of representing the country or city where it was made'. Indeed, in the Renaissance Italian context, the gendering of citizenship through dress was not based solely on sex: Florentine *giovani* (young men who could be from eighteen to thirty-five) were excluded from political life until the age of thirty and were subject to public opprobrium because of their association with excessive fashion, femininity and homosexuality, all perceived as 'socially disruptive activities' (Currie 2000: 170).

As Landes and Jennifer Jones have shown, concerns about dress and legitimate political participation in France were present even before the Revolution. The exclusion of women from public life during and after the Revolution stemmed in part from a strong cultural association between women and fashion, frivolity and luxury, which was seen to be exemplified by Marie Antoinette (Jones 1996: 25, 47–8). In *Women and the Public Sphere*, Landes has argued that the liberatory discourses of enlightenment and republicanism classified public women in France as illustrative of the worst excesses of both the *ancien régime* (represented by the salonnieres) and the revolutionary terror (represented by the women of the mob). The new political discourses arising from the Revolution, in which only what was universal could be claimed for truth or reason, associated women and their interests with particularity and, as such, reduced them to the status of special interests, defined as at odds with the common good, the general will (Landes 1988: 44). Landes's account of how, at the beginning of the modern liberal state in France, women were defined outside foundational categories such as the public, the rational subject and the citizen is echoed by Victoria de Grazia who associates the development of modern practices of consumption, including those associated with dress and fashion, with the transformation of concepts of public and private and the constitution of the modern political domain from which women were excluded (1996: 17–18). Bound up with this transformation was an anxiety about women's role and participation in the public domain, an anxiety often coded in concerns about women's appearance. As Rousseau (1968: 88) put it, 'a woman outside of her home loses her lustre, and, despoiled of her real ornaments, she displays herself indecently . . . Whatever she may do, one feels that in public she is not in her place'. The paradox Rousseau offers here, of authentic ornaments being those which are not visible, is symptomatic of a view which saw women in public as at best inappropriate and at worst morally objectionable if the woman resorted to decoration and fashion.

This association between women, fashionable adornment, and exclusion from political participation also had implications for men's dress. In his study of masculine dress in England from the seventeenth to the nineteenth centuries, David Kuchta argues that male dress performed significant semiotic and ideological work in establishing notions of legitimate political authority. Revising the theory of 'the great masculine renunciation' as the dominant account offered to explain the relative drabness and uniformity of modern men's fashion (first advanced by J. C. Flugel in 1930), Kuchta argues that this renunciation 'began in the early eighteenth century as an aristocratic response to the political culture that emerged after 1688 and continued into the early nineteenth century motivated by a rivalry between aristocratic conservatives and middle-class reformers' (1996: 71). After the Revolution of 1688, the Restoration court's adoption of French finery and fashion excess gave way to a more modest sartorial style among aristocratic men. As one Frenchman noted in 1698, 'generally speaking, the English men dress in a plain uniform manner' (cited in Kuchta 1996: 60). This change in style was due to an emerging association between modest dress and public virtue and, as Kuchta argues, 'encouraging and embodying public virtue was a prime concern of England's political elite, who feared that encouraging luxury would lead to England's moral and political decline' (1996: 62). This construction of a modest masculinity through a restrained style of dress worked to define the character necessary for participation in the polity:

> Political participation in the nation, then, was defined in terms of a masculine renunciation of luxury, and this definition explains why vanity and luxury were such dominant definitions of femininity. If displaying masculinity was inherently tied to political legitimacy, displaying femininity was intimately linked with political exclusion. (Kuchta 1996: 65)

When the political hegemony of the aristocracy was challenged from the late eighteenth century by reformers and radicals such as Thomas Paine and William Cobbett, this challenge drew on the existing language of public virtue associated with modest masculinity in order to claim the right to political participation (Kuchta 1996: 67). In doing so, reformers still distinguished themselves from those whose association with fashion and luxury metonymically coded their 'legitimate' exclusion from the political domain (such as women and foreigners).

As Mirzoeff (1995: 58) has concluded, 'Just as the French Revolution found it difficult to detach the new notion of the body politic from the individual body of the king . . . so later reformers have found this gendered construction hard to escape'. Feminist theorists have often insisted on the irredeemably masculine nature of the modern body politic, given its basis in ties of fraternity (Pateman 1988; see also Mirzoeff 1995: 62). Moira Gatens has argued that, historically, the metaphor of the body politic was constructed from an image of the masculine body 'which reflects fantasies about the value and capacities of that body' (1996: 25). There are two key aspects of citizenship that have worked historically to exclude women from the category and hence from full participation in the body politic: the citizen as speaker/deliberator in the political domain; and the citizen as defender of the state (Fraser 1989: 126). If citizenship is envisaged within a Habermasian model, the capacity for rational debate is a primary requirement and, as has been previously discussed, the capacity for debate and consent has been configured as a masculine capacity in the modern body politic (see Fraser 1989; Yeatman 2001). The other aspect of citizenship, the citizen-soldier, has, historically, been similarly gendered. As Gatens (1996: 23–4) notes:

From its classical articulation in Greek philosophy, only a body deemed
capable of reason and sacrifice can be admitted into the political body as an
active member . . . Constructing women as incapable of performing military
service and so incapable of defending the political body from attack . . . is
sufficient to exclude [women] from active citizenship.

During the French Revolution, one of the arguments for introducing a
national uniform, with no distinction between civilian and military, was
that 'in a Republic, all the citizens compose the military and should thus
wear a type of dress which allows them to be ready for the first alarm'
(cited in Harris 1981: 307). Despite the fact that some Frenchwomen
dressed in the uniform of the National Guard (Harris 1981: 293), women
were never seen as full citizens like men who could perform military
service for the nation. Indeed, the new sense of nationhood was bound
up with this conception of the citizen-soldier: as the artists advocating
the adoption of civil uniforms stated, a national uniform 'would announce
to everyone immediately one's citizenship and prevent the French from
being confused with people of other nations still branded by the shackles
of servitude' (cited in Harris 1981: 306).

Citizenship's link with nation, nationality and nationalism, however,
predates the emergence of the modern nation state and forms of dress
have long been deployed to actively construct and reinforce this link or,
to put it in Benedict Anderson's (1991: 6) terms, to imagine the political
community. Currie (2000: 163–4), for instance, has noted both the
importance of dress for identifying citizens in Italian renaissance cities,
where the connection between dress and spatial limits was especially
important in the clearly divided *quartiere* of an Italian city, and a recurring
anxiety about the breakdown of such a 'geography of dress' (across
classes, between cities, between nations). From the fourteenth to the
nineteenth centuries, as Gilles Lipovetsky (1994: 32–3) has argued:

each [European] territorial state . . . persisted in differentiating its forms of
dress through special elements that distinguished them from those of its
neighbours. In its own sphere, fashion registered the rise of the fact and feeling
of nationhood in Europe, starting in the late Middle Ages. In exchange, by
producing national forms of dress, fashion helped reinforce the awareness of
belonging to a single political and cultural community.

Nira Yuval-Davis and Pnina Werbner (1999: 1) have noted that
although modern notions of citizenship and nationalism historically have
coexisted in a single social field, 'democratic citizenship's overt stress
on rationality, individuality and the rule of law has frequently been in

tension with, and even antithetical to, nationalism's appeals to communal solidarities and primordial sentiments of soil and blood'. An emphasis on this historically contingent articulation of citizenship with concepts such as nation and democracy has distinguished recent examinations of citizenship, such as that by James Donald (1999: 101, 98) who asks whether bearing the rights and obligations of state membership necessarily entails a cultural identity. In response, Donald (1999: 99) proposes that 'The position of citizen *must not* have a substance' (emphasis in original). Like the utterance of the pronoun 'I', 'so "the citizen" too denotes an empty space. It too can, in principle, be occupied by anyone' (Donald 1999: 99). This position marks a point of departure between a (disembodied) political theory of citizenship and its history: as all the chapters in this book make plain, whether or not citizenship *should* have an identity, historically it always has. Despite (or because of?) the dream of a disembodied citizen in the political imaginary we have inherited, the position of citizen has always been an embodied one.[7] And as Lauren Berlant has argued concerning the ongoing exclusions from full citizenship for some kinds of bodies, only a privileged subject – or what she terms the 'iconic citizen' – can posit citizenship as an empty space: 'today many formerly iconic citizens . . . sense that they now have *identities*, when it used to be just other people who had them' (1997: 2, emphasis in original).[8]

Concerning the current interest in citizenship, Cindy Patton and Robert L. Caserio (2000:1) have observed, 'Multiple disciplines with multiple motives have converged on this word, so banal and yet so ineffable'. It is perhaps this ineffability that is part of the attraction in recovering or refiguring citizenship, an ineffability due in part to citizenship being increasingly recognized and located in the everyday, banal experiences of modern subjects. May Joseph (1999: 4, 16), for instance, in examining the citizen 'as a performed site of personhood' enacted in the complex spheres of everyday life, notes: 'Notions of citizenship are infused with public images, official definitions, informal customary practice, nostalgic longings, accrued historical memory and material culture, comforting mythologies of reinvention, and lessons learned from past rejections' (1999: 5). For Berlant (1997: 10, 56), too:

> The practices of citizenship involve both public-sphere narratives and concrete experiences of quotidian life that do not cohere or harmonize. Yet the rhetoric of citizenship does provide important definitional frames for the ways people see themselves as public, when they do.

By emphasizing the importance of everyday performance to contemporary forms of citizenship, recent accounts such as those by Joseph and Berlant offer suggestive avenues for examining the deployment of practices of dress in the presentation and self-understanding of citizen-subjects, particularly those whose claims to citizenship are tenuous or contested within the body politic where they are located. The idea of citizenship as 'a performing sphere that transforms the abstraction "the people" into individuated political subjects and participating citizens,' in Joseph's words (1999: 15), emphasizes the importance of practices of subject-formation – of which dress and the presentation of the self are good examples – in participation in the polity. The means by which citizens are (ad)dressed, as Stephanie Hemelyrk Donald argues in the case of contemporary China in this volume, may well exemplify complex and contradictory meanings of, and identifications with, the nation and its history.

Melanie White and Alan Hunt (2000: 109) have argued that 'citizenship has no necessary political content; citizenship is as compatible with political repression as it is with radical egalitarianism' while Berlant has proposed that 'citizenship is a status whose definitions are always in process. It is continually being produced out of a political, rhetorical, and economic struggle over who will count as "the people" and how social membership will be measured and valued' (1997: 20). These observations are especially relevant to the chapters in this volume which examine very different political formations and ideologies within which citizenship was and is formulated, expressed and embodied.

Beginning with an examination of that stereotype of the French Revolution, the *sans-culotte*, Richard Wrigley establishes several threads, which run through other chapters in the book in relation to very different national and historical contexts, such as the paradoxical relationship between the visibility of dress practices and the instability of meanings associated with them. The items of dress associated with the sans-culotte – the *bonnet rouge*, the *pantalon* and the *carmagnole* (short jacket) – worked to establish this figure as the exemplary popular militant even as they were open to subversion, contrivance and satirical representation. Despite the fact that by March 1794 the presumed authenticity of the *sans-culotte* costume was believed to have been thoroughly compromised by its subversive misuse, residual meanings of popular insurgency continue to circulate around this recognizable figure. In particular, the association between popular militancy and authenticity, which the *sans-culotte* stereotype seemed to guarantee by its deployment of working dress, carried an effective historical resonance. From the donning of working dress by politically disaffected nobles in nineteenth-century Russia (Ruane) to the adoption of blue shirts by the Spanish Falangists in the 1930s to echo the common dress of the working man (Vincent), the wearing of clothes associated with labour have depended on binary oppositions between artifice/authenticity, illegitimate rule/legitimate popular movements to represent an authenticity of political purpose and subjecthood believed to be readily apparent to both wearers and observers.

Sometimes the capacity of clothes to carry desired political meanings could be more formally deployed in national contexts in order to mobilize new senses of the (emerging) nation, as Christine Ruane and Regina Root argue in the instances of Russia and Argentina, respectively. Ruane follows the shifting relation between the Russian state and modernity through the institution of a dress code by Peter the Great and its modifications and reversals leading up to the end of the Tsarist state in 1917. When Peter the Great outlawed Russian dress in 1701 in favour of European (German) clothing, it was to signify the monarchy's commitment to modernization (which in the visual economy of the time could only be figured as foreign). Later rulers negotiated this problematic binary in order to refigure Russian national identity within a modernizing nation. Under Catherine the Great, for instance, the development of women's court dress offered a kind of synthesis between European and Russian styles of dress; while the Westernized uniforms worn by upper-class men remained unchanged (until 1882), it was women's bodies that were intended to carry new meanings of a modern Russian court. Just as in Russia, so too in nineteenth-century Argentina. Following independence from Spain, 'dress played an important role in the configuration of a national subject' (Root). But again, just as adopting forms of dress could signify either endorsement or protest in relation to existing power structures in Russia, so too in Argentina dress could serve as a way of signalling support for the ruling party (for instance, through the favouring of certain colours) or the rhetoric of dress could be strategically deployed as a means of political protest. Through an examination of magazines at the time, Root argues that fashion writing, through working as a metaphor for political change and renovation, could defy official censorship, challenge traditional and tyrannical practices, and speculate on a developing national identity and the formation of a new body politic.

The political deployment of fashion and the discourse of fashion is also the focus of my own chapter in this volume on the Edwardian suffragette movement in Britain. Like Root, I argue for the capacity of fashionable dress to constitute a form of political critique, in this case through the suffragettes' emphasis on a stylish feminine appearance in the performance of political protest. Challenging their exclusion from a masculine body politic, suffragettes insisted on their claims to citizenship not by drawing on a rhetoric of abstract personhood but by drawing attention to their sexual specificity as women, most notably through forms of dress. In the process, suffragette dress undermined the boundaries between a private sphere of consumption and a public sphere of politics. Fashion was a form of agency for suffragettes, I argue, enabling and enhancing the women's acts of protest.

Besides the French Revolution, the 'uniformed' 1920s and 1930s in Europe is arguably the most significant historical period for the study of dress, gender and citizenship and is represented in this volume by three chapters. Simonetta Falasca-Zamponi and Mary Vincent examine Italian and Spanish fascism, respectively, while Tammy Proctor reminds us of another significant uniformed movement, in the form of the Scouts and Guides movement. In all three cases, the significations of youth (including vitality, activity and continuity), were central to defining the movements represented by the uniforms. Examining the worldwide Scouting move-ment in the interwar period, Proctor finds conflicts between the discourses of imperialism and internationalism played out not only through the rhetoric of leaders but through the uniform practices of different regions. Uniforms, which as Proctor notes, signified conformity and loyalty as well as a distinct form of adventurous masculinity associated with the Scouts, triggered conflicts of meaning when worn by white and non-white bodies, or when adapted by Scouts in the light of cultural, religious or economic differences: 'For decades, British males had been justifying their power and forming their identity around the idea that they were manly and males in the colonies were effeminate, and the concept that each could be Scouts on equal footing was hard to accept' (Proctor). Similarly, the Guiding movement was riven with divisions concerning appropriate dress and behaviour for girls, exemplified by debates about nomenclature which demonstrated the gendering implicit in notions of 'scouting' and 'guiding'. In Britain, khaki was seen as too militaristic in connotation to be worn by girls and young women who instead wore uniforms dominated by dark blue; in the United States, however, which insisted on naming the movement 'Girl Scouts', the girls wore a khaki uniform, like their male counterparts.

The gendering of uniforms is also a focus in Vincent's chapter on the Falangists in Spain in the 1930s and 1940s. The adoption of the blue shirt by Falangists was not only a form of self-conscious homage to Italian fascism but also conveyed a range of meanings associated with a mascu-linity of youth, action and patriotism. The informality and affordability of an item such as a blue shirt, associated with the working man, aligned the movement with street-fighting: 'the cadres were on the streets, openly agitating, demanding to be seen' (Vincent). When adopted by women within the movement, however, the meanings of the blue shirt changed: 'For men, donning uniforms meant fighting and dying at the front. For women, the blue shirt was redefined to mean service' (Vincent). The women of the Seccion Femenina, the Falangist organization for women, did not participate in street fighting, they sewed and nursed for the movement. Unlike the women fighting in the Republican militias, Falangist women did not wear trousers. Through a careful demarcation of dress codes and forms of service, the Nationalists maintained a strict gender order, which they identified with a 'natural' social order based on the family, Church and state. Conflicts concerning the changing role of women in Spain, however, at least in part attributable to the expanding range of duties and roles offered in the Seccion Feminina, were also encoded in changes and contradictions in the women's dress practices, according to Vincent.

While in Italy the designated colour of women's shirts was changed from black to white in 1932, the gendering of Italian fascism was more bound up with distinguishing between authentic and inauthentic forms of masculinity (and the politics to which they gave rise) than between masculinity and femininity. As Falasca-Zamponi argues, the black shirt adopted by the squads of the early fascist movement was intended to signify a distinction from the suits and top hats worn by traditional politicians. Representing action, combat and violence, the fascist black shirt helped define the movement against a parliamentary politics considered 'feminine'. In the fascist political imaginary, the citizen-soldier formed a part of a virile body politic and the black shirt stressed the erasure of individuality within this body corporate formed by the citizenry under the leader. Within this paradigm, Falasca-Zamponi argues, fashion – with its association with consumption, material pleasure and individual satisfaction – was antithetical to citizenship; the black shirt, ensuring uniformity and anonymity, defied fashion and self-expression.

If the black shirt in Italian fascism was a means of denying difference or covering up bodily specificity, so too, Margaret Maynard would argue, was the practice of gifting blankets to indigenous Australians in the nineteenth and early twentieth centuries. Although the meanings of this practice shifted over the course of its implementation, the issuing of blankets by European settlers to Aborigines worked to obliterate most forms of traditional attire and formed an important means by which the dominant culture sought to impose its authority on indigenous people as 'colonial subjects' rather than citizens. Noting the importance of dress codes in traditional notions of the 'civilizing' process, Maynard goes on to contrast the practice of blanket issues with the visibility of overtly political dress adopted by Aboriginal activists and protestors today: both instances can tell us much about the negotiations around (and resistances to) the recognition of the full citizenship of indigenous Australians.

The contemporary performance of citizenship through dress is also the subject of the final chapter by Stephanie Hemelryk Donald on the invented tradition of Children's Day in China. Given that Children's Days around the world are 'all as much about how a nation likes to think about itself as they are about the rights of children', Hemelryk Donald looks at how this celebration of cultural citizenship in contemporary China enables children to articulate their relation to the state, its norms and histories, through practices of dress. Combining western fashion with revolutionary signifiers and the 'exotic' dress of minority cultures, Children's Day spectacles graphically display some of the disjunctures of contemporary China, 'an authoritarian collective society in transition to a market economy with socialist characteristics.'

The contemporary examples examined by both Hemelryk Donald and Maynard testify to the continuing imbrication of dress with the meanings and practices of citizenship and with representations of the body politic. Lipovetsky (1994: 6) has argued that fashion has become the organizing principle of modern collective life, which he takes not as 'the sign of the decadence of the democratic ideal' but rather sees as presenting 'an opportunity for democracies' (1994: 7). Lipovetsky's audacious argument makes a refreshing change from condemnations of 'politics-as-theatre' (1994: 6) and a view which can only see the resurrection of the king's body in every visualization of the body politic. Lipovetsky's (1994: 10) defence of fashion as 'the ultimate phase of democracy' – because of the importance he assigns to 'the role of the frivolous in the development of critical, realistic, tolerant consciousness' (1994: 10) – is not necessarily reflected in the accounts of the multi-accentuality of dress and fashion in *Fashioning the Body Politic*, but it nevertheless warrants serious considera-tion as it insists on the importance of material practices in the formation of citizen-subjects. As Peters has argued, now that the state is larger than a face-to-face gathering of citizens, visual or symbolic representation should not just be seen as a necessary evil of the modern nation state. Rather, the positive possibilities of representing the body politic should be imagined and implemented (1993: 565–6): 'To address a citizenry that lives in something larger than an ancient city-state, some vision of the social totality must be provided. To condemn style in politics per se is to miss how such visions could be democratic and participatory' (1993: 566).

That the democratic potential of such visions of a stylish politics remains largely unrealized, however, was illustrated by a recent episode in Australian politics featuring the dress of a woman in public. It reminded me again of how dress, gender and citizenship may highlight the parameters of the political imaginary. On the night of the Western Australian state election, One Nation (a populist right-wing, anti-immigration and anti-indigenous rights party) seemed to have polled well and won several seats in the Legislative Council. One Nation's leader, Pauline Hanson, buoyed by the news, made a spectacular entrance to the voting tally room which dominated media coverage of the election for most of the ensuing week. Ostensibly reporting the return to electoral favour of One Nation, reportage actually focused most scrutiny on Hanson's appearance and, in particular, the dress she had worn in the tally room: a colourful, halter-neck full-length party dress. 'The dress' appeared in photographs, cartoons and caricatures and was discussed by both political commentators and fashion gurus; the national broadsheet newspaper, *The Australian*, ran a large front-page photograph of Hanson (dwarfing a smaller photo of the Labor Party leader who had in fact won the state election in a landslide), with a story titled 'Lazarus in a floral frock' (12 February 2001: 1). While Hanson had clearly intended to make a statement with her appearance, the media attention to this episode illustrates well the fact that women's capacity to 'flesh out' the body politic remains problematic, despite the presence and agency of women within the political domain. As the *Australian*'s cartoon best illustrates, the fleshy materiality of the woman's body, in combination with her 'flashy' (read 'cheap') dress – which so alarms the male politicians in the background (the Prime Minister and Treasurer, respectively) – recalls Rousseau's censure of the woman in public as indecently displayed. While I personally find repugnant everything Hanson stands for, I am dismayed by the savagery that often characterizes press and cartoon representations of her because of what it suggests about women's precarious position within the body politic. In an era when spin doctors and style consultants have become *de rigeur*, Hanson's fashion sense is still metonymically associated with inauthenticity and illegitimacy in the political domain. As the *Australian*'s cartoon shows, male politicians may have their facial features caricatured, but their dress is thoroughly unremarkable, it is unmarked in the sense that it provides the norm against which deviations (like floral frocks) are measured. Hanson, however, has used the normative dress of politicians to her own advantage, to position herself as a fresh alternative to the (drab) political mainstream; as she told one journalist, 'On election night people told me I looked so bright and everyone else looked so dull and boring' (*The Australian* 13 February 2001: 1). The clash of meanings associated with Hanson's floral frock, I would argue, again shows us that there is always contestation over how the body politic is fashioned and by whom.

Notes

1. In the state parliament of Western Australia, for instance, women clerks in the 1990s were still not permitted to wear trousers in the Legislative Council chamber.
2. For accounts of this tradition, see, for instance, Martin Jay (1993) and David Chaney (1993).
3. The artist and deputy Jacques-Louis David was commissioned by the Committee on Public Safety to design such a uniform (Hunt 1984: 75–6; see also Harris 1981).
4. As Lipovetsky notes, this decree was largely symbolic, marking formally the end of sumptuary laws which in fact had not been strictly enforced for a considerable period prior to the revolution (1994: 30–1).
5. Interestingly, a motion to make the wearing of the *bonnet rouge* compulsory for Jacobins was opposed by Robespierre and Petion, who 'felt that there were certain inconveniences attendant upon adopting a new symbol of patriotism, thinking that the tricolour *cocarde* and the slogan *vivre libre ou mourir* should be sufficient for supporters of the constitution' (cited in Harris 1981: 292). See Wrigley (1997) for a comprehensive discussion of the conflicting usages and interpretations of the liberty cap.
6. See also Mirzoeff's discussion on the proposed Hercules statue (1995: 78–80).
7. See Peters (1993: 564) on 'subjectless' citizens in the political theory of Rousseau and Kant.
8. To be fair, Donald (1999: 99) anticipates this critique of his position by feminists: 'They dismiss the idea of a desirable but unachievable universality as an alibi for ignoring, or even colluding in, actual inequalities and domination.'

The Formation and Currency of a Vestimentary Stereotype: The *Sans-culotte* in Revolutionary France

Richard Wrigley

The term *sans-culotte* is one of the most well-known examples of the use of vestimentary vocabulary to identify a distinctive mode of collective political identity. Within the historiography of the Revolution, there is an ongoing debate about the social constitution of the *sans-culotte* movement, and how this effects our understanding of the nature and extent of their political engagement (see Soboul 1958; Andrews 1985; Rose 1983; Cobb 1970).[1] Albert Soboul argued that the *sans-culottes* were at heart a genuinely popular phenomenon, creators and beneficiaries of a new political culture of radical democracy. Subsequent commentators have disputed this, pointing out, on the one hand, the socially heterogeneous constitution of the *sociétés populaires* of the local *sections* of Paris, and, on the other hand proposing that such activists made up a kind of incipient local political cadre. These scholarly arguments are in a sense merely an extension of the contestation that surrounded the arrival and the demise of *sans-culottes* from the revolutionary stage. Indeed, the image of the *sans-culotte* – men of the people, wearing *bonnet rouge* (red woollen caps), *pantalon* (loose trousers), *carmagnole* (short jackets) – is best known through retrospective satire and caricature (Jouve 1978; Bindman 1989; Langlois 1988; Leith 1989; Hould and Leith (eds) 1990; Naudin in Vovelle (ed.) 1997). The pungency of such images' visual and discursive rhetoric has, however, been an obstacle to recognizing the various antecedents and tributaries that fed into the image, and the contested uncertainties that surrounded the adoption and currency of versions of *sans-culotte* dress.

This study will explore aspects of the formation and currency of the *sans-culotte* type with the aim of understanding some of the ways in which this vestimentary ensemble functioned as a site for the assertion and challenging of political values. We will see that the stereotype was considerably less stable than usually presumed. Dress was a powerful and multifarious index of revolutionary ideas but, here as elsewhere, one cannot separate questions of the currency of a type of dress from the interpretations that it elicited.[2] Indeed, in seeking to focus on the image of the *sans-culotte,* and more specifically its vestimentary dimension, a key consideration is that its constitution, and in due course dissolution, occurred without any legislation or official direction.[3]

Annie Geffroy has argued that the currency of *sans-culotte* costume as a form of political self-identification can only be understood in the light of a pre-existing discourse:

> Si le pantalon devient à la mode en 1792, je pense que c'est parce qu'il fournit une explication respectable à un désignant socio-politique déjà bien installé dans la langue, plutot que l'inverse. Le 'costume des sans-culottes' part d'un vêtement populaire, mais le transforme en symbole; il le fait [faut?] donc décoller de ses déterminations sociales. (1986: 586; see also Geffroy 1985: 157–86 and Reinhard 1971: 214, 420)

> (If trousers became fashionable in 1792, I think this is because they provided a respectable explanation for a socio-political indicator already well-established in language, rather than the reverse. The 'costume of the sans-culottes' is based on popular dress, but transforms it into a symbol; it should therefore be detached from its social determinations.)

Geffroy's argument is also consistent with the fact that elements of what was to crystallize as the *sans-culotte* vestimentary stereotype are in evidence in prints and drawings showing contemporary revolutionary scenes well before the spring of 1792.[4] The consolidation of the image of the *sans-culotte* was only possible because a set of conventions for representing men of the people already existed, which it was possible to harness to new political ends (see Sonenscher 1989: chapter 10).

Geffroy has meticulously and revealingly mapped out the changing meanings of *sans culotte* (without breeches) and *sans-culotte* (a person without breeches) during the later eighteenth century and the early years of the Revolution. Until February 1792, the term *sans culotte* was primarily used in a mocking sense carried over from the later *ancien régime* as a way of satirizing people's failed claims to respectability. To be deemed 'sans culotte' was equivalent to lacking an essential sign of proper dress, and therefore to be consigned to society's lower ranks.[5] In the early years of the Revolution, the term was given a political dimension, being employed to distinguish *propriétaires* (property owners) and *honnêtes gens* (respectable people) – legitimate beneficiaries of the new political order – from their social inferiors. The establishment of meaning within a binary polarity was to remain a fundamental strategy in revolutionary rhetoric. For example, Robespierre contrasted *sans-culottes* and *culottes dorées* (Soboul 1958). It is only after February 1792 that the term begins to be given a positive, polemical meaning to invoke a constituency that was claimed to be united by its espousal of a politics of radical populism.[6] After the invasion of the Tuileries palace on 10th August 1792, it occupied the foreground of political vocabulary until the spring of 1794, when the *sans-culottes'* presence on the political stage was eclipsed, coming to be synonymous with the militant politics of the Parisian sections (see Soboul 1958 and also Genty 1987). However, throughout this period, as will be noted later, old and new meanings continued to co-exist in frictious tension.[7]

Although historians continue to argue about the social constituency and political agenda of those gathered under the rubric *sans-culotte*, it is nonetheless the case that, as a vestimentary phenomenon, it has almost been taken for granted. That is, it has been presumed to have a fairly clearly defined inception and demise.[8] In what follows, I emphasize the extent to which pre-existing conventions for representing men of the people in the later *ancien régime* and the early Revolution feed into the *sans-culotte* stereotype.[9] Essentially, what we find is a set of representational elements that are at once more eclectic and less novel than has usually been presumed to be the case. To this extent, the new political function of the *sans-culotte* stereotype can be seen as having a significant degree of continuity with pre-existing conventions for dealing with the representation of men of the people.[10]

A hitherto unexplored antecedent for the politicized notion of the *sans-culotte*, and one that also relies on an item of dress as its key referent, is the term *bonnets de laine* (woollen caps), and its currency between 1791 and the summer of 1792.[11] This looks back to the *ancien régime* and the association of the woollen cap with male artisans and labourers. It was also one of the semantic and vestimentary tributaries that were to feed into the later, much more widespread emblematic phenomenon of the *bonnet rouge* as liberty cap (see Wrigley 1997: 131–69). In the early history of the Revolution, the term *bonnets de laine* acquired a specific meaning, being used to refer collectively to men from the faubourg Saint-Antoine who had been active in the taking of the Bastille in the summer of 1789. Moreover, after 1789, the weight of reference was inherently retrospective, in so far as the taking of the Bastille became consolidated as a foundational moment of popular activism.[12] References to *bonnets de laine* exemplify the tension between innovation and redesignation in the formation of new vocabularies for defining the revolutionary landscape, its institutions and allegiances. The case of *bonnet(s) de laine* anticipates that of *sans-culotte(s)* in that the constitution of this political language predominantly relied on changing the meaning of already existing terms: antithesis and inversion are more in evidence than neologism.[13] The two terms also share an essentially distanced relation to their vestimentary referents.

In the spring of 1791, references to *bonnets de laine* exemplify the increasingly polarized and fragmented language of politics – that is, with specific regard to what sort of people were, or should be, legitimately involved in political activity, both organized and spontaneous. On the one hand, we find satirical references to the faubourg Saint-Antoine as *le faubourg de la gloire* (the glorious faubourg), which dispute the notion that *chez un peuple libre, la véritable gloire consiste à porter un bonnet de laine, à marcher en sabots et sans culottes* (with a free people, real glory consists in wearing a woollen cap, walking in clogs and without breeches) (Marchant, cited in Geffroy 1985). We can see here usage of the *ancien régime* form of mocking reference to vulgar clothing, a state of demeaning undress signalled by the comic and shameful absence of *culottes*. On the other hand, there are also positive references which, within a legitimizing but containing narrative framework, rely on the idea of a kind of cross-class collaboration at times of emergency or national crisis, as in the case of the construction of the arena for the Fête de la Fédération in July 1790,[14] in which people identified by their *bonnets de laine* lend their physical vigour to patriotic activities. In the context of the highly charged arena of revolutionary politics, the ideological resonance of such a narrative could assume a momentous, potentially destabilizing import, in so far as the 'people' threaten to take on a more established and independent political role.[15]

Examples of the polarized language of contestation surrounding the visibility of *bonnets de laine* can be found in accounts of the translation of Voltaire's remains to the Panthéon on 11 July 1791. References to the presence of men from the faubourg Saint-Antoine in contemporary commentaries on this occasion are to some extent explained by the fact that the procession set out from the site of the Bastille, on the edge of the faubourg. Commentaries on the pantheonization of Voltaire illustrate a sense of the way in which figures from the 'peuple' could be represented as integral to the cohesively enthusiastic spectacle of such celebratory and commemorative occasions. For example, in his *Courrier des LXXXIII Départements*, Antoine Gorsas (12 July 1791 no. 11) previewed the event by describing part of the procession as follows:

> La Bastille sera portée concurramment par des Bourgeois, des ci-devant gardes françoises avec leurs uniformes, et des braves citoyens du faubourg St-Antoine, vulgairement appelés Bonnets de laine. (12 July 1791, no. 11: 170) [16]

> (The [model of the] Bastille will be carried successively by Bourgeois, former French guards with their uniforms, and valiant citizens of the faubourg St-Antoine, vulgarly known as woollen caps.)

Here, the 'vulgar' nominative appellation of *bonnets de laine* is given patriotic legitimacy by highlighting their privileged role in sharing the responsibility for carrying the model of the Bastille, and also by qualifying them as 'braves', alluding to their heroic actions on 14 July 1789.

Gorsas also pointed out that those people 'vulgairement appelés bonnets de laine . . . s'honorent de cette dénomination glorieuse' (vulgarly called woollen caps are honoured by this glorious title) (13 July 1791, no. 12: 185). In his subsequent euphoric report on the day's events, he played up the presence of *bonnets de laine* from the faubourg Saint-Antoine, but also noted that *bonnets de la liberté* were worn by many spectators. When it came to carrying the sarcophagus onto the site of the demolished Bastille, extra help was needed, and spontaneously provided:

> tout-à-coup une foule de peuple se précipite; mille bras s'empressent de s'en saisir, et milles têtes parées du bonnet de la liberté, se précipitent pour le porter effectivement à travers d'une allée de peupliers et de chênes. (13 July 1791, no. 12: 185) [17]

> (all of a sudden a crowd of people threw themselves forward; a thousand arms strained to take hold of it, and a thousand heads wearing the liberty cap, threw themselves forward to carry it across an alley of poplars and oaks.)

The terminological slippage between *bonnets de laine* and *bonnet de la liberté* is symptomatic of the coded way in which the popular was assimilated into political language. Given the problematic nature of the press as a documentary source for information on festivals, this tacit identification of *bonnets de laine* as liberty caps tells us more about revolutionary rhetoric than it does about the existence of any self-conscious policy on the part of the faubourg Saint-Antoine men themselves. Indeed, as one might have expected, references to the unifying effects of patriotic enthusiasm are complemented by royalist commentaries which are at once sarcastic and baffled, where the occasion is dismissed as *burlesque et magnifique* (burlesque and magnificent) (*L'Ami du roi*, 13 July 1791, no. 194: 775–6).[18] That the term *bonnets de laine* was still pivoting between a meaning associated with a backward-looking satire and taking on a new political function is illustrated by the fact that Charles de Villette, writing in the *Chronique de Paris* in July 1791, defended the people who were given this name by asserting that such caps were, in fact, proudly worn by men from the faubourg because they were a *symbole de la liberté* (symbol of freedom) (12 July 1791, no. 193: 781).[19] However, he ensures that this symbol operates on a national level, rather than tieing it to the local identity of the faubourg Saint-Antoine: 'Depuis que la France a recouvré son souveraineté, cette coiffure est la couronne civique de l'homme libre et des Français régénérés' (Villette 1792: 186) (since France recovered her sovereignty, this headgear is the civic crown of free men and regenerated Frenchmen).

Despite Gorsas's claim that the *bonnets de laine* embraced the idea that their headgear had taken on the role of liberty cap, it is surely more accurate to see this as a form of political rhetoric, in which the active political role of ordinary inhabitants of the faubourg Saint-Antoine was given a dignified cultural legitimacy by reference to a Roman emblem. On the one hand, the term *bonnets de laine* slides homophonically into *bonnet de la liberté*. On the other hand, the idea of the cap of liberty as an allegorical attribute is shifted to signify the enfranchisement of those that wore them. To this extent, such terminological elision marks a deeper political transition, corresponding to the invention of a language which could conceive of and recommend the role of popular activism, albeit in terms which restrict such activism within a vision of united patriotic endeavour.

Within the larger field of political language, the terminology of dress played an important role in articulating this transition. The way that the common *bonnets de laine* of artisans from the faubourg Saint-Antoine were given a collective emblematic role is paralleled in commentaries on the procession by references to the way in which items of ordinary clothing, and especially working clothes, were elevated to a ceremonial status. Thus, the journal *La Bouche de fer* described the presence of a contingent of printers 'bien retroussés et dans leurs costume de travail' (well enwrapped in their working dress), between the chariot bearing Voltaire's sarcophagus and copies of his works. They had made themselves paper caps, on the front of which was the inscription 'liberté de la presse' (freedom of the press), on the rear 'vivre libre ou mourir' (live free or die), and gathered around a tricolore banner with the words 'confédération universelle des amis de la vérité' (universal confederation of the friends of truth) (*La Bouche de fer*, 12 July 1791, no. 90: 4–5).[20] *L'Ami du roi* noted a hybrid form of dress sported by 'des forts de la halle, en equipage militaire, mais en vestes couvertes de farine, et en grands chapeaux blanchis de la même manière' (market porters in military outfits, but in jackets covered in flour, and in large hats similarly whitened) (*L'Ami du roi, des français, de l'ordre, et sur-tout de la vérité, par les continuateurs de Fréron, sous la direction de M. Montjoye*, 13 July 1791, no. 194: 775–6).[21] The context of the festival gave these clothes a new meaning, transforming them into a form of celebratory costume. Whether the wearing of such dress in the festival is to be seen as a sign of spontaneity, or, rather, as the result of a deliberate decision to display collective pride in the distinctive trappings of professional labourers, placed at the service of the celebration of one of the Revolution's great pioneers, these examples suggest that, within the ceremonial space of the festival, and also the discursive space of commentaries on such events, ordinary dress was acquiring an increasingly politically resonant visibility. It is significant that, in the case of the market porters, the promotion of such forms of costume is closely linked to the phenomenon of popular militarization, something that also applies to the proliferation of *sans-culotte* costume.[22]

Working dress had been used as a form of officially condoned ceremonial attire in the later eighteenth century, but the profoundly different context provided by the Revolution inevitably changed the meanings of such forms of public display.[23] The key issue in these texts from the summer of 1791 is, I would argue, the idea of popular self-representation.[24] This is exemplified in disputes over the obligation to acquire and pay for a uniform in order to serve in the Garde nationale (see Genty 1987: 28–9). Prudhomme raised this point in referring to, and speaking for, the masons and *forts de la halle* in the procession:

> Ils n'avoient point d'uniformes, et n'en étoient pas moins remarqués. On dit qu'on va les habiller. Tant pis! on n'en fera que des gardes nationales ordinaires; ils cesseront d'être des hommes, et à coup sûr, ils n'en deviendront pas meilleurs patriotes. (*Révolutions de Paris*, n. 105, 9–16 July 1791: 5)[25]

> (They had no uniforms, and were not the less noticed. It is said that they are going to be given uniforms. So much the worse! This would only make them ordinary national guards; they would cease to be men, and they would certainly not become better patriots.)

Indeed, it was precisely the issue of the refusal of uniform which Prudhomme, in November 1793, cited as a defining moment when sketching a typological genealogy for *patriotes par excellence, de ces républicaines nés* (patriots *par excellence*, born republicans). He claimed that this could be traced back to 1790: 'On nommait alors les hommes de ce groupe 'bonnets de laine', et il s'agissoit du vrai peuple républicain qui faisait son service en habit de travail' (at this time the men of this group were known as 'woollen caps', and it referred to the true republican people who did their national guard service in working clothes), despite the disdain of the (royalist) *habits bleus du roi* (king's blue uniforms) and (bourgeois) *lafayettistes*.[26] These comments only make sense, of course, in the light of the later crystallization of the stereotype of the *sans-culotte* as exemplary popular militant. They nonetheless point back to a phase in the Revolution when the visibility of popular political activity was legitimized through a vocabulary in which the vestimentary became emblematic, in a way that was polemically construed as signalling a form of political authenticity.

This is also found in Gorsas's account of the invasion of the Tuileries on 20 June 1792, where he picks out a group of coalmen in order to assert the virtue of honest, and ingenuously unwashed, labouring men. The establishment of their symbolic status is defined within a binary opposition to the cosmetic dissimulation of *aristocrates*:[27]

> Vos figures, noircies par un travail qui fournit aux riches qui vous dédaignent les moyens de faire convertir en mets succulens les viandes des plus grossières; *ces figures symboliques de la vertu*, qui ne cherche pas à farder ses couleurs, en imposoient à tous ces Achilles parfumés du Palais Royal, dont le teint est aussi froid que leurs limonades, et le coeur aussi mou que les bisques qui repaissent leur frêle individu. (*Courrier des LXIII départements*, n. 22, 22 June 1792: 334, my italics) [28]

> (Your faces, blackened by a labour which provides for the rich who disdain you the means to transform coarse meat into succulent dishes; these symbolic figures of virtue, who do not seek to disguise their colours, command the respect of all these perfumed Achilles from the Palais Royal, whose complexions are as cold as their lemonade, and whose hearts are as soft as the fish soup which nourishes their feeble constitutions.)

For all Gorsas's enthusiasm, his adoption of an emblematic register inscribes a degree of necessary distancing, achieved by means of linking popular participation in revolutionary action to a pre-existing discourse of the virtue of labour. Indeed, one of the defining strands underpinning *sans-culotte* ideology was the idea of productive work, revalorized in aggressive political terms. As the *Journal des sans-culottes* asserted in 1792:

Les sans-culottes, hommes féroces et superbes, font la majorité de la nation, les sans-culottes soutiennent seuls l'état, les sans-culottes fournissent les défenseurs de la patrie, vous habillent, vous nourrissent, ils peuvent se passer de vous et vous ne pouvez exister que par eux, vous consumez, et ce sont eux qui produisent. (no. 1: 3)[29]

(The sans-culottes, ferocious and superb men, make up the majority of the nation, the *sans-culottes* sustain the state, the *sans-culottes* provide defenders of the motherland, dress you, nourish you, they can do without you and you only exist because of them, you consume, and it is they who produce.)

Such rhetoric pushes the idea that the morally desirable condition of transparency was most irreducibly evident in the form of men of the people engaged in political activity. Remarks such as Gorsas's on the events of 20 June 1792 highlight the way that working dress was taken to be a sign of such transparency by virtue of its grubby quotidian lack of artifice. Yet in April 1792, the idea that working dress had become a political symbol was resisted. A letter from Gorsas to Palloy regarding the preparations for the festival of Liberty honouring the liberated soldiers of the Châteauvieux regiment ironically plays on the need for precisely this kind of palliative representational artifice. Gorsas notes the likely protests at *Palloy's projet bizarre* (bizarre project) to have a stone model of the Bastille carried *par des véritables sans-culottes* (authentic *sans-culottes*). Although he mocks the unease at the spectacle of common men of the people participating in the procession, his recommendation of caution to Palloy – so as not to play into the hands of satirical commentators – registers a recognition of the need to translate the popular into a stylized, codified form (BNF – MS Nouv. Acq. Fr. 308 fol. 278).

It is perhaps not surprising that accounts of festivals and moments of political crisis promote the emblematization of ordinary dress. For example, the events surrounding the invasion of the Tuileries on 20 June 1792 – a key moment in the radicalization of revolutionary politics – in fact see dress being represented in manifold emblematic ways. As Annie Geffroy has noted, although the vestimentary element most notoriously connected with this episode is the *bonnet rouge* as donned by Louis XVI, accounts of the massed deputations from the faubourgs St-Antoine and St-Marcel procession through the Assemblée Nationale on 19 June also contain another pungent but puzzling vestimentary ingredient (1985: 175–6).[30] This reportedly took the form of a pair of old and torn black *culottes* with *tricolore* ribbons attached being paraded on the end of a pike, creating a threateningly emblematic trophy. Significantly, on the same occasion, commentaries note that the slogan *Vive les sans-culottes* appeared on banners.[31] The meaning of the term can be seen to be pivoting between its previous deprecatory sense and as a way of asserting the existence of a new constituency. As Richard Twiss observed, the people carrying this 'standard' wore breeches; 'sans-culottes' was 'the name that has been given to the mob' (cited in Ribeiro 1988: 86).[32] Indeed, for the *Révolutions de Paris*, the 20 June became the *Journée des sans-culottes*.[33] The notion of *sans-culottes* as a mobilized collectivity was thus named, at least in reported form (as emblems and *tableaux* in festivals often had labels or placards), at the same time as it was visually evoked in the antithetical form of a pair of black *culottes*, whose symbolic function was signalled both by their having been hoist on a pike and the attached ribbons. Moreover, the way that the meaning of the term *sans-culottes* was established within a strongly polarized binary vocabulary was doubly evident in that reports also refer to the pairing in the procession of the *culottes* with the attached inscription *vive les sans-culottes* and a calf's heart skewered on a pike with the label 'coeur d'aristocrate' (Geffroy 1985: 175, quoting *Moniteur*, 22 June 1792, XII: 718; *Journal des débats*, 22 June 1792: 218).[34] In this text, the *culottes* antithetically substantiate the slogan *vive les sans-culottes*, in a way that is at once formalized and improvised, literal and allusive, as the calf's heart spells out a complementary kind of brutal triumphalism.[35] The pungency of such descriptions is, I would suggest, precisely a response to the disturbing spectacle of the quotidian being infused with emblematic significance. That this is so might be seen as being confirmed by the attempts to consign it to the realms of satire. The *Mercure universel* referred to the *culottes* as a 'caricature' (21 June 1792, cit. Pfeiffer 1912: 84/280), and even Gorsas, who loquaciously enthused over the events of the 19–20 June saw in the parading of 'un guidon analogue à son honorable misère' (a pennant analogous to their honorable poverty), 'une vieille culotte noire' (an old pair of black breeches), evidence of 'la gaité française et cette originalité piquante qui distingue la nation' (French gaiety and this piquant originality which distinguishes the nation) (*Courrier des LXXXIII départements*, 22 June 1792, no. 22: 336). The rest of his remarks treat the procession as having a pronounced carnivalesque flavour.[36]

The prevalence of this kind of contested semantic manipulation can also be found in evidence in the spring of 1792 in references to one of the *sans-culotte*'s 'popular' avatars. This is the soiled woollen cap worn by the theatrical character Janot in Dorvigny's *Les battus qui paient l'amende* (*The Downtrodden who Pay the Fine*), a tremendously popular Parisian vaudeville first performed at the boulevard theatre of the Variétés

Amusantes during the winter of 1779–80, and still vividly remembered in the Revolution, especially during the early months of 1792, when the *bonnet rouge* was coming to be associated with exponents of militant populist politics, notably the Jacobin club (see Wrigley 1996). Janot's cap had been soiled by the contents of a chamber pot poured from a first-floor window by the disapproving father of his paramour, Suzanne; he spends the rest of the play trying ineptly and unsuccessfully to obtain retribution, ending up being fined for his pains, hence the title of the piece. Janot and his cap were recalled during the spring and summer of 1792 either to vaunt the progress made in the active participation of the 'downtrodden' in political life, or else to decry the appallingly vulgar nature of would-be patriots and their champions. Janot's soiled woollen cap points, so to speak, both back to its comic connotation of unhygienic commonness, and also to the crystallization of the *bonnet rouge* as an item of challengingly novel political symbolism. But the descriptive energy of both types of commentary relies on a recognition of the transformation of a piece of humdrum clothing into a tremendously powerful symbol – whether inspiring or threatening – associated with the intervention of *le peuple* in political activities.

One indication of the process of terminological evolution in question is the way that, from 1791, the collective terms *bonnets de laine* and *sans-culottes* come to be treated as equivalent. In February 1791, Hébert's *Père Duchesne* cites *bonnets de laine* and *sans-culottes* together, but as separate entities: 'Honneur, mille millions de tonnerre, au grand général La Pique, grand bruleur de moustaches, de barbes de capucins, le plus digne de la confiance des cinquante mille bonnets de laine et des cinquante mille sans-culottes!' ('Honour, a thousand millions of thunder, to the great general Pike, great burner of moustaches, of capuchin's beards, the most worthy of confidence of the fifty thousand *bonnets de laine* and the fifty thousand *sans-culottes*') (No. 38, 28 Feb. 1791, cit. Geffroy 1985: 163). The novel nature of this terminology is registered in the equivocal way it is invoked in a review of Jean-Jacques Barbier's *La Prise de la Bastille* published by Gorsas in his *Courrier des LXXXIII Départements* in August 1791. The mix of social classes in the audience was euphemistically evoked: 'Car tout y était, jusqu'à ces citoyens des faubourgs, que MM. de l'aristocratie ont baptisé *bonnets de laine* et quelque chose de plus ou de moins' ('For all were there, down to the citizens of the faubourgs, who have been baptized by Messieurs of the aristocracy woollen caps and something more and less') (28 August 1791, cited in Lacroix 1909: 658–9). Here these terms are treated as polemical and deprecatory inventions, thus denying any positive identification with them. By nivôse an II (December 1793/January 1794), the convention of referring to *bonnets de laine* from the faubourg Saint-Antoine had been superceded by the phrase 'sans-culottes du faubourg Saint-Antoine' (Tuetey 1890–1914: 110).

In the aftermath of the second invasion of the Tuileries palace on 10 August 1792, and the effective removal of Louis XVI from political power, to be superceded by the declaration of a republic, the term *sans-culottes* shifted from the contested margins of the political landscape, to a more central, prominent position. However, it remained a term that was employed and defined in a variety of ways.

A complement to the ways in which we have seen working dress being treated as emblematic in the summer of 1792 are the attempts to find a legitimating historical pedigree for *sans-culotte* costume. Reflecting on the rise of popular political involvement in July 1792, Mercier invoked the historical precedents of the 'Gueux' ('Poor') in Holland, who revolted against their Spanish oppressor, Philip II, as well as the Greeks and Romans, 'tous gens sans culottes' ('all people without breeches') (*Chronique de Paris*, July 1792, p. 62, cit. Pellegrin 1989b: 162; see also Sonenscher 1989: 344). In a paean of praise to the *sans-culottes* from the same period, references embraced Spartacus, the Romans, the Swiss, the Dutch, Christ, Mohammed, Rousseau, Homer, Shakespeare, and Franklin (*Journal des sans-culottes*, [1792] no. 1: 4). The scheme for republican costume proposed by the artist and *conventionnel* Sergent in 1793 invoked working dress – 'Ce costume n'est autre chose que l'habit journalier des Hommes de la campagne et des Ouvriers des villes' ('This outfit is nothing other than the daily dress of Men of the countryside and Workers of the towns') – implying that his design amounted to the elevation of the dress of the common, working man to quasi-official status. Yet he also claimed it as equivalent to the honorific Roman toga.[37] In discussing the etymology for *sans-culottide* in a report on the introduction of the republican calendar on 24 October 1793, Fabre d'Eglantine pointed out that *aristocrates* were mistaken in assuming that the term *sans-culotte* was inherently demeaning, for it had Gallic origins, part of France having been known as 'la Gaule nonculotté' (breechless Gaul): 'Quoi qu'il en soit de l'origine de cette dénomination antique ou moderne, illustrée par la liberté, elle doit nous être chère; c'en est assez pour la consacrer solennellement' ('Whatever may be the case regarding the origin of this term, ancient or modern, made illustrious by liberty, it should be dear to us; this is enough to consecrate it solemnly.')[38]

Although a degree of legitimacy, and accepted currency was achieved by the term in the wake of the 10 August 1792,[39] there was still no formal legislative or official codification of *sans-culotte* costume. This is consistent with its identification with the Parisian *sections*, whose political culture was in the nature of an aggregate of local pressure groups. The nearest equivalent would be an occasion such as the Section des sans-culottes voting that its president should present an address to the Convention wearing *bonnet rouge* and 'pantalon' (Soboul 1958: 651). Equally, and perhaps surprisingly, it is rare to find *sans-culottes* included in the descriptions of festival programmes and processions. When they are present as part of the processions, they are auxiliary to monumental allegorical elements. Thus, in the festival on 10 nivôse an II (30 December 1793), honouring military casualties in general, and in particular those from the taking of Toulon, the 'Char de la Victoire, portant le faisceau national, surmonté de la statue de la Victoire' ('The Chariot of Victory, carrying the national fasces, with the statue of Victory on it') was to be surrounded by '50 Invalides et de 100 braves sans-culottes en bonnets rouges' ('fifty veterans and 100 valiant *sans-culottes* wearing *bonnets rouges*');[40] it is likely that it was only the caps that were uniform. *Sans-culotte* costume also appears in the carnivalesque festivals and processions associated with dechristianization. In these, it was often worn under religious vestments that were to be cast off, revealing the 'true' *sans-culotte* beneath (see Ozouf 1977: 345).

The idea that *sans-culotte* costume enjoyed a distinctly restrictive currency is consistent with 'revisionist' accounts of the movement, which argue that the *sans-culottes* were more of a political cadre or oligarchy than a mass movement. According to this view, summarized by Patrice Higonnet: 'le sans-culottisme deviendrait, pour modifier l'expression de Soboul, une démocratie révolutionnaire idéologisée, plutot qu'une manifestation véritablement populaire' ('sans-culottism became, to adapt Soboul's expression, an ideologized revolutionary democracy, rather than a truly popular manifestation') (Soboul 1958: 424). This reinforces the idea that *sans-culotte* costume was a form of unofficial political uniform whose utilization was probably confined principally to club meetings, and participation in deputations.[41]

The extremely limited adoption of *sans-culotte* costume in the Convention corresponds to the fact that it was identified with the local, and increasingly rival, power base of the *sociétés populaires*. Those who wore the same dress in the Convention as they did in *sociétés populaires*, such as Omer Granet from Marseille, Chabot[42] and Thibaudeau, were noted as standing out (although we must acknowledge that references to this are retrospective and therefore of uncertain reliability).[43] Only Armonville allegedly wore the *bonnet rouge* in the Convention (Quicherat 1879: 630).

The implicit incongruity between the degree of respect for authority expected of those in the national assembly, and the odour of street politics attaching to the *bonnet rouge* is exemplified by Mercier's retrospective claim that, when Chabot appeared in the Convention *en sans-culotte*, he held his cap 'honteusement' (shamefully) in his hand (Bonnet et al. (eds) 1994: 113).[44] When Chaumette encouraged the members of the Conseil Général of the Commune de Paris to wear clogs, this was as part of the war effort, in response to the chronic shortage of clothing and equipment, notably shoes, for the struggling revolutionary army, rather than a recommendation that popular dress be adopted as such (*Moniteur*, XIX, n. 96, 6 niv. an II / 26 December 1793: 42). When prominent figures took to wearing *sans-culotte* costume, this was seized on as a sign of suspicious exaggeration, a conclusion that was repeatedly and vehemently rammed home as such figures fell victim to censure, arrest, or execution, most notoriously Philippe Egalité, the king's regicide cousin, the former duc d'Orléans,[45] and Hébert, the voice, through Père Duchesne, of intransigent *sans-culottisme*.[46] After Thermidor, there was a wholesale repudiation of 'maratisme', in which modesty and simplicity of dress was castigated as dishevelled dirtiness and repugnant filthiness, constituting a kind of hierarchical aesthetic rationale for the unworthiness of its associated populist politics (Barailhon 1795: 3).[47]

A measure of *sans-culotte* costume having achieved a normative function (if not being ubiquitously adopted) is, precisely, evidence of its subversion, which is recorded as occurring between late 1793 and the spring of 1794. Detailed police reports filed for the Minister of the Interior give us an unusual degree of detail on how *sans-culotte* costume was misused. We have, of course, to acknowledge that it was the business of the police agents who compiled these reports to be able to provide information on the vagaries of *l'esprit public*, above all when dissent was manifest – they were looking for troublemakers; reports are least detailed when they are able to report calm and solid consensus.[48] Nonetheless, these texts provide a considerable degree of precision regarding the currency of *sans-culotte* costume, and more specifically evidence of its misappropriation, since for all their bureaucratized sloganizing, when it came to delineating the features of suspect individuals, they are extremely precisely observed in matters of physical appearance and dress.[49]

During this period, the *sans-culotte* outfit – *carmagnole*, *pantalon*, and *bonnet rouge*, but sometimes only one or two of these elements[50] – was put to subversive use, in order to provoke and insult people who had presumably become habituated to its status as a sign of republican rectitude. In some cases named individuals were noted as deliberately concealing their dubious political credentials by adopting *sans-culotte* costume. In December 1793, the *ci-devant* marquis d'Audelot 'se promène en sans-culotte; il ne lui manque que le bonnet rouge pour que ceux qui ne connoissent pas le royaliste le prennent pour un patriote, qu'il ne sera jamais' ('walks about as a sans-culotte; he only lacks a *bonnet rouge* for people who don't know him as a royalist take him to be a patriot, which he will never be') (Caron vol II: 36, 7; niv. an II / 27 December 1793). The implication is that the more complete the costume, the more it was likely to be the result of contrived concealment. As we noted in 1792, the type of the *sans-culotte* was also linked to that of the *forts de la halle*. In September 1793, a police report warned that, amongst 'plusieurs personnes très mal vêtues' ('very poorly dressed people'), who were in fact suspected of being 'des personnes très comme il faut', there were some who had dressed up as 'forts de la halle' ('market porters') (Caron vol I: 157; 22 September 1793).

By March 1794, *sans-culotte* costume was reckoned to have been comprehensively compromised by its subversive misuse:

Les aristocrates ont absolument pris le costume républicain. On assure que les deux tiers des bonnets rouges et des carmagnoles sont des scélérats avérés qui ne cherchent qu'à corrompre l'esprit public et qui, par leur costume, en imposent aux vrais sans-culottes. (Caron vol V: 213; 20 vent. an II / 10 March 1794)

(Aristocrats have absolutely adopted republican costume. We are reliably informed that two thirds of the bonnets rouges and short jackets are the most avowed scoundrels who only seek to corrupt public morale and who, by their costume, intimidate true *sans-culottes*.)

Opinion therefore turned against men in such costumes:

Méfions . . . des bonnets à poil, des bonnets de police, des pantalons et des carmagnoles. C'est avec ces symboles insignifiants qu'ils se sont glissés, depuis l'affaire du deux septembre [prison massacres], dans toutes les sections, qu'ils se sont emparés des places les plus importantes, et qu'ils cherchent à arrêter dans sa course le char de la Révolution [par] des mesures exagérées' (Caron vol V: 225–6, 21; vent. an II / 11 March 1794).

(We must scorn [military] busbies, police caps, trousers and short jackets. It is with these insignificant symbols that, since the affair of the second September [prison massacres], they insinuated themselves into the sections, that they

secured the most important positions, and that they seek to halt the chariot of
the Revolution in its course by exaggerated measures.)

A few days later it was reported that: 'On insulte hardiment les citoyens
vêtus en carmagnoles' ('Citizens dressed in short jackets are brazenly
insulted') (Caron vol V: 441–2; 30 vent. an II / 20 March 1794). However,
beyond the shifting status accorded to the essentially stylized ingredients
of *sans-culotte* costume, it is important to note that, with the establishment
of a ubiquitous regime of surveillance, dress in general had become a
site for apprehensive scrutiny, and moreover that this applied to the most
ordinary items of dress.

This repudiation of *sans-culotte* costume in the spring of 1794 was
complemented by observations that there had been a relaxation of
republican dress codes: dressing down was no longer obligatory in order
to conform – willingly or opportunistically – to the vestimentary status
quo.[51] Nonetheless, we continue to find references to people adopting
the outfit well in to 1795. In an essay on dress in the *Décade philosophique*, Amaury Duval, a resolute republican, recorded observing an
ostentatiously stylish *muscadin* (previously known as a 'fat' (fop))
teetering down the Champs-Elysées in discomfortingly tight *culottes*,
followed by a group of five or six 'prétendus sans-culottes en pantalons
et vestes' (would-be *sans-culottes* in trousers and jackets). It was the
former sight which disturbed him, since it seemed to be a throwback to
pre-revolutionary moeurs: 'Je crus avoir rêvé la révolution' (I thought I
had dreamt the Revolution) (*Décade philosophique* vol. 2: 139–40; vol.
3: 527).[52] The survival of '*sans-culotte* style' was little more than a bitter
reminder of lost ground. Nonetheless, it seems to have been possible to
continue wearing elements of *sans-culotte* dress, notably the bonnet rouge
throughout the later 1790s, if at the risk of insult. In 1795, the *conventionnel* Armonville was mockingly described as tenaciously refusing to
abandon his bonnet rouge, to the extent of eating and sleeping in it
(*Annales patriotiques*, 10/11 March 1795: 10, cited in Bonnet et al. (eds)
1994: 1395 note). At the end of the 1790s, such items of dress are
disparagingly referred to as 'relics', implying that they are merely obsolete
and impotent vestiges of a past age, hence no longer threatening (Beau-
varlet, *Caricatures politiques* (1798), cited in Ribeiro 1988: 84).

By way of conclusion, I would like to turn to three images of *sans-
culottes*, and test them as a potential source for what they might help us
understand about the nature of this form of politicized dress. This is
necessarily a fragmentary sampling of the complex problems involved
in analysing the visual representation of *sans-culottes*.[53] The images have

been chosen because they correspond to three significant strands within the rather limited repertoire of *sans-culotte* imagery.[54] All are prints; there are, in fact, almost no paintings of men 'en sans-culotte' (the nearest one might get to this are occasional portraits).[55]

Godefroy's etching *Le Jongleur Pitt soutenant avec une loterie l'équilibre de l'Angleterre et les subsides de la coalition* (*The Juggler Pitt maintaining England's Balance and her Subsidies for the Coalition with a Lottery*) (1794) (Fig. 2.1), is one of many anti-British images from this period. On the right, Pitt's left ankle is held by an athletic *sans-culotte*, who raises his right hand in a sign of warning and admonition. His idealized muscular legs and arms suggest that Godefroy had some awareness of the heroic conventions of history painting (the box-like space which contains the figures is also directly linked to current compositional conventions). Although the *sans-culotte* acts from a position in the corner, he is not an incidental character, but more a powerful personification of the French Republic, nonchalantly throwing his gawky adversary off

Figure 2.1. Godefroy: 'Le Jongleur Pitt soutenant avec une loterie l'équilibre de l'Angleterre et les subsides de la coalition' (The juggler Pitt maintaining England's balance and her subsidies for the coalition with a lottery), etching, first half of 1794.

balance, to the dismay of King 'Georges Dandin'. This image is interesting because it shows the combination of two representational modes: the extreme caricature applied to Pitt, and the more idealized treatment of the *sans-culotte*. The *sans-culotte* wears an apron, with a hammer tucked into his belt, thus evoking the continued presence of residually emblematic eighteenth-century iconographical conventions for representing male artisans. However, there is a further level of meaning here, in that aprons and hammers were also the attributes of *sapeurs* (sappers). Thus, the image inscribes a sign of national militarization, celebrating the heroic endeavour of this personification of the *peuple* as French People.

In another image from the same period, Antoine-Denis Chaudet's *Le Charlatan politique, ou le léopard apprivoisé (The Political Charlatan, or the Leopard Tamed)* (Fig. 2.2), the delineation of two *sans-culottes* is strikingly different. They emphasize the caricatural more than the heroic, with the result that there is some ambiguity in how we might read them. In the middle distance, we see the head of the République also wearing a liberty cap, topped by the tricolore, placed on the prow of the 'vaisseau

Figure 2.2. Antoine-Denis Chaudet: 'Le Charlatan politique, ou le léopard apprivoisé' (The Political Charlatan, or the leopard tamed), etching, first half of 1794.

de la République Française'. They are heavily muscled, but in a way that suggests plebeian 'Hercules forains' rather than the conventions of academic drawing. Yet beneath their short-sleeved jackets they wear loose-fitting long shirts which, in the manner of high art drapery, part to reveal the body beneath – not the elegant outlines of an academically idealized anatomy, but massive hips and thighs. Their faces are coarse, their joints thickened, and they wear sagging stockings and heavy clogs; they are placed in the left and right-hand corners, in a way that seems like a parodic echo of the use of repoussoir figures in history painting. We might also read the figures as echoing the earlier satirical use of the term *sans culotte*, for they are not clothed in any kind of stylized popular dress; rather, they literally illustrate a state of comic undress. That this comic rendition of *sans-culottes* was not deemed subversive, but rather a legitimate element in caricature, is demonstrated by the fact that both prints were subsidized by the Comité de Salut public (Committee of Public Safety) as part of a campaign of anti-British propaganda (Hould 1988: 29–37).

These two images exemplify the way that representations of the *sans-culotte* are predominantly either markedly idealistic, or virulently caricatural – a polarization that parallels what Geffroy calls the 'légende noire' and 'légende blanche' surrounding the historiography of the *sans-culotte* (see Geffroy 1985; Leith 1990; Bindman 1989). Forging an image of a *sans-culotte* or cognate types seems to rely on two main sets of conventions: those governing the representation of the heroic male body, as associated with history painting; and the varied kinds of exaggeration found in caricature, which are analogous to the theatrical modes of burlesque and vaudeville. They also employ quite different strategies for dealing with the symbolism of *sans-culotte* dress. In Chaudet's image, the *sans-culotte*'s costume is tailored to emphasize his athleticism. By contrast Godefroy's *sans-culottes* are much more stylized. The exaggerated features of their ill-fitting clothes conform to the image's satirical idiom; even so they are capable of a comic mastery over the dehumanized English.

The print, *Dansons la Carmagnole* (Fig. 2.3), a frontispiece to a 1793 almanac, illustrates the residual presence of the earlier deprecatory meaning of 'sans culotte'. On the one hand, for all that the figure wears a woollen cap (presumably red), and is armed with the popular pike and sword, this image of a daintily dancing *sans-culotte* seems deliberately to refuse any more tangible evocation of the physical power of the 'peuple armé' (and it is set in a vaguely rural, rather than obviously urban, context). Rather, we notice the presence of exaggerated ragged tears in his clothes (which contrast with his neatly laced shoes). To this extent, the image

LA RÉPUBLIQUE

EN VAUDEVILLES. /

Précédée d'une Notice des principaux événemens de la révolution,
pour servir de Calendrier à l'année 1793.

France

A PARIS,

Chez les Marchands de nouveautés.

1 7 9 3.

Dansons la Carmagnole.

Figure 2.3. Anonymous: 'Dansons la Carmagnole', etching, frontispiece, *La République en vaudevilles. Précédées d'une notice des principaux événemens de la révolution, pour servir de Calendrier à l'année 1793* (Paris, 1793).

represents an equivocal confluence of the new positive meaning of *sans-culotte* with its pre-revolutionary antecedent, the disparaging stereotype of the risibly underdressed 'sans culotte'.[56] This semantic discordance was remarked on at the time. In one of the police reports from November 1793 published by Caron, the term *sans-culotte* was used licentiously in a way that holds on to the eighteenth-century usage noted by Geffroy, rather than, or perhaps deliberately instead of, its new politicized meaning.[57]

* * *

As a form of costume, the *sans-culotte* had a short career, only being actively adopted between 1792 and 1794. We have seen, however, that for all its intended polemical simplicity as a form of political statement, it drew on, and generated, a complex semantic baggage surrounding the representation of working men, specifically the men of the artisanal centre of the faubourg St-Antoine, and the emblem of the *bonnets de laine*. A sampling of the currency of *bonnets de laine* in 1791 underlines the latent ambiguities that fed into the *sans-culotte* stereotype, and which were exploited in the rhetorical contestation that accompanied its crystallization during the course of 1792. As Annie Geffroy has argued, the history of *sans-culotte* costume owes more to the dynamic, frictious evolution of revolutionary language than it does to mere stylistic vestimentary innovation. It has only been possible to touch on the ways in which the multi-layered richness of this discourse also found expression in visual imagery. Nonetheless, even within the limits of an exposition of three prints, it is clear that the representation of the *sans-culotte* was anything but consensual, and drew on divergent referential ingredients, exemplifying the contestatory nature of such imagery, and the multi-layered symbolic power of dress.

After 1794, the phenomenon of the *sans-culottes* remained present in the language of politics, but predominantly in the form of, on the one hand, satire and caricature, and on the other, of the mythologization of the republican cause. In due course, nineteenth-century historical genre painting consolidated and recyled visual figures for the ferocious, sanguinary nature of the *sans-culotte* stereotype (Chaudonneret 1988: 313–40). While it has proved to be extremely difficult to recover any empirical history of the utilization of *sans-culotte* costume, this study has demonstrated that any enquiry into the episodes in the politics of revolutionary dress must always be conceived of as embracing a critical reading of interpretative texts and commentaries on vestimentary codes, as well as trying to evaluate the highly problematic resource of visual imagery.

* * *

I am extremely grateful to Colin Jones for helpful comments and to Philippe Bordes for his constructive criticism of an earlier version of this text, which also contained material that will form a separate, complementary article on Jacques-Louis David's *Serment du jeu de paume* and the representation of a man of the people in 1791.

Notes

1. For a recent summary of the historiographical question, and references

to the main contributory studies, see Higonnet, 'Sans-culottes', in Furet and Ozouf (eds) 1988.

2. The best single account of dress and the Revolution is Devocelle 1988 – alas unpublished. See also Ribeiro 1988, Pellegrin 1989a and 1989b. A fundamental study, which will inform any further work on eighteenth-century and revolutionary dress, is Roche 1989.

3. Eliel states that the *carmagnole* was banned when Bonaparte became First Consul (1989: 93), referencing Harris 1981: 286. However, no supporting reference is given here.

4. In the print 'époque du vendredi 19 Février 1791' (*Révolutions de Paris*, 1791: n. 32, p. 29), showing men from the faubourg Saint-Antoine, we find, in the bottom left-hand corner, a man wearing a cap, striped trousers, short jacket, and carrying a pike (BNF – HC, no. 10650). A similar figure appears in a 1791 drawing by Louis Lafitte (1770-1828) (BNF –HC, vol. 125, n. 11002, Qb1 1791), showing Louis XVI and the royal family in June 1792, being escorted back into Paris after their interception at Varennes. The broad-brimmed hat, sloping backwards over the shoulders, identifies this figure as a *fort de la halle* (market porter), discussed below (note 21) in relation to antecedents for the *sans-culotte*. On Lafitte, see Heim, Béraud and Heim (1989: 249).

5. On the cognate role played by hats and their absence, see Sonenscher 1987.

6. Geffroy notes that *sans-culotte* is not used in the pamphlets reprinted in Aulard, *Société des Jacobins* between February 1790 and July 1791 (1985: 180, note 7). George Rudé dated the shift from old to new meanings of *sans-culotte* to June 1792, i.e. the invasion of the Tuileries (1959: 12).

7. For example, a satirical response to the prominence of the term's new meaning:
'Mais aujourd'hui sans qu'on me hue / Je me promène dans la rue, / Que je sois ou non culotté, / Vive, vive la liberté!' (*Le Réviseur universel et impartial et bulletin de Madame de Beaumont* 1792: 2).

8. To this extent, the idea that the costume was instigated by the appearance of the actor, Simon Chenard, in a prototype *sans-culotte* outfit, at the festival of Liberty of Savoy in October 1792, as commemorated in a painting by Louis-Léopold Boilly (Musée Carnavalet), is anachronistic, and erroneous. On Boilly's picture, see Siegfried (1995: 41–2) and Ribeiro (1995: 146–7). The assumption that the painting corresponds with the festival is, however, problematic. Chenard wears a hat, not a *bonnet rouge*, which would have been *de rigueur* in late

1792. This opens up the idea that the picture was in fact made later, the cap being omitted as a way of eliding any explicit reference to the heyday of the Republic, with the result that the image is shifted into the domain of portraits of actors in character. Copia's print after the picture was announced in the *Journal de Paris* on 7 February 1795 (price 6 *livres*). The Musées d'art et d'histoire at Auxerre possess an album of studies by A.X. Leprince, showing Chenard in forty-eight of his leading roles (not, however, including this festival). I am grateful to Micheline Durand for her extremely helpful c o r r e s p o n d e n c e .

9. See Sonenscher (1989) for a brilliantly illuminating re-reading of the language of *sans-culotterie*, not in terms of historians' interpretations of the course of the Revolution, but rather its relation to the world of artisanal labour.

10. This article deliberately focuses on male *sans-culottes*, because it is they who dominate revolutionary texts and images. The topic of female *sans-culotte* seems not to have attracted a comparable degree of attention, except in so far as female participation in revolutionary political culture was seen as anomalous. The subject requires further enquiry.

11. As yet, I have not located any images which explicitly incorporate the *bonnets de laine*.

12. Indeed, as Raymonde Monnier has shown, in 1791 the faubourg was less actively at the forefront of organized public political action, rather than spontaneous protest, than in the early days of the Revolution. For example, in elections in June 1791, voting turn-out in the faubourg was relatively low compared to other areas of Paris, and the general tenor of the participation in the new revolutionary political culture was still predominantly bourgeois, and did not involve any organized popular militancy (1981: 120).

13. For detailed explorations of the complexities of the Revolutionary lexicon, see the exemplary studies that make up the *Dictionnaire des usages socio-politiques (1770–1815)*, (1985–88).

14. See *Essai sur la méthode à employer pour juger les ouvrages des beaux-arts du dessin, et principalement ceux qui sont exposés au Salon du Louvre, par une société d'artistes* (Paris, 1791), pp. 7–8), cited in Bordes (1985: 73). Lynn Hunt notes a similar example of this in July 1793 applied by Fouché to times when 'liberty was in danger' (*Archives parlementaires de 1787 à 1860*, dir. I. Maridal, E. Laurent first series (1787–99), vol. 68: 73, cited in Hunt (1984: 101). This could be seen as a dramatic, newly politicized version of the idea of special cultural events as exceptional moments of class

convergence. On the example of the Salon as a pre-revolutionary site for the symbolic reconciliation of social difference, see Wrigley (1993: 88–90).

15. For later development of this discourse, see Muller (2000: 93–112).
16. The literature on this occasion is summarized in David Dowd (1948: 48–54) and bibliography, and Tourneux (1890–1913: vol. 2).
17. Brissot explained the cohesive role played by 'l'enthousiasme qu'a inspiré cette cérémonie aux amis de la liberté et au peuple' (*Patriote françois*, 13 July 1791, no. 703: 50).
18. In Fontenai's *Journal général de France*, the word 'burlesque' is also used to describe the occasion, suggesting that it would have provided Rabelais with ample matter for a new chapter to add to his account of the exploits of Gargantua and Pantagruel (16 July 1791, no. 166: 692).
19. Significantly, when reprinted in Villette references to *bonnets rouges* were edited out (for example, 1792: 182), presumably so as to minimize what might have retrospectively appeared as the progressive intervention of militant *sans-culottes* and Jacobins for whom the *bonnet rouge* had, by this date, become a rallying sign.
20. This was the paper of the Cercle social, of which the 'Amis de la Vérité' was the public manifestation (Andress 2000: 121). Hence, this would seem to be a self-congratulatory reference to a group of the Cercle's adherents. On the Cercle social, see Kates (1985).
21. During the Revolution, inscribing headgear is a recurrent enunciatory device. On 22 prairial an III, demonstrators from the faubourg Saint-Antoine wrote on their hats 'du pain et la constitution démocratique de 1793' (Schmidt, 1867–71, vol. 2: 343).
22. On the *forts de la halle* as *les aînés de la Révolution* (the elders of the Revolution), see *Arch. Parl.*, vol. 44: 551–2. In an address to the Assemblée on 4 June 1792 by a deputation of *forts*, it was proposed that, at the head of the army, *l'arche sainte de la loi* be carried by the *forts*, in the manner of the Hebrews. The term 'les aînés de la liberté' was also used in a description of a banquet on the Champs Elysées, 25 March 1792, where *Vainqueurs de la Bastille* fraternized with *forts* (*Courrier des LXXXIII Départements*, n. 26, 26 March 1792: 409, and n. 28, 28 March 1792: 440–1, and suite, n. 29, 29 March 1792: 458). Once again, we find the celebration of an inversion of power relations in the celebration of: *cette classe si dénigrée de l'ancien régime, et traitée de bonnets de laine et de sans-culotte, sous le nouveau*. On the close-knit community of the forts, see Garrioch (1986: 119, 124, 253).
23. Working clothes had been an element in *ancien régime* ceremonies

such as the laying of the foundation of Ste Geneviève 1764, which included masons wearing jackets, aprons, and white stockings, their hats decorated with ribbons and cockades; see Gruber (1972: 28).

24. This remains the case later, as in the the use of costume associated with defunct *corps de métiers* as part of a carnivalesque festival procession which also included religious dress, adopted so as to provide a parodic spectacle. See Pellegrin (1989b: 125–6) on a festival at Poiteirs on 20 frimaire an II (10 December 1793).

25. In his next issue he reported that they were to have their uniforms paid for, but that they resented this, preferring to pay for themselves (n. 106, 16–23 July 1791: 90).

26. Lafayette was the head of the Garde nationale. *Révolutions de Paris*, 15 brumaire an II [5 November 1793], n. 214, p. 77–8, cit. Devocelle (1988, vol. 1: 77–8).

27. *Aristocrate* was an all-purpose pejorative term for counter-revolutionaries.

28. Mercier also noted amongst the 'bataillons populaires' 'les charbon-niers qui n'avaient pour armes que leurs bâtons, et pour drapeau qu'un sac à charbon attaché au bout d'un gourdin' (Bonnet *et al.* (eds) 1994: 152).

29. On the representation of work and workers, see Milliot (1995); Proust (1973: 65–85); Sewell Jr, in Kaplan and Knoepp (eds), (1986: 258–86).

30. On the *bonnet rouge*, see Wrigley (1997), Pfeiffer (1912).

31. See also 'Fameuse journée du 20 juin 1792', in *Révolutions de Paris*, n. 134: 348, with caption 'Réunion des citoyens du faubourg St Antoine et St Marceau allant à l'assemblée nationale présenter une pétition et de suite une autre chez le Roi'.

32. Twiss's observation fits with the point made by Jones and Spang, drawing on Roche's analysis of popular dress before the Revolution (1981: 189), that the artisans, shopkeepers, servants, and petty officials who made up the social core of revolutionary *sans-culottes*, in fact tended to wear breeches rather than *pantalon* (1999: 47).

33. 'Les citoyens du faubourg St-Antoine et St-Marcel chez le Roi, lui font une pétition, Louis 16 prend un bonnet rouge et le met sur sa tête en criant vive la Nation et buvant à la santé des sans-culottes', *Révolutions de Paris*, no. 154: 554, BNF – HC: t. 127, no. 11176, Qb20 juin 1792; 59.B.23615. Similarly, Fontenai encapsulated the significance of the day as one of a simple, lamentable conflict: 'On a vu les Sans-Culottes lutter contre leur Roi constitutionnel, et l'assiéger dans son château avec des piques et des canons' (*Journal*

général, 21 June 1792: 698).

34. Other versions give 'le peuple est las de souffrir' ([Weston] 1793: 33). An alternative way of reading the incident is that this brandishing of a *culotte*, was intended as a satire on the status quo, using the association of *culottes* with respectability and therefore authority, that is to say recalling with the essential meaning of *sans-culotte*. Indeed, perhaps one could see this latter reading as consistent with the cultural trope of the 'battle of the trousers', shifted from a matter of domestic conflict to the public political arena.

35. As noted by Leith (1990) and Geffroy (1988), a fascinating example of iconographical euphemism is Villeneuve's print, *L'Amour sans culotte* (Cabinet des Estampes, Bibliothèque Nationale de France, Paris: QB1 10 Novembre 1793, ill. Geffroy 1988: 593). This shows a pair of culottes hoist on an arrow by a winged cupid who wears a liberty cap. The image has the motto: 'Quand l'amour en bonnet se trouve sans culotte, la liberté lui plaît il en fait sa marmotte.'

36. On this phenomenon, see Stallybrass and White (1986) and de Baecque (1993: 303–74).

37. 'Costume Républicain (de Sans-culotte), adopté, proposé & dessiné par Sergent, Député de Paris à la Convention Nationale. Ce costume n'est autre chose que l'habit journalier des Hommes de la campagne et des Ouvriers des villes, il n'y auroit de différence entre les Citoyens que dans la qualité des Etoffes. Toutes les articulations ne sont plus gênées par des attaches; il est de forme demi-circulaire, et se jette sur les bras ou les épaules.'

    'Il pourroit n'être porté qu'à 21 ans, âge où les Citoyens commencent à exercer leurs droits, et tiendroit lieu de la Robe Virile des Romains. Ce Dessin à l'aquarelle porte 12 po. de large, sur 14 de haut' (*Description des ouvrages de peinture, sculpture, architecture et gravure exposés au Sallon du Louvre, par les artistes composans la Commune générale des Arts, le 10 Août 1793, l'An 2e de la République Française, une et indivisible* [n.d.]): 18–19). The drawing is lost.

38. P.F.N. Fabre d'Eglantine, *Rapport fait à la Convention nationale . . . au nom de la Commission chargée de la confection du calendrier* [24 October 1793], cited in Guillaume (ed.) (1984: 704), cited in Sonenscher (1991: 115).

39. The Section du Jardin-des-Plantes changed to its name to 'des Sans-culottes' on 13 August 1792; it reverted to its original name on 10 ventôse an III / 8 February 1795. A decree of 7 fructidor an III / 24 August 1795, replaced *sans-culottides* by *jours complémentaires*. In

the royalist press, the term's currency was acknowledged through bitter parody; for example, after 10 August 1792, the *Gazette de Paris* created the euphemistic neologism 'invêtus salariés' (Condart 1995: 298).

40. See *L'Ordre de la marche de la fête qui aura lieu décadi prochain 10 nivose, l'an 2e de la République une et indivisible, en mémoire des armées françaises, et notamment à l'occasion de la prise de Toulon*: 1.

41. For example, when Chenard sang the *Marseillaise* in the Convention and also at place Louis XV in 1793, he is noted as having worn a *carmagnole* and clogs (Ch. Moisset in *Dictionnaire de Biographie française*, vol. 8: 223–6).

42. Chabot is shown wearing a *bonnet rouge*, but not *pantalon* in 'La balance des abus' (described in *Journal de Paris* 23 April 1792), ill. Langlois (1988: 216–17, 247).

43. On Granet, see Pellegrin (1989b: 97). Granet was sufficiently notorious to have been drawn in one of Lesueur's gouaches (Musée Carnavalet, Paris). On Thibaudeau, see Pellegrin (1989b: 175).

44. By contrast, when Chabot was *en mission* in Amiens, he addressed the people from the cathedral pulpit 'coiffé d'un énorme bonnet rouge' (Vicomte de Bonald 1908: 202–3, where he gives as his sources histories of Amiens by Dussenval and Calonne).

45. No directly contemporary source has ever been cited to back up the claim that the duc d'Orléans wore *sans-culotte* costume. The only source for this seems to be Madame Tussaud's memoirs, which, if reliable, indicate that, at a date left imprecise, he adopted a more chic alternative to *sans-culotte* costume proper: 'a short jacket, pantaloons, and a round hat, with a handkerchief worn sailor fashion loose round the neck, with the ends long and hanging down . . . the hair cut short without powder *à la* Titus, and shoes tied with string' (1838: 177, cited in Ribeiro 1988: 85). The representation of a similar kind of outfit in an anonymous print from 1790, *Hommage à la Constitution* (Musée de la Révolution française, Vizille, 1984–87) suggests that Mme Tussaud's recollections relate to a period before that characterized by *sans-culotterie* (Jourdan 1995: 505). Other connections of the duc to revolutionary dress include his having sent his sons in Garde nationale uniform to meetings of the St Roch district (Quicherat 1879: 626). In a letter (24 March 1792) from the comte de Fersen to the king of Sweden, the duc d'Orléans and his sons were described as having walked beneath the king's window in the Tuileries wearing *bonnets rouges* (Gazeau de Vautibault and H. Daragon, *Les Orléans au tribunal de l'histoire*, 7 vols (1888–1892),

vol. 5: 135–8, cited in La Marle1989: 628–9).

46. Although these examples would seem to go against Geffroy's assertion that 'aucun parlementaire ne s'est, sous la Révolution, présenté dans le 'sanctuaire des lois' en pantalon', she is surely correct to make the point that when individuals are accused of wearing *sans-culotte* costume in the Convention, we should probably take this to mean that they were 'mal vêtu' (poorly dressed), rather than kitted out with *bonnet rouge, pantalon,* and *carmagnole* (1985: 167). Pellegrin notes the vestimentary anbivalence evident in the inventory of Saint-Just's effects, which included trousers in blue cloth and white silk, several *culottes*, a *bonnet de police*, and a number of hats (1989b: 160–1).

47. On the alignment of a repugnant form of politics with a dirty, ugly body and dress, see de Baecque (1988: 61–70).

48. The reports were published by Caron (1910–64). On the mindset and bureaucratic procedures exemplified by these reports see Cobb (1970: 3–48).

49. This mode of description can be found beyond such official realms; for example, the journal *Le Babillard, journal du Palais royal et des Thuileries* (June–October 1791), which employs almost exactly the same style of picking out both exemplary and dubious public speakers, though driven by a hard-edge constitutionalist outlook. Meticulous scrutiny of dress had become a widespread skill, driven by uncertainty as much as suspicion, and the urgent need to know what socio-political identity lay behind visible outer layers. The journal's aim was 'répandre les principes de la constitution, inspirer le respect pour les lois, faire connoître l'opinion publique, démasquer les factieux de tous les partis' (*Prospectus*, pp. 1–2).

50. As Devocelle has noted, during this period, the ensemble was rarely visible in its totality in the street and in assemblies (1991: 314). Devocelle analyses this point more fully in his mémoire de maîtrise (1988: 76–81).

51. '[O]n peut aujourd'hui s'habiller décemment même avec goût; plus de bonnets rouges, plus de tutoiement affecté; on peut aller aux spectacles, et chez les filles, sans y être insulté par les sans-culottes ou par les satellites de l'armée révolutionnaire' ('Extrait d'une lettre de la frontière, en date du 29 mai 1794', in Browning (ed.) (1885: 364). See also a text from April 1794: 'Le luxe n'est point le goût, et en dépit des pantalons, des bonnets rouges, des cheveux coupés et des moustaches, il est permis à des républicains de porter d'élégants culottes, des chapeaux d'une forme heureuse, une chevelure ou brille

la main délicate et légère du perruquier' (cit. Walter 1948: 410, quoted by Ribeiro 1988: 70). The belief that *sans-culotte* costume had been a contrived vestimentary façade surfaces after Thermidor: 'distinguez donc l'homme de bien / Du paresseux et de vaurien / Et des faux patriotes! / Peuple honnête et laborieux, / Ne vous déguisez plus en gueux; / Remettez vos culottes' (A. Dauban, *Paris en 1794 et 1795* (1869): 539–40, cited in Pellegrin 1989b: 151). The second verse points out the economic drawbacks of the impoverishment of costume.

52. On the prevailing post-Thermidorian socio-political typology – largely vestimentarily cued, see Siegfried (1995: 70–84).

53. As ever, cost has, unfortunately, closed off the possibility of including a wider range of imagery, and thereby developing this aspect of the material.

54. Leith has discussed the image of the *sans-culotte*, but without paying attention to its early development (1990: 130–59).

55. Portraits of men *en sans-culotte* are almost non-existent. Certain instances are problematic. For example, the anonymous portrait (spuriously attributed to Greuze in an anecdote emanating from the family of Mme Tranchant, from whom the picture was bought in 1901), *Portrait du jeune Alloy en sans-culotte* (Musée des beaux-arts, Orléans), shows a man, traditionally identified as François Alloy, wearing a *bonnet de police*, with loose shirt and jacket with a double collar. The story that Alloy put on 'sans-culotte' costume in order to carry a message to Louis XVI at Versailles must be erroneous on the basis of chronology (the king had left Versailles in October 1789, long before the arrival of the *sans-culotte* phenomenon). For all that, there is a residual congruity with the proposed idea that the wearing of such outfit was connected to formal, official occasions. See O'Neill (1980 vol. 1: 193). I would like to thank Annie Defarges for her assistance.

56. A similar instance of this is the anonymous drawing *Sans culotte parisien* (Musée Carnavalet, Paris) (ill. Pellegrin 1989b: 164), which also has torn clothing, and a rather effete down-at-heel demeanour.

57. André Saintanac, a surgery pupil, interrogated by the Tribunal révolutionnaire on 5 Prairial an II was cleared of any connection to aristocratic gatherings, 'mais a reconnu qu'en badinant avec une femme de la section des Lombards sur le mot sans-culotte, il avait été arrêté par le comité de cette section' (Tuetey 1890–1914 vol. 9: n. 2325).

-3-

Subjects into Citizens: The Politics of Clothing in Imperial Russia

Christine Ruane

In December 1701 Peter the Great, tsar of Russia, issued the following decree:

> . . . all residents of the city of Moscow including those serfs who come to the city to trade, but excluding the clergy and agricultural laborers, must wear German dress. Outerwear must consist of French or Saxon coats, and underneath men must wear camisoles [sleeved vests], breeches, boots, shoes, and German hats. And they must ride in German saddles. Women of all ranks – women of the clergy, wives of officers, musketeers, and soldiers – and their children must wear German dress, hats, skirts, and shoes. From this day forward no one will be allowed to wear Russian dress, Caucasian caftans, sheepskin coats, pants, or boots, nor will anyone be permitted to ride in Russian saddles. Finally, artisans will not be allowed to make or trade [in these goods]. (Polnoe 1830: 4: 182)

With these words Peter began nothing less than a cultural revolution in his realm, the impact of which was still being felt 200 years later when the Romanov dynasty collapsed in 1917. Peter's sartorial revolution began as a revolution from above. This eighteenth-century Russian tsar imposed his will upon his *subjects* who would not become *citizens* until the twentieth century. Yet, what started as an imperial command in 1701 became part of a genuine cultural revolution from below in the nineteenth century. All Russians, including the peasants who had been specifically excluded in Peter's decree, appropriated European fashions and ethnic costume to fashion new identities for themselves. By providing greater choices in clothing this democratization of male and female dress allowed Russians of all ranks to participate in the movement away from an autocratic social, cultural and political system toward a more democratic one. In other words, Peter's sartorial revolution helped to facilitate

Russians' transformation from subjects into citizens during the early years of the twentieth century.

Peter the Great's Sartorial Revolution from Above

The inhabitants who lived within the boundaries of the Muscovite state at the end of the seventeenth century came from a number of ethnic and racial groups and their clothing reflected that cultural diversity. Tatars, nomadic peoples of Siberia, Ukrainians, Poles, and Lithuanians, each with their own culture and costume, found themselves subjects in the Russian Empire. But even those people who inhabited the Russian heartland were descendants of a number of Slavic and Finnish tribes which all had their own distinct form of dress. Thus, the clothing worn in Muscovy represented a number of sartorial systems whose purpose was to identify individuals by marking their ethnicity, religion, gender, and place of residence within the Muscovite realm.

All of this changed with Peter the Great. As a child, the future tsar became entranced with the motley group of Western European mercenaries and artisans who inhabited the 'German' or foreign quarter in Moscow. It was there that the tsar became acquainted with Western technology, dress, and manners. One of Peter's first acts as tsar was to take an extended trip to the German states, the Netherlands, England, and France in 1697 to see the wonders of Europe for himself. Peter returned from this trip a 'true believer' in the superiority of Western technology and culture, determined that he would make Russia a member of that wider world of European military power and culture.

One important way to achieve his goal was to make European clothing the dress code of Russian politics and business, which is precisely what he did in 1701. Peter understood that in order for his subjects to become Europeans, before they could absorb the technology, let alone the European cultural world, first they had to look the part. Peter's dress reform replaced the loose, flowing garments of Muscovy with clothes that hugged and revealed the body. Men wore breeches, vests, and tight-fitting coats. Women bared their bosoms and replaced their elaborately decorated headdresses with wigs. These new clothes became the 'uniform' for all men and women at any court or government function.

Practically overnight, Peter the Great changed the visual landscape of Russia in complex ways. Those who supported Peter wore European fashions and saw themselves as progressives in the fight against ignorance, superstition, and backwardness. European clothing served as a symbol of the monarchy's commitment to modernization defined as Westernization. Those who harbored a mistrust of Peter and his policies refused to wear the new clothes and were quickly banned from court. From the very beginning of Peter's sartorial revolution, European fashions became linked with the concepts of modernity and progress. Wearing Russian or any other kind of non-European clothing came to represent traditional, pre-modern attitudes. This split between Russian tradition and Western modernity created a fissure in Russian life for it meant that 'progress' or 'modernity' could only be seen as foreign and not as a Russian product. No better symbol of this fissure could be found than the creation of two sartorial systems within the Russian empire.

At the same time, Peter introduced a new gender order into Russia, one imported from Western Europe as well. The court became a site for new forms of sociability. Prior to the eighteenth century Muscovite courtiers had been segregated by gender for much of the day. Now male and female members of the aristocracy gathered together to play cards, dance, and gossip. These new forms of sociability allowed both men and women greater freedom to interact with one another thereby changing social expectations for both sexes. Thus, European dress became a key way of separating 'liberated' aristocrats from those who held to the old gender norms. Once the monarchy fashioned for itself a European image and lifestyle, the nobility had no choice but to accede to the new cultural politics or lose its own social power and status.

Having reorganized court life, Peter encouraged the nobility to build European-style palaces replete with European furniture, carriages, and gardens. Russian dress seemed out of place in such settings, so all government servitors from the highest to the lowest now had to abandon their traditional forms of dress. Government officials designed Western-style uniforms for servants to the court, civil servants, and members of the Russian military. By creating a uniform for all levels of service that carefully delineated rank within government service, the Russian government spread the influence of these new clothes beyond Russia's elite living in the two capital cities. As the Russian nobility began to build European dwellings in the countryside, following the lead of the court, they brought European furniture and fashions with them, thereby exposing Russian provincials, both nobles and peasants, to the new cultural and gender order (Hughes 1998: 186–202 and 248–97; Roosevelt 1995).

Peter's successors continued his cultural revolution. The Russian court became known for its extravagant displays of wealth and privilege, which became part of the monarchy's attempt to secure its own power and prestige (Wortman 1995). The emperors and empresses introduced the latest fashions into Russia through their attention to dress. Empress

Elizabeth, Peter's daughter, was reported to have 15,000 dresses in her closet on the day she died in 1762. These government expenditures on luxury goods set the example, which the Russian nobility tried to emulate. Eighteenth-century men and women shared a love of adornment. Both sexes spent a great deal of money and time acquiring the latest fashions and accessories to dress *comme il faut*. Because both sexes were spending such large sums of money on dress, in 1782 Catherine the Great created new court uniforms, which were supposed to discourage some of this extravagance. Men's uniforms were modelled after those worn in other European courts. Women's court uniforms combined design elements of the Russian sarafan, a kind of jumper, and the exceptionally long sleeves typical of Muscovite female dress with European high fashion. Female courtiers were also required to wear Russian-style headdresses. The resulting confection was called 'Russian' court dress and was worn by all women at court until the end of the dynasty in 1917 (Shepelev 1991: 185–9).

Catherine's reform of women's court dress indicates a significant shift in the government's dress code inherited from Peter. Up until the late eighteenth century, there were two styles of dress – European and Russian. Uncomfortable with this rather sharp division, the government intended women's court dress to represent visually an imperial synthesis of Western technology and culture with Russian might and ambition, so the gowns combined Western and Russian design elements into a harmonious whole. Thus, the dresses served as a visual symbol of deeper abstract forces at work. The government hoped to create a thoroughly Westernized court, but one that was still Russian at the same time. It was an attempt to imbue European culture with a Russian sensibility. It is also important to note that it was women courtiers who reflected this new synthesis. Men's uniforms were not redesigned – they were supposed to look completely Europeanized. It was women's bodies which were intended to represent national identity and thereby heal the social and cultural breach created by Peter the Great.

The Democratization of Dress in Russia

Cultural historians have remarked upon a phenomenon that occurred in nineteenth-century Europe, which they have labelled the democratization of dress (Roche 1994; Perrot 1994). Inexpensive textiles, the invention of the sewing machine and proportional systems of measurement created a ready-to-wear fashion industry that allowed individuals outside the elite to buy cheap copies of *haute couture*. Around the same time, the rise of romantic nationalism across Europe fostered contradictory impulses in terms of dress and fashion. On the one hand, intellectuals in their efforts to articulate their ethnic identity romanticized 'the people', a process that included attempts to catalogue and preserve ethnic dress. The common man and woman were expected to preserve those customs and qualities that made each ethnic group unique. On the other hand, 'the people' were abandoning ethnic dress in favor of cheap fashions that permitted them greater social mobility and freedom. Thus, the democratization of dress, however incomplete and contradictory, was a key component in the development of nationalist and democratic politics in nineteenth-century Europe.

In Russia, this process of democratization took place in many over-lapping stages, but it began with nationalism. In the late 1820s and 1830s Tsar Nicholas I attempted to use the rhetoric of romantic nationalism to serve the cause of preserving the autocracy. 'Official Nationality' based upon the principles of Orthodoxy, autocracy, and nationality became the ideology that guided Nicholas and his government. And while Nicholas' formulation of romantic nationalism rejected democratic politics as its goal, it did call for a rethinking of what it meant to be Russian (Riasanovsky 1959; Wortman 1995: 247 and 277).

Nicholas's call to define 'Russianness' did not remain confined to government circles, but the educated Westernized elite participated in these discussions as well. Thoroughly Europeanized in outlook, dress, and lifestyle, these men and women were the heirs of Peter's cultural revolution. By the early decades of the nineteenth century, Peter's cultural heirs had become uncomfortable with their cultural isolation from the bulk of the Russian population. One writer characterized the split between the elite and the peasantry in rather dramatic terms:

> In order to understand the truth, it is necessary only to look at the poor, half-wild existence of this country's inhabitants where no industrial development has penetrated, and, then, at the contented and luxurious life of the government where manufacturing and trade flourish. On the one side, poverty and none of life's necessities; on the other, a contentment with everything and even superfluous luxury; there, rank coarseness and ignorance; here, civility, education, refined taste, and politeness . . . in short, there stands a rough son of wild Mother Nature and here stands an educated citizen of civilized society. (*Opisanie* 1829: 28 and 32–3)

Thus, a growing number of educated Russians felt a pressing need to discuss their alienation from their ethnic heritage and the majority of the population.

Writers were some of the earliest intellectuals to take up the question of Russian identity. During the 1820s and 1830s, the society tale became a popular genre (Shephard 1981: 111–62). Primarily tales of love and seduction, the action in these stories takes place at the balls, salons, and spas of Russia's Westernized elite. The society tales, which were very popular, publicized the manners and mores of the elite for those who lived outside of that charmed circle, but who wanted to imitate the lifestyle of their social betters. At the same time, writers such as Alexander Pushkin and Mikhail Lermontov criticized the shallowness of high society, which often manifested itself as a preoccupation with European finery. The male protagonists were portrayed as dandies who amused themselves gambling and dueling, while their female counterparts were completely absorbed with shopping, fashion, and illicit love affairs. The narrator in one society tale made a fairly typical observation: 'In the old wooden shopping arcades there were crowds of ladies every day; the merchants displayed the *most fashionable* gauzes and other materials; the ladies of all ages appeared at each new ball in new gowns with fancy new bits' (Gan 1996: 7, emphasis in original). Many writers and intellectuals were troubled that this glittering world of Russian high society came at a very high price. The backbreaking labour of Russian serfs, the Russian 'people', provided the financial resources upon which this world was built. Those who could afford fancy French fashions depended upon the labour of those dressed in Russian peasant dress.

The critique found in these tales laid the foundation for a full-blown public debate about the impact of Westernization upon Russian national identity in the late 1830s. Unhappy with the government's programme of Official Nationality, which continued to foster this artificial divide between an Europeanized elite and a tradition-bound peasantry, two groups of thinkers proposed radically different plans for healing the breach in Russian society. The first group called themselves Westernizers. As the name suggests, they believed that Russia's path to greatness lay in the continued influx of Western European ideas and technology into Russian life. In contrast to the government's view, the Westernizers proposed that modernization should not be confined to the elite, but should benefit Russians of all social ranks. They openly argued for a more democratic form of political life in Russia. The second group was labeled Slavophiles. They argued that it was precisely Peter's reforms that were preventing Russia from realizing her own national destiny which was distinct from that of Western Europe. Peter's reforms had cut Russia off from all of those qualities that had made her great. The Slavophiles strove to define a romantic nationalism which healed the breach between the elite and the peasantry by emphasizing those qualities that they believed made Russia a unique and distinctive civilization.

These debates raged in the salons and the press, but clothing also played a role. One of the Slavophiles, Konstantin Aksakov, began wearing Russian dress to the soirees that he attended to demonstrate his rejection of Westernization and his solidarity with 'the people'. In fact, Aksakov's attire made him the butt of jokes (Walicki 1989: 238). Nevertheless, elite men's choice of Russian dress came to be seen as a form of political protest by violating the government-mandated dress code for state and social occasions, and more importantly, by rejecting government spons-ored modernization in favour of Russian social cohesiveness. This act of male sartorial defiance became a potent symbol which other prominent intellectuals used during the nineteenth century. The art critic, Vladimir Stasov, who tried to popularize Russian folk art, appeared at social gatherings dressed in ethnic costume. But perhaps the most famous individual to abandon European dress was Leo Tolstoy. His decision to wear peasant clothing publicized his rejection of what he felt was the hypocrisy and dissolution of aristocratic life, and his embrace of the truly noble life of ordinary Russian peasants.

Elite women also used ethnic dress to claim a limited political role for themselves. In 1855 Russia went to war with Turkey who in turn called upon France and Great Britain to help defeat the Russians. During the Crimean War Russian noblewomen abandoned their French fashions and began to wear Russian dress to public gatherings. They selected these clothes to express their patriotism and solidarity with the Russian war effort. A government apologist, Nikolai Grech, quickly criticized elite women's 'misguided' patriotism and demanded that they resume wearing European dress. He stated categorically that a Russian sarafan should not be worn in society. This mixing of symbols from European and Russian cultures was anathema:

> Jumping around during a polka or waltzing in the style of dress of the empress Natal'ia Kirilovna [Peter the Great's mother who lived during the seventeenth century] is absurd and funny . . . Wear sarafans and ribbons only when they suit you and to please your husbands. But do not think that patriotism consists of this: a beautiful hat interferes with healthy thoughts and a French corset stifles a Russian heart. ('Kostium' 1856: 114)

In other words, for the elite, clothing no longer served as a marker of ethnic identity. Those qualities which identified aristocratic men and women as Russians resided in their hearts and souls, not in their clothing.

By the middle of the nineteenth century, ethnic dress appeared completely out of place at elite gatherings. While wearing Russian dress in polite society remained a potent political symbol for both government supporters and detractors, most Russians rejected it as too radical a step. As elsewhere in Europe, the trend was for ordinary Russians who stood outside of the elite to copy the dress and manners of the Westernized aristocracy. Their sartorial emancipation meant that it was no longer possible to judge as easily a person's place in society by their clothing. The gulf between the elite and 'the people' had begun to break down. But, nationalist concerns accompanied this social anxiety. Government assurances to the contrary, how could Russians be Russian if they wore copies of Parisian *couture*? Peter's original plan was for the peasantry to preserve ethnic identity in dress, but as the impact of Westernization spread to the countryside, this became increasingly untenable. It was these social and national anxieties that preoccupied Russians as they tried to create a modern society.

The Sartorial Transformation of Russian Cities

The first phase of this democratization occurred in Russia's urban centers. Prior to the nineteenth century, Russian cities were little more than administrative and military outposts, but as the empire expanded both territorially and commercially, the pace of urbanization quickened. A new social phenomenon appeared, the *raznochintsy*. These individuals were the descendants of priests, bureaucrats and others who had achieved an education and found employment as writers, doctors, lawyers and teachers. Joined by businessmen, they became the core of a new urban middle class. Because the 'uniform' for government and business was European dress, anyone who wanted to work in Russian cities found that they needed to dress accordingly. People of the middle ranks – professionals, businessmen, and minor government clerks – needed well-tailored garments in order to advance their careers, but they frequently found that their meager wages did not permit them to spend much money on clothes.

Once again, it was Russia's writers who captured the plight of these men and women. The literature from the 1830s and 1840s is filled with individuals of modest means trying to improve their station in life only to be thwarted by their inelegant clothing and financial insecurity. The best example comes from Nikolai Gogol's famous short story, 'The Overcoat'. The hero, Akaky Akakievich, was a reclusive government scribe who was not promoted due to his rather peculiar habits of dress and manner. According to Gogol:

[Akaky] never gave a thought to his clothes. His frock coat, which was supposed to be green, had turned a sort of mealy reddish . . . And, somehow, there was always something stuck to Akaky Akakievich's frock coat, a wisp of hay, a little thread. Then, too, he had a knack of passing under windows just when refuse happened to be thrown out and as a result was forever carrying around on his hat melon rinds and other such rubbish. (Gogol 1960: 71)

Because of his irregular dress, Akaky's more sophisticated co-workers tease him mercilessly and he remains stuck in a dead-end job. Tired of walking around in a threadbare coat, which does not keep him warm, Akaky decides to order a fashionable overcoat from a local tailor, but the garment worker makes him a new coat with a collar of cat fur! Akaky's laughable attempts to improve his wardrobe make him a celebrity at the office, but he mistakes his popularity for a belief that his life has changed for the better. His luck quickly changes. His coat is stolen which leads to a mental and physical breakdown. The clerk soon died but his spirit haunted those who had made his life so miserable.

In this story, Gogol lays bare the intimate connection between elegant clothing and social advancement. Akaky's uncouth appearance makes him a marginal figure both at work and on city streets; no one notices him except to snicker. In order to be seen and taken seriously, Akaky tries to improve his appearance through his purchase of an overcoat, but even though he spends his entire savings, he cannot afford real luxury or elegance. Gogol deftly illustrates the social anxiety that many Russians of the middle ranks felt as they tried to imitate the dress and manners of polite society. The story also makes clear that by the 1840s when Gogol published his story, European fashions had become *de rigeur* for all inhabitants of Russia's cities, not just high government officials and nobles.

It is also no coincidence that Gogol's hero is male. During the first half of the nineteenth century, men were just as preoccupied with their attire as women were or perhaps even more so. Because professional and social advancement depended upon good grooming and attention to dress, men who wanted to succeed needed to pay close attention their self-image. Gogol suggests that an individual's abilities to work hard mattered less in the Russian bureaucracy than personal appearance and deportment. And while Akaky's concerns with purchasing a new overcoat may appear silly or unmanly to modern readers, his very livelihood depended upon the creation of a new image for himself. For Russian men with families to support, clothing expenditures were not luxuries but rather essential expenditures.

Gogol's hero had to seek his revenge as a ghost for there was little opportunity for protest of any kind in autocratic Russia. And yet, the Westernized aristocracy joined by the newly emerging middle class became increasingly restive in the nineteenth century. Tired of leading circumscribed lives in an autocratic state, in the late 1850s and early 1860s a group of young Russians fashioned a more active role for themselves. Called Nihilists by their elders, they demanded active lives devoted to scientific inquiry and helping 'the people'. To signal their emancipation, they abandoned the elegant manners and costume of their parents in favor of greater simplicity. Nihilist women cut their hair, wore unadorned woollen dresses, smoked cigarettes and looked at the world through blue-tinted spectacles. Men, too, grew careless in their dress. This defiant rejection of their parents' values sent shock waves through Russian society. Taking their cue from Aksakov and the Slavophiles, the Nihilists chose to shock through their choice of clothing, but this time they used Western dress instead of ethnic costume. They created new identities for themselves by reordering elements of European dress. What they came up with was a look that had been created by bohemians and intellectuals in Western Europe. Nevertheless, this radicalism in dress, this anti-fashion statement, shocked polite society in Russia as it had done in Western Europe.

Nihilism marked an important moment in the history of clothing and political protest in Russia (Brower 1975). Russian social and political activism now had a uniform just like other forms of public service. Those who committed themselves to transforming Russia abandoned fashion, making their protest against injustice visible on their bodies. These simply dressed men and women contrasted sharply with government courtiers and military officers who continued to wear brilliantly coloured and highly decorated uniforms. As Nihilism evolved into different forms of political radicalism, all members of the Russian revolutionary underground signalled their rejection of society by adopting some form of this radical uniform. For the revolutionaries, sartorial splendor now came to be associated with moral, economic and political corruption.

The Nihilists' defiant rejection of elegant clothing served as a model for other groups to follow for it showed how fashion could be manipulated not just by the government or the aristocracy, but by all social groups who were interested in creating a new self image. One such group was the Russian bourgeoisie. The sartorial habits of this new class were varied, reflecting the social complexity of this new class. A portion of the bourgeoisie wanted to flaunt its new wealth by mimicking the lifestyles and dress of the aristocracy. These men and women tried to break into high society through ostentatious displays of wealth and luxury. Some members of the aristocracy merely laughed at the *nouveau riche*. Nevertheless, these transgressions caused consternation; the boundaries between these two groups were proving to be rather porous. Other middle-class types who could not afford *haute couture* tried to make a virtue out of a necessity. They rejected the ornamentation of government uniforms and favored instead dark suits, white shirts and ties. Females followed French fashion, but modestly and with understated taste. No longer content to mimic the aristocracy or follow government orders, the Russian middle class tried to create their own self-image.

Gender, too, played an important role in Russian sartorial developments in the second half of the nineteenth century. Peter the Great had introduced the European gender order into Russia, which was hailed at the time as a genuine emancipatory step, but a century later critics found it wanting. Male and female intellectuals criticized the empty lives of elite women who spent their days primping and gossiping to the detriment of their husbands and children. Some elite women longed for greater independence to lead rich and rewarding lives like their brothers and husbands. Influenced by feminists in Western Europe, Russian elite women initiated a women's movement in the mid-nineteenth century demanding the same opportunities, rights, and responsibilities as men. Because elite women's lives had long been associated with the pursuit of high fashion, many feminists sought to free themselves from fashion. They adopted the Nihilist uniform for women. By the 1890s feminists had organized a dress reform movement similar to the one which had started in Western Europe. Articles and pamphlets appeared chronicling the crippling effects of high fashion on women's bodies and spirit (Stites 1978).

Having created a place for themselves visually in the social landscape, the new bourgeoisie and the women's movement began to demand political representation within the Russian polity. No longer content to serve as government servitors, the middle ranks demanded some form of political system which could represent their particular class interests. Feminists wanted access to higher education as well as political rights. Thus, by the end of the nineteenth century, Russia had developed liberal, conservative and revolutionary political movements that gave voice to the profound social and economic transformation that the empire was experiencing.

As long as Russians had to rely on tailors and dressmakers to sew custom-made clothing, wearing European fashions was an expensive affair. By the 1870s retailers and manufacturers had created a ready-to-wear fashion industry which prided itself on the mass production of cheap copies of French fashion. There were Russian fashion magazines to publicize what was *à la mode* and boutiques, department stores and second-hand clothing markets in which to buy the clothes. The development of a domestic fashion industry was part of a larger industrialization programme that Russia was undergoing in the second half of the nineteenth century. Peasants, emancipated from serfdom in 1861, left their agricultural work and migrated to Russian cities to work in factories and artisanal workshops. While there was much poverty among these workers, there is also evidence that suggests that they gave up their homespun garments in favour of ready-to-wear fashions for themselves and their families. Just like the middle class, workers wanted to express their emerging identity as proletarians. One worker, Semen Kanatchikov, who later joined the revolutionary underground, wrote of how his new clothes helped him to think of himself as a worker:

> My struggle against 'human injustice' in no way prevented me from becoming more accomplished in the 'worldly' social graces . . . I had bought myself a holiday 'outfit', a watch, and, for the summer, a wide belt, gray trousers, a straw hat, and a pair of fancy shoes. In a word, I dressed myself up in the manner of those young urban metalworkers of that period who earned an independent living and didn't ruin themselves with vodka. (Zelnik 1986: 71)

Kanatchikov's radical politics grew out of his refashioning of himself. His growing pride in his skill as a metalworker gave him the confidence he needed to improve his social skills and appearance. Having experienced such a radical transformation personally, Kanatchikov wanted other workers to share in his upward mobility. It was this desire to improve all workers' lives symbolized by the ability to wear modern city clothes that drew him and others like him into politics.

By the early years of the twentieth century, one writer, G. Vasilich, bemoaned the visual transformation of urban spaces:

> In general in the last few years the streets of Moscow have taken on a more 'Europeanized' appearance. A kind of 'chic' has appeared among the crowds in the street whereas in old Moscow the population had no understanding of fashion. The dress and customs were regulated by tradition, daily comfort and personal choice. But, the tendency toward impersonal 'fashion', valued only because everyone follows it, is already growing with substantial progress in city life. This collective culture is leveling city dwellers by making them resemble factory-made products. Bowler hats, coats, monotonous in their black coloring – are conquering the Moscow streets. Long-waisted coats, Russian shirts, service caps and colorful shawls– all have disappeared and have gone to the suburbs. This leveling of the various strata of the city population testifies

to the general democratization of culture. Beneath the mask of imitation the yearning of the urban lower classes appears to join with the powerful flow of world culture. 'Russian dress' is worn only by the Old Believers in the eastern part of Moscow, and even there 'German dress' is sometimes worn for church services. (Vasilich 1912: 7)

Vasilich is documenting the important sartorial transformation that Russia was undergoing. Colourful peasant costumes had given way to the black coats and bowler hats of modern industrial capitalism. Dressed in basic black the bourgeoisie exhibits no individuality. There is an impersonal uniformity about them, just like the goods they manufacture. For Vasilich the rise of modern capitalism represents a clear unmitigated loss for Russia. Gone are the colour and uniqueness of Russia's former way of life. Furthermore, the middle class is joined by the lower classes who mimic the bourgeoisie in their sartorial habits and yearn to become a part of modern European culture. This social levelling is cause for concern because it blurs the boundaries between the bourgeoisie and the proletariat. Both groups have given up their Russian identity in favour of 'impersonal fashion', a situation which Vasilich like other nationalists deplores.

Sartorial Changes among the Peasantry

The problem of social levelling was more widespread than even Vasilich was willing to acknowledge. By the second half of the nineteenth century peasants were beginning to acquire a taste for European finery and this trend shocked both the government and many members of educated society who looked to the peasantry to preserve what was special and good about Russian ethnicity. The key moment in this visual transformation of the peasants was their emancipation from serfdom in 1861. The end of serfdom was a disappointment for the peasantry for it did not give them control of the land, nor did it allow them full freedom of movement with the empire. Nevertheless, the emancipation marked an important transitional moment in Russian agricultural workers' identity from serf to peasant.

In 1873 a government commission published its findings on the state of agriculture, a decade after emancipation. Local reporters who included landowners, local and state officials, priests, and teachers from the forty provinces of European Russia described conditions in their area. The vast majority of these officials commented that most peasants had begun wearing 'city clothes' – European dress, and many accused the peasants of dandyism or foppery [*shchegol'stvo*] (*Doklad* 1873: I; 225–52).

Figure 3.1. A Russian family portrait from the 1890s.

According to a Novgorod official, 'Luxury in dress is at scandalous proportions. It is not uncommon for a peasant to lay waste to his household and barn in order to buy his wife a 100 ruble dress and to clothe himself in city clothes' (*Doklad* 1873: I: 225). One reporter from Podol'sk province detailed the changes that had occurred:

> All clothes with the exception of undergarments are made from manufactured materials and cloth. Shoes are sewn to fit the foot more closely and in more attractive styles. Homemade straw hats are worn only in the hot weather; caps . . . are the usual headgear. In inclement weather a few use store-bought felt hats and in the winter sheepskin hats made from local sheep costing one ruble fifty or more. Young men wear wool ribbons in their straw hats. Ribbons are also used as neckties with turndown collars. Lately the use of vests has spread everywhere. Women wear calico skirts and aprons; traditional dress is only worn by the old women. In general, women's clothing is factory-made rather than homemade. This dandyism is particularly noticeable near the cities and

sugar factories. Peasants not only wear factory-made clothing, but they even buy linen. Practically every little trading outpost has a shop with these beautiful items. (*Doklad* 1873: I: 243–4)

It may strike modern readers as laughable that woolen ribbons, hats, and shoes could be considered foppery, but these statements indicate the deep concern that educated Russians felt about changes in peasant dress. On the one hand, peasants symbolized backwardness and ignorance, the antithesis of modern life. Indeed, Peter the Great and his successors had specifically excluded the peasantry from participating in the government's Westernization program except as bonded laborers. At the same time, this exclusion meant that the rituals of peasant life preserved Russian uniqueness. But, the emancipation inexorably changed rural life and allowed Russian peasants to begin to craft their own identities. And they did this by buying ready-to-wear garments and accessories. Just like the workers in the cities, peasants knew that by wearing city clothes they would be treated with greater respect and dignity.

Peasant demand for 'city clothes' continued unabated during the second half of the nineteenth century. Young men left the countryside to work in the urban factories and sweatshops, but they returned to their native villages to find wives. In order to be considered an eligible mate for an industrial worker, young women were expected to have dowries that included city clothes. One statistician inventoried peasant women's dowries in Moscow province. She found one which included ten stylish coats and capes made from fur, satin and other fabrics, five woolen, ten silk and twenty-five cotton dresses, forty shirts and high-quality underwear. None of this clothing was handmade, it had been purchased in Moscow. Furthermore, the lack of handmade garments meant that many women grew up without ever learning how to sew, which prevented them from making traditional costumes (Gorbunova 1882).

It is important to stress that, for the peasantry, the working class, and even the bourgeoisie the nineteenth century marked a time of transition. All of these groups were in the process of becoming distinct social classes and this transition remained uneven and incomplete. Younger peasants and workers were more likely to purchase Western dress than their elders who were reluctant to give up their old ways. Certainly peasants located hundreds of miles from the nearest town did not have ready access to European fashions. Many peasants and workers too combined ethnic and European clothing in their dress, combining a handmade shirt with factory-made trousers and cap. Others wore European fashion only on holidays and for special events. But what had happened was the desire to purchase these goods had taken hold. These new social groups were in the process of defining themselves in new terms. They saw themselves as dynamic, modern, and progressive, and they wanted their image to reflect this dynamism. Of the two sartorial systems available to them, only European clothes expressed those values, which is why peasants and workers made financial sacrifices to purchase factory-made straw hats, calico skirts, and other fashion goods. So long as Russian ethnic dress remained tied to a romantic view of the past, a past frequently defined as backward and traditional, this clothing could not represent the social aspirations of a modernizing Russian nation.

The Nationalist Response

Despite the uneven nature of these developments, the anxiety about social leveling was palpable. The transition from an agricultural to an industrial economy was a painful one which caused enormous social dislocation. By the early twentieth century, examples of this social dislocation were everywhere. Some merchants and industrialists rivaled the old aristocracy in their displays of wealth. Dripping in diamonds and furs, they flaunted their new riches at city nightspots. Working-class ruffians and prostitutes appeared on street corners and other public spaces to mock the dress and manners of respectable Russians in their own outrageous costumes (Neuberger 1993; Bernstein 1995). Peasant 'fops' came to the city on shopping sprees only to be conned into buying outdated fashions by conniving salespeople. In all of these cases, which were widely reported in the Russian news media, these individuals transgressed the boundaries of the new class society that was emerging.

The social tensions brought about by urbanization and modernization occurred at the same time as colonial expansion. In the Baltic, Russian Poland, Ukraine, and the Caucasus, the government initiated an intense Russification campaign. Russian language and culture claimed precedence over the native languages and cultures. Russians moved into areas of Central Asia previously outside of imperial control and established colonial rule over these people. This campaign had racist overtones as the Russians portrayed themselves as an enlightened force whose mission was to bring civilization to the supposedly backward and barbaric peoples of Central Asia. These colonial encounters helped to fuel a resurgence of Russian nationalism in the second half of the nineteenth century. Government administrators, ethnographers, linguists, and other scholars took great pains to identify and classify the cultural differences between Russia and her colonial subjects. Invariably, Russian culture emerged as superior to that of any of the subject peoples (Weeks 1996).

By the second half of the nineteenth century, the role of the Russian government had changed. While the government remained committed to its programme of industrialization and technological innovation, its social and political programmes reflected a growing conservatism. Faced with the enormous social dislocation which its own policies had brought about, the government refused to sanction any political changes that would have helped ease the situation. In other words, the Russian government under Alexander III and Nicholas II refused to share power with representatives of the new social system which it was responsible for creating. Despite the best efforts of the government to squelch political reform, a political opposition movement developed. This opposition movement reflected the dynamism of the new social system under construction. Liberals and revolutionaries demanded that the government begin to share political authority with them. Workers, too, began to organize trade unions and joined the revolutionary parties, all of which were illegal. Having crafted new social identities, these individuals wanted to emancipate themselves even further from government tutelage and participate in the creation of a modern Russian nation. Casting off their status as subjects, they demanded their rights and obligations as citizens.

Transgressive social behaviour, political activism and nationalist concerns about Russian identity fuelled a renewed interest in clothing as an expression of social and cultural identity. The government, concerned with the loss of Russian customs and traditions particularly among the peasantry, advocated for the first time in almost a hundred years the introduction of ethnic design elements into European clothing. While women at court continued to wear 'Russian dress' throughout the nineteenth century, men's apparel had never included native designs. In 1882, Alexander III introduced a new uniform for all Russian military forces. Since Peter the Great's dress reform, Russian army uniforms had closely resembled those worn by other European and, especially Prussian, armies. Alexander now introduced 'the Russian caftan' as part of a new look for his soldiers. This reform was intended to remind officers and soldiers alike that they were defenders of the tsar and their motherland (Shipov 1901; Glinka 1988: 86–9). In the same year, judges at a Russian industrial exhibition took up the government's campaign and chided clothing manufacturers for failing to manufacture clothing which expressed Russian national identity:

Above all, almost all of these luxury goods ... were lacking any kind of typical national characteristics and revealed themselves as slavish and insipid imitations of the tyrannical lawmakers in Paris, Vienna and other cities. Fashion and taste terrorize the elite of all European societies, but in particular the newly rich but poorly educated classes (bourgeois upstarts, *les parvenus*), who with particular cupidity throw their money after every expensive new fashion. (Bezobrazov 1884: IV: 378)

The judges claimed that Western Europeans managed to include ethnic elements in their dress; it was only Russians who failed to do so. By drawing attention to this deplorable situation, they hoped that the manufacturers would introduce folk elements into their clothes. At least then the bourgeois upstarts would look Russian!

Figure 3.2. Nicholas II dressed in the garments worn by his ancestor, Tsar Alexis for the 1903 ball at the Winter Palace.

Perhaps the most famous example of the government's attempts to manipulate the politics of clothing in Russia came during the reign of Nicholas II. The tsar, who wore Russian dress whenever he could, gave what was to be the last ball ever held in the Winter Palace in February 1903. The purpose of the ball was to mark Peter the Great's founding of St Petersburg in 1703. Nicholas personally disliked Peter and his policy of Westernization. So, rather than celebrate Peter, the tsar turned the evening into a celebration of Peter's father, Aleksei, and the Muscovite world in which he lived. Everyone invited dressed in the costumes of the seventeenth-century Muscovite court. In other words, they dressed in those clothes that Peter the Great had outlawed two hundred years earlier. The evening was a stunning success. Nicholas wore robes that had belonged to Aleksei, while the other guests wore copies of Muscovite court costume. The garments were richly embroidered and accented with fur and jewels (Ferro 1991: 34–6; Ometev and Stuart 1990: 116).

The evening was full of irony. The ball occurred in St Petersburg, Peter's window on the West, rather than in Moscow, the ancient Russian capital, where tsar Aleksei had lived. Guests supped and danced in the Winter Palace, a graceful example of Western European architecture, not in the Moscow Kremlin. Tailors and dressmakers, trained in French haute couture, attempted to create copies of Muscovite court dress. In a final twist, the tsar had invited photographers to record the brilliant evening for posterity. Using a fake background designed to resemble a Kremlin palace, the photographers snapped portraits of each guest in Muscovite regalia.

This juxtaposition of Muscovite and European elements revealed the true nature of the evening – it was a costume ball. Nicholas and his court could no longer put on Russian dress and look authentic. Two hundred years after Peter had introduced European clothing into Muscovy, Russian clothing had become costume worn only for masquerades and special national celebrations. The lives of urban Russians had become so thoroughly Europeanized that traditional Russian dress appeared out of place. Only peasants could wear traditional clothing for everyday dress, and even they were abandoning ethnic dress as well. And even though Nicholas had intended the ball to be an assertion of Russian national culture and dress, the evening demonstrated definitively the success of Peter the Great's sartorial revolution two hundred years earlier. Once the ball was over, the participants went home, took off their costumes, and dressed themselves in European fashions. These were the only clothes in which they felt truly comfortable.

The evening also served to underscore a political message. Nicholas II believed in autocracy as the only way to govern Russia. For him autocracy meant the ability to wield political power without any intervention from his subjects. Russians were to implement the imperial will, not participate in its creation. So when Nicholas stepped into his forefather's clothing and had himself photographed for posterity, it was this image of the all-powerful autocrat which he wanted to project. It was Nicholas alone who would determine Russia's path.

Nicholas' assertion of autocratic power and national pride in 1903 came too late. At the same time that he was trying to recreate himself as a Muscovite tsar, the political opposition was gaining strength. In 1903 the liberals announced the formation of the Liberation Movement whose purpose was to wrest political power from the tsar and place it in the hands of an elected parliament. Meanwhile, the revolutionary parties demanded political and social equality for all Russians. The women's movement and the nationalists also clamored for political representation. In 1905 government troops fired upon a peaceful demonstration of workers and their families. This fundamental breach of trust between the government and the people set off the Revolution of 1905. The Liberation Movement forced the government to hand over some of its power to elected representatives of the people, but this power sharing did not satisfy either side. Nicholas II continued to rule as though he were the sole source of authority, ignoring the new legislature when he felt like it. The Russian population was no longer willing to remain the passive recipients of autocratic authority, however. These men and women had fashioned a new dynamic image of themselves which reflected the complex transformation Russia had undergone in the 200 years since Peter's reforms. Instead of being satisfied by the political compromise reached in 1905, the new social classes – landowners, bourgeoisie, workers, and peasants – women, and nationalists demanded their rights as citizens to shape their own destinies. This political crisis continued unabated for twelve more years. In the end it was the Russian people who succeeded. The vast autocratic edifice came crashing down in February 1917. Russians had finally become citizens.

Conclusion

Peter the Great's dream was to make Russia into a modern European power. To achieve his goal, he initiated a series of reforms intended to begin that transformation. A central feature of Peter's programme was the introduction of European dress into Russia in 1701. Despite the importance of the tsar's decree, few scholars have attempted to understand the impact of Peter's sartorial revolution for Russian history. This essay nas tried to rectify that situation by suggesting the ways in which changes in dress were linked to the larger social and political transformation Russia was undergoing in the eighteenth and nineteenth centuries.

Socially, the introduction of European fashions facilitated the transformation of Russia from a system of estates to one of classes. The court set the tone for what was fashionable and anyone who wanted to advance had to wear the appropriate clothes. Each new class – the nobility, the bourgeoisie, the proletariat, and the peasantry – replaced its Muscovite garments with newer clothes borrowed from the West. And while there was pressure to conform to the new dress code, Russians adapted Western clothing to their particular situation. The Slavophiles, the Nihilists, bourgeois parvenus, working-class hooligans and prostitutes are all examples of how Russians learned to manipulate Western clothing to serve their own interests and to fashion new identities for themselves. These new, dynamic images gave these newly emerging classes the courage and the confidence to seek a greater role in Russian political life. Proud of whom they were, they claimed their rights as citizens to help govern the Russian state.

Peter's sartorial revolution also changed the social relations between the sexes. Dressed in clothes intended to reveal the body rather than conceal it, Peter's courtiers gathered together to dance, play cards and gossip. These innovations led to a more profound change in gender relations. First, as in Europe, men's role became increasingly involved with the public world of business and commerce whereas women's role centered on home life. Second, during the late eighteenth century men abandoned colourful, richly decorated clothing for dark suits while women's dress became increasingly more elaborate. The new domestic ideology declared that clothing was women's occupation alone; men were not to concern themselves with fashion. Despite this ideology, Russian men remained deeply concerned with dress throughout the nineteenth century primarily because their occupational and social advancement depended upon understanding the rules of good grooming and deportment. At the same time, many Russian feminists rejected the pursuit of high fashion. No longer fashionable dolls, they wanted to lead rich and full lives, but in order to do that they had to fight for political and social equality. Russian feminists joined their male counterparts in demanding a new gender order in the new Russian polity.

Finally, Peter's introduction of Western clothing facilitated a complex redefinition of Russian ethnic identity. Initially, Russians who wore French fashions and lived in opulent, Europeanized palaces felt themselves to be outsiders in their native land. But the government-led campaign to associate European culture with progress paid off. Increasingly, Russian rituals practiced only among the peasantry came to be seen as a marker of backwardness. Ethnographers, anthropologists and geographers took up the study of Russian dress and rituals. Russian folkways became the object of scientific study, not of lived experience. For city folk, Russian clothing became frozen in time, preserved in museums. The only Russians who continued to dress in traditional garb were peasants, but even they were wearing cheap copies of European fashions by the beginning of the twentieth century. Once Russian dress ceased evolving, it became costume worn only for balls or national events. Thus, what constituted ethnic identity underwent an important correction. Ethnic identity in Russia no longer depended upon a particular style of clothes. Russians could remain true to themselves because Russianness found other forms of cultural expression. And even though there were attempts to revive ethnic design elements, they ultimately failed. In the end, Peter had proved correct – a French corset could not stifle a Russian heart. Far from stifling Russians, French fashions freed them to image themselves as citizens.

−4−

Tailoring the Nation: Fashion Writing in Nineteenth-Century Argentina
Regina A. Root

Clothing has functions so apparent that they become easily dismissed, trivialized, or forgotten altogether. But the same coat that keeps out the elements can also distinguish one's social class as well as one's political affinities. In nineteenth century Argentina, several influential writers used the apparent triviality of fashion to import revolutionary ideals, using what seemed to be innocuous descriptions of clothing and fashion trends. Going far beyond the reporting of innovations in the fashion industry and the detailing of new articles of clothing, these writers imbued everything from pantaloons to petticoats with radical significance in the spectacle of an emerging public sphere.

Figure 4.1. Federalists and Unitarians dance a 'cielito' to celebrate independence from Spain.

At no time in Argentine history would the rhetorical use of fashion gain more prominence than it did during the period following independence from Spain. During this period, dress served as a way of identifying members of opposing parties at a time when the political spectrum found itself divided between two tendencies, the Unitarians and the Federalists. The Unitarians, led by the intellectual elite of Buenos Aires, looked to the institutions of Europe for a progressive and liberal design for a centralized Argentine republic. They wore the latest European fashions in hues of light blue and green. The Federalists who opposed the Unitarians, many of them landowners from outside Buenos Aires who desired the autonomy of their local leaders, sported crimson clothing. Federalist men donned moustaches and sideburns while Unitarian men sported U-shaped beards to indicate party support.

During the Federalist regime of Juan Manuel de Rosas (1829–52), light blue and green, deemed Unitarian colors, would be suspect and, ultimately, illegal. In an effort to procure order in a period of civil strife, the Rosas government implemented a series of dress and conduct codes that outlawed many of the fashions associated with the European-oriented Unitarians. By government decree, Rosas mandated that all citizens wear a crimson insignia, regardless of gender, class or race.[1] Police records from the period document the imprisonment and, in some cases, the execution of those individuals who transgressed these laws.

Icons of Federalist power so permeated the etiquette of daily living that simple gestures, such as the type of fan or vest or dinner plates used, served as indicators of partisanship, indifference or rebellious animosity. Women's gloves that revealed crimson-hued portraits of Rosas, for instance, allowed ladies to direct an admirer to kiss her extended hand *and* the dictator's face. Some men positioned political allegories inside their top hats so that, when bowing to make a formal greeting, they might display the underside of their hat and their thoughts on government. Because this canonization of taste occurred alongside the rise of feelings of nationhood, many intellectuals stressed the importance of assigning customs a pivotal role in the development of an Argentine republic.

With great ease, the writers and statesmen of the Rosas period linked the creation of uniquely Argentine customs to the goals and ideals of an emerging republic. While some argued that the collective regulation of cultural identity would ensure national stability and industrial progress, others maintained that the development of customs would elevate and renovate the character of the Nation. Some even discussed the necessity of creating a fashionable order comprised of young intellectual males. The virtuous dress of this elite, argued the editors of *El Mártir o Libre*

(*The Martyr or the Free Man*), would serve all Argentines as an archetype of moral fortitude and righteousness. Narratives on customs and the morality of dress played an important role in the configuration of a national subject.

At the same time, however, the rhetoric of fashion served as a means to defy censors and to challenge the traditional and tyrannical practices of the period. Because government censors often thwarted open political discussion, fashion emerged as a metaphor for political change and renovation. In this chapter, I will demonstrate how intellectuals of the opposition depended on a protocol of unveiling to introduce topics that, presented in any other forum, would have been censored. Using the work of Roland Barthes as a guiding thread, we will see how fashion writing served as a viable means of political protest. *La Moda* (*Fashion*) of Buenos Aires disguised its ideological leanings and patterns for national reform in the descriptions of appearance and dress. *El Iniciador* (*The Initiator*), a magazine published in Montevideo would carry on this tradition when *La Moda* was closed down in Buenos Aires. Immediately following the fall of Rosas, women writers co-opted the vocabulary of fashion previously used by their male predecessors in order to press their status as citizens and push for education reform. The female editors of *La Camelia* (*The Camellia*) embarked on an ambitious path to restructure and democratize society of the post-Rosas period, resorting to fashion description to make some of their most vital points.

Configuring the National Subject

In *The Empire of Fashion*, Gilles Lipovetsky (1994) pursues the evolution of modern democracy through the history of dress. He traces the rise of nationalist sentiments to the creation of national forms of dress in Europe of the Middle Ages. Fashion, he argues, 'helped reinforce the awareness of belonging to a single political and cultural community.' He continues:

> As a collective constraint, fashion actually left individuals with relative autonomy in matters of appearance; it instituted an unprecedented relation between individuals and the rule of society. (Lipovetsky 1994: 33)

While emerging customs seemed to grant sovereignty to the individual, they also required that the citizen relate him or herself to society at large. Lipovetsky would argue that this shift in responsibility to the individual made it possible to configure a civil and political identity for the national subject.

In nineteenth-century Latin America, the rhetoric of fashion would contribute to the creation of a national identity and the formation of a model political body. The establishment of new customs in the realm of literature, it might be argued, served as a means to liberate symbolically a pre-national subject from Spanish domination. In his article on 'Fashioning Cuba', Norman Holland has demonstrated how nineteenth-century fashion narratives played a role in constructing aesthetic and political identities in pre-Independent Cuba. Drawing from the rich descriptions of dress found in Cirilo Villaverde's *Cecilia Valdés*, Holland illustrates how portrayals of national style organized a host of characters within a framework of ethnic pride. He writes:

> Though Cuba's stratified, colonial society hardly seems to resemble the Enlightenment democracy of the European bourgeoisie, the novel's preoccupation with fashion constructs an inclusive social contract in which all participants are invited to dress and dance. (Holland 1992: 150)

While Villaverde's novel does not revolutionize the status quo of colonial Cuba, it does bind each character to specific codes of behavior and a network of national consumption, offering a presage of a national subject for independent Cuba.

Other regions of Latin America made similar calls to dress and dance, and many narratives explored the make-up of the imagined political community that was to dominate after Spanish rule.[2] Long after Independence, a newspaper published in Montevideo, Uruguay entitled *El Corsario* (*The Corsair*) summoned its Latin American readership to establish national customs in order to paint layers of distinction in a sea of confusion. When expressing its vision of young America, its editors appropriated a corporeal metaphor. In one instance, a new republic was personified as a young, independent man who had emerged from battle against Spanish domination only to realize his sad underdevelopment. 'Unfortunate days,' the Montevideo newspaper proclaimed, 'but so natural in the life of all young societies'[3] (no. 1: 1). *El Corsario* would characterize the continent as an unformed, if not malformed, body. Dispossessed of its past cultural identity, a country could not run on its military glory alone. The editors explained:

> Literature, the arts, customs are all elements that still do not figure into this body that we call society. One might say that the social body does not live but in an incomplete and mutilated state, for all its members have worked on developing one part alone: the arm. This life of action is physical and

tempestuous by nature; the life of intelligence, beautiful and tranquil, may be discovered only in the distance. (no. 1: 2)

Society, the editors argued, could lead its warriors to a peaceful existence by instituting a series of changes that aimed to decorate the body politic not with weapons but with the ornaments of progress and virtue. Such an argument no doubt also addressed the civil strife of the Rosas period. Later issues of *El Corsario* extended this analysis to the emerging Argentine nation, wrought with civil strife and stagnated by lack of direction. In a series of satirical portrayals of the Rosas regime, leading government figures appear in disheveled cloth and join the burlesque rituals of carnival. Argentina, it would seem, lacked virtuous and 'civilized' rulers.

Many writers and artists have used organic metaphors in literature and art throughout time to allude to a national body. Nicholas Mirzoeff (1995) theorizes that representations of the body politic undergo change when the citizens of a nation attempt to transform government. This modification of the state undoubtedly leads to a shift in representations of the body politic. Mirzoeff demonstrates that a regenerated body politic prominent in the visual arts represented the transformations brought about by the French Revolution. During this moment, there was a shift from the traditional representation of the state, as symbolized by the monarch, to allegorical representations depicting interacting men and women and metaphors derived from sexual reproduction. With the rise of constituency, 'the constant calls for unity which permeated the political scene were matched by an artistic effort to resolve the contradictions of the nation into one durable image' (Mirzoeff 1995: 75).

Mirzoeff expands the traditional presentation of the body politic to incorporate a theory of reception. After all, he writes, 'The involvement of the spectator is the key to successful representations of the body politic. The Body politic is after all a myth which can ultimately be sustained only by consensus' (Mirzoeff 1995: 93). The reception of changing images of the body politic played a central role in the discussion of fraternity politics during this period. He writes, 'Central to the dissemination of meaning was the incorporation of the audience in radical constructions of the state as participants in the body politic, rather than as passive spectators' (Mirzoeff 1995: 58). Mirzoeff believes the ever-transforming body politic 'became entirely dependent upon visual representation' (Mirzoeff 1995: 60). In the case of Latin America, however, we shall note that politicized images of governing bodies occurred at the level of literary representation as well.

Many of the newspapers and magazines published by the opposition during the Rosas period would highlight the need to create new customs that would allow Argentina to exude a more 'upright' cultural identity. For the most part, narratives on customs and fashion emphasized the importance of improving Argentina's moral state through dress. The pages of *El Mártir o Libre* argued that the status of nations rested on the respectability and decorum of its subjects.

> A Republic that is born into the political orbit, that begins to form its customs and its tastes, must measure the extent of its spending within the limits of its resources. Dress and the decoration of rooms are external indicators of the qualities of the people who possess them, and therefore it is all the more respectable when the magnificence of its dwellers is displayed. (no. 9: 2–3)

If the objects consumed and displayed by a nation were vested with ideological meaning, then these possessions might be used to bring together the citizens of an emerging republic in a national dress and dance. Seemingly frivolous details, whether suits or handkerchiefs, could also become symbols for status and power, which in turn promised to help the republic gain the respect of foreign nations.

The promise for national greatness depended on the moral stance upheld and disseminated by the country's leaders. Luis Saavedra, the editor of *El Grito de los Pueblos* (*The Cry of Nations*), argued that happiness and order would prevail in Argentina if the patriotic citizen realized his role in organizing the moral and political foundations of the country. Caricatures that depicted Rosas as a barbarian in farmer's wear, preparing to dissect Unitarian bodies or make unethical pacts with demonic figures, cast a dark shadow on the traditions adopted by Argentines. Saavedra proposed a more positive model for the nation. He writes,

> Good morals and honest customs are the solid foundations upon which the happiness and prosperity of a nation rests. Consequently, the governing bodies of a nation must devote themselves to the reform of vices and the domestic customs of the citizens they represent. (*El Grito de los Pueblos* 1831: 1–2)

According to Saavedra, a nation could lead its citizens to moral and economical prosperity merely by instituting a set of civil codes that exuded integrity and goodness. By establishing new customs, the national subject would embody a new spiritual ideal. If citizens adopted a set of preferences that defined them and their ideals, they would be able to correct any national flaws with ease.

La Mariposa (*The Butterfly*), a society weekly published in Monte-video, Uruguay, called on the power of narrative to help configure the national subject. Literary meditations on customs and etiquette, its editors argued, would help unravel the true character of a nation while disseminating a political agenda that promised to transform flawed communities into virtuous nations. One article entitled 'Customs' reads:

> The customs . . . of individuals from all segments of society are subject to the influence of literature. Literature is the only medium that can indicate an improvement in customs and one that can improve these customs without foregoing their purity. This is the best way to propagate knowledge and to disseminate moral and divine precepts. (no. 18: 139)

A literary work focused on the customs of a nation would benefit the nation by ascertaining strengths and by exposing moral flaws, not to mention that it promised to initiate a literature of national scope. G. P., the anonymous author of 'Customs', argued that literature had functions not unlike a hand-held mirror. It allowed the reader or the subject to assume the role of spectator, to gaze upon his own reflection and to form a judgment on the national characteristics he wished to embellish or conceal. Literature, he writes, is 'the mirror that reflects the customs and the styles of the individuals who possess them. It allows everyone to observe clearly what is ridiculous and harmful, to correct the image in the mirror and in so doing, to improve on customs' (no. 18: 138–9). If a legislator used his endowments to pass laws and change the direction of the country, then surely a writer could manifest the ideals and symbols of adornment for the nation's social body in his narrative (18: 137).

Without a doubt, many Latin American intellectuals of the nineteenth century attributed an important ideological role to narratives on customs and etiquette. The rhetoric of fashion, having initially served as a means to configure a national subject, evolved into a device used by ideologues to plot the nation's course and to disseminate progressive political agendas. In their attempt to inspire individuals and evoke images of national pride and change, some authors relied on metaphors appropriated from the realm of fashion. Fashion writing seemed tailor made for political discourse, an idea that we will explore in further detail in the following sections of this essay.

Fashion Writing

In *The Fashion System*, Roland Barthes (1967) reminds the reader that fashion writing does not simply recreate some already existing garment.

He writes that 'the function of the description of fashion is not only to propose a model which is a copy of reality but also and especially to circulate Fashion broadly as a meaning' (Barthes 1967: 10).

Barthes assigns to fashion description three more functions that are specific. The first and primary one is 'to immobilize perception at a certain level of intelligibility', that is, to filter out the static innumerable but less suitable interpretations (Barthes 1967: 13). But description does not only limit possibilities. Language can relay information about colour and spatial dimensions that a drawing or photograph simply cannot capture. Fashion writing, Barthes argues, can emphasize specific features – whether a collar or a hem line – which allows the garment to unfold in a calculated manner according to its own logic.

Barthes points out that the transition from the visual to the written is hardly seamless. The ideology of the fashion group can be found in rhetoric, emerging through the act of naming and assigning function (for instance, silk=summer). Barthes postulates that written language

> conveys a choice and imposes it, it requires the perception of this dress to stop here (i.e., neither before nor beyond), it arrests the level of reading at its fabric, at its belt, at the accessory which adorns it. Thus, every written word has a function of authority insofar as it chooses – by proxy, so to speak – instead of the eye. The image freezes an endless number of possibilities; words determine a single certainty. (Barthes 1967: 13)

The writer constructs her own garment when she assigns function and value to the otherwise neutral article. It is here that we can see that fashion itself is a carefully constructed language, tailor-made for political discourse.

Vested with the structure and authority of language, the written garment becomes a site of rhetorical connotation. Fashion exhibits 'nebulous' qualities that go beyond grammatical coherence to the core of a latent signified. Barthes helps us unveil the characteristics of this rhetorical guise inherent to the ideology of fashion. He writes:

> Connotation generally consists of masking the signification under a 'natural' appearance, it never presents itself under the species of a system free of signification; thus, phenomenologically speaking, it does not call for a declared operation of reading; to consume a connotative system (in this case the rhetorical system of Fashion) is not to consume signs, but only reasons, goals, images . . . (Barthes 1967: 231)

Because 'literature is what it signifies' (Barthes 1967: 228), fashion writing constitutes a genre that rests on a unique, if not paradoxical, axis. The rhetorical connotations inherent to fashion writing are neither implicit nor explicit in nature. They are hidden, perhaps like the political unconscious proposed by Frederic Jameson (1981). For Barthes, the meaning of a fashion narrative is not read. It is received (Barthes 1967: 232).

Fashioning the Modern Nation

In May of 1837, a literary society to be known as La asociación de la joven generación argentina (the Association of the Young Argentine Generation) was founded by Esteban Echeverría. Meeting in a Buenos Aires bookstore, this group of young intellectuals, later named the Generation of 1837, sought to explain and to criticize their country's past and present failures. With their faith placed firmly in ideas of progress, these enlightened Argentines began to devise a programme for the modern nation. Nicholas Shumway writes, 'Theirs was a generation of writers who apparently felt that progress lay in the right words, the right beliefs, and the right constitution' (Shumway 1991: 126). Shumway points to a biblical verse, more specifically the words of Saint Paul, that the generation used to elucidate their strategy for a New Argentina: 'Let us therefore cast off the works of darkness, and let us put on the armour of light' (Romans 13: 12). This metaphor granted ideas the status of weapons and expelled from the national body any unenlightened practices or beliefs. The generation portrayed the openness to new ideas as analogous to national strength. A democratic spirit would protect the integrity of the nation like a strong armor forever withstanding the impotence of tyranny. Shumway writes, 'By the right words, Argentina would be saved' (Shumway 1991: 127).

In hopes of importing the European enlightenment to Argentina, these intellectuals founded *La Moda*, an imitation of the French periodical that later became a force of violent opposition in Paris, *La Mode*. Published in Buenos Aires during the regime of Juan Manuel Rosas, the weekly magazine had a life of twenty-three issues (from November of 1837 to April 1838). In an effort to secure the publication of the magazine, *La Moda* listed its editor as Rafael Jorge Corvalán, the son of Rosas' aide-de-camp, despite the fact that the real editor of the magazine was Juan Bautista Alberdi. Alberdi was an independent thinker who affiliated himself more with the intellectual underpinnings of the Romantic movement than with the countering ideals of the Rosas regime[4] (Myers 1995: 44). Under the banner headline of '¡Viva la Federación!', *La Moda* identified itself as the 'Weekly Gazette of Music, Poetry, Literature and Customs'. Without a doubt, the Federalist slogan at the top would have appealed to government censors. When most volumes were bound, however, the slogan at the top was easily cropped and cast aside into the garbage bin.

If, as Valerie Steele suggests in *Fashion and Eroticism* (1985), changes in fashion precede rather than follow great historical events, then surely the men of *La Moda* were setting the scene for an end to the tyrannical reign of Rosas. Because an avowedly political journal would have been censored, and because few would associate fashion with politics, what better medium was there to import enlightened European ideas than to, quite literally, cloak them in a fashion magazine? *La Moda*'s prospectus would reflect upon the state of fashion in Europe and Argentina, elaborating on the social value of each so long as it was one of the intelligent, 'simple and healthy notions of democratic and noble politeness' (no. 1: 1). To help its readers appropriate these manners, the magazine proposed ways in which the Argentine man could tailor fashionable trends to his more practical needs. The adoption of foreign styles, however, was only a path to enlightenment and not an end in itself.[5]

The first issue of *La Moda* began by merely detailing the latest French fashion from the pages of *Petit Courrier des Dames* and *Gazette des Salons*, without including any readily apparent social commentary. Yet if read with a careful eye, the commentary initiates a subtle play with the political nature of colour and history. When presenting the latest in French home decoration, one fashion column highlights the crimson and greenish tones, which given the political climate would no doubt have been a daring interplay of the colours that represented Federal power and the Unitarian opposition (no. 1: 2). The author guides the reader from Paris into the homes of Buenos Aires, asking us to reconsider the old-fashioned armchairs that once belonged to the country's Spanish grandfathers. If one exhausts all the fashion possibilities, he writes, there is no recourse but to return to ancient customs (even if they date to the Middle Ages) and to initiate another cycle of trends. The classic armchair of Buenos Aires, described as a mass of crimson cloth attached to the frame by rusty nails, may have made a powerful allusion to the expired qualities of the seats of power held in Buenos Aires. The pages of *La Moda* would continue to record the fashion dictates of the day, while providing a forum for change, commenting on the need to restore and, ultimately, to replace the old.

Under the heading 'Fashions of Buenos Aires', the editors defined the new Argentine as one who patterned himself after Europe, while altering his accessories so as to dress in step with national style.

Our fashions are, as we all know, nothing more than alterations of European style. However, this modification is one that is executed artistically by intelligent men. In these pages we will present their testimonies, highlighting the latest modifications of this elegant crowd. (no. 1: 3)

In light of later issues, this article would demonstrate the double focus of *La Moda*'s discourse. Francine Masiello explains:

On the one hand, elegance of style symbolized European civilization and represented a dramatic break with the unsavory crassness of Rosas' regime, suggesting that if fashion could be imported acceptably from England and France, then ideas about liberal reform could also cross the Atlantic. On the other hand, fashion discussions drew attention to appearance and frivolity, to the faulty design of the garments chosen to cover the national body. In a country lacking dominant ideas or customs, fashion came to signal a weakness of the cultural imagination. (Masiello 1992: 23)

Just as the Unitarian intellectuals were to alter Parisian fashion for an Argentine climate, so too would they tailor French and English liberal ideals for Argentine consumption. Artistic modification was taking place at the level of discourse, allowing for an increasingly political reading of most descriptions of fashion.

La Moda's first article on women's hairstyles provides us with an intriguing example of the nuances of fashion during this period. 'Women's Fashions – Hairstyles' began with a discussion on the importance of democratic ideals in all areas of national culture, including grooming habits. Criticizing the lack of dominant ideas, fashions and customs, the author would direct the reader's attention to the values of progressive democracy rather than to the outlandish hair styles worn by the women of Buenos Aires. In order to distance themselves from the styles worn under Spanish domination, the fashionable women of Buenos Aires had taken to wearing an enlarged hair comb, called a *peinetón*, to mark their presence in the public sphere.[6] The article reinforced the belief that one's gaze should not rest on the enlarged peinetón or the crimson ribbons in a Federalist supporter's hair. Instead, citizens must direct their gaze to the virtues of democracy inherent to those simple hair fashions with lines down the middle. The writer then engages a more daring hair-do.

The lighthouse, or let us just call it that, on which we must rest our eyes in order to escape the chaos of antithesis that envelops us – in legislation, morality, education, science, art, as well as Fashion – is democracy. (no. 3: 3)

If the citizens of Argentina could only visualize the prize of a just political constitution and not be diverted by the flattering crimson ribbons adorning heads everywhere, then the country might embark on a democratic path similar to that undertaken by France, England and the US. In admiration of North American politics, the anonymous writer argued:

> Democracy stands out there as much in dress and manners as it does in the political constitution of the United States. Placed on an identical route, we might observe the same laws. A fashion, like any custom or institution, will be all the more beautiful for us the more restrained, the more simple, the more modest it be, and the less it has armed itself with insulting pomp against the honorable average citizen. (no. 3: 3)

Because the article on hair fashion came forth with dangerous leanings, *La Moda* carefully voiced support for Federalist policies in the article that immediately followed. 'Political Fashions', a report on the symbolic uses and display of Federal red, bordered on full-fledged patriotic support for Rosas. Although the author acknowledged that the color disgusted some Argentines, he also concluded that those repulsed people should still wear it, as the popular majority had chosen it. 'Political Fashions' complimented Federalist politics to such an extent that, according to José A. Oría, the presented information could have done little else to please Federal censors (Oría 1938: 38). The article read:

> When a political ideal adopts a color as its emblem and this ideal reigns triumphant, the color used symbolically quickly becomes voguish in the eyes of the public. All individuals wish to flaunt on their garments the color that expresses the thoughts and interests of the majority. In this way, it achieves the double success of gaining both public approval and fashionability, which is another form of public sanction. This is the case with the color scarlet, emblem of federalist ideals; at once it is a political and voguish color. With confidence, the population wears this color on its clothing and on the national flag, thus depending on a double authority which it would be ridiculous to ignore. (cited in Masiello 1992: 24)

For the editors of *La Moda*, the might of popular accord had determined the dictates of fashion. The scarlet insignias and vests were a mere reflection of the times, part of a larger process that called on men of might to follow blindly a path set by Rosas. Yet the context of a fashion magazine allowed for a particularly critical reading of Rosas and the immutable Federal uniform. If popular decree espoused a given 'fashion', then it would follow that one trend might easily be deposed by another, more cultivated, alternative.

In the midst of absolute stagnation, fashion writing promised change and progress. *La Moda* dedicated its fourteenth issue to the concept of movement and flow. The cover story made *flow* synonymous with *customs*, and attributed varying gradations of flow to the countries of the world. Within this paradigm, Argentina contrasted with its Spanish ancestors in that it exhibited the characteristics of a vital flow, a concept that promised a civilized future for all of its citizens. The article explains:

> He who dares to lose himself in the labyrinth of customs and manners of nations, or the popular, indigenous and domestic uses of fashion, will be reminded of the sheer numbers of those who weigh on the Earth. He will find that those who blindly obey the course paved for them are not unlike the water of a river that gently flows because a stream propels it. That is why the Englishman has mercantile flow; the Frenchman, scientific flow; the Turk, sensual flow; the Spaniard, listless flow; and we, who make such an effort to move ahead, progressive flow. (no. 14: 1–2)

If Argentina did not answer the call for national reorganization, its people would halt the natural rhythm of progress. By contrasting a young Argentina with an apathetic Spain, *La Moda* asked its readers to consider the cultural ramifications of ignorance and stagnation.

Using the pseudonym of Figarillo, Alberdi would combine humour with a didactic approach in an attempt to cultivate an intellectual life in Buenos Aires that would foster democratic ideals. His weekly column in *La Moda* berated the lack of interest in new ideas. The mission of the fashion magazine was utterly hopeless, he wrote, if its words were a sermon in a desert, devoid of a sympathetic ear. How could *La Moda* instruct the nation in the fine art of elegance when its citizens ran from change and progress in a way that sheep, long sheltered from the elements, run from the open spaces of the pampas? Alberdi believed that the inattention to ideas and national customs stemmed from the lack of a proper education.

In comical form, Figarillo engaged the reader in a series of dialogues that posited the popular voices that supported Rosas in a civilized setting. Each column carefully observed the speech and mannerisms of the stereotypical characters of society and issued judgments that aimed to help 'civilize' them. Figarillo declared, 'If in Buenos Aires there exists the ridiculous, then there also exists a critic who destroys this ridiculousness' (no. 4: 3). Figarillo would teach the city-dwelling *gaucho*, well versed in the easy rhymes of popular song, about the cadences of the minuet. He would also issue quips to his wife who, instead of going to an elegant ball in proper attire and with distinguished guests, had invited country relatives and hired help along. Doña Rita Material, the first character to make her appearance in Figarillo's column, gossips about the disguised wealth of the butcher's daughter and 'says *replubic* for republic and *threate* for theatre.' Figarillo ends the column with irony, 'I do not know if this will be progressive, for I know not what progress is' (no. 4, p. 3). A later column in *La Moda* would explain more clearly the elements of style and good taste with an 'ABC' directory, further under-scoring the didactic intent of some of the fashion writing of the period.

One reader who claimed to represent the interests of the people called into question the virtues of formal dress and etiquette in a letter to the editor. Signing as 'One of the People', his condemning words appeared on the cover of the fifteenth issue. He writes, 'Politeness, far from being a virtue, is the most contemptible of the vices. I would desire courtesy for my enemies, for my slaves, but never for my compatriots' (no. 15: 1). He further disputed the positive qualities of civilized customs by main-taining that they feminized men of might. 'One of the People' continues:

> The strong youth is the beautiful youth. Little does it matter to know how to remove one's hat when one knows how to die for liberty on the battlefields . . .
> The cream of society, that luxury of Argentine youth, is a group of young people who are industrial, patriotic and warrior-like. This segment of society makes up its heroism, its strength and its glory. Public temples shine with the flags stolen from enemies of the nation with strong arms, not elegant ones. (no. 15: 1–2)

National glory emanated from the aesthetics of war, not from the elegance of civilized customs, the letter to the editor suggested. For this reader, the battlefield was more beautiful than a flower, and a warrior certainly more important than a gentleman.

A later column by Figarillo entitled 'Signs of a Gentleman' responded to the letter by reminding readers that the idea was not to *be* a gentleman. One only had to look like one. Figarillo's comical bulletin presented a novel approach to image politics of the period, suggesting that fluid identities were indeed possible under a system that had not been designed to take this opportunism into account. He writes, 'Even if you have all the courage in the world, no one will think you are handsome if you do not wear a large sword, fierce expression, an enormous moustache, insulting glares' (no. 15: 2). One need only remember Daniel Bello, the noble character found in the best-selling nineteenth century Argentine novel *Amalia* (Mármol 1979 [1851, 1855]). In this novel, Bello is a Unitarian who disguises himself as a high-ranking Federal. Appropriating

Figure 4.2. Federalist soldiers or 'corazeros' patrol the countryside.

the dress and behaviours of the ruling powers, he gains acceptance and power from the Federalist regime and then serves those Unitarians who need his assistance in order to escape Rosas' cruelty. *La Moda* reminded its subscribers of that same power, asking them to bear in mind that God alone could expose the core identity of a given individual. Although clothing could serve as an indicator of the powers governing the nation, it could not determine the ideals of the heart.

Masquerading their editorial and political stance under the guise of frivolity and entertainment, Unitarian ideals thus entered into the realm of public discourse. 'If frivolity was their public pose', Shumway reminds us, 'in private the members were deadly serious' (Shumway 1991: 128). An anonymous author writing for *La Moda* proclaimed that liberty was not to be achieved by perfume alone (no. 21: 3). In expressing their desire for progress and more perfect institutions, the young Argentines of *La Moda* daringly challenged the current regime and embarked on an ambitious path, but one from which there was no return.

By March 17, 1838, *La Moda*'s editorial staff issued a warning to its subscribers and critics. Such a signal could only mean the editors were under fire with the Rosas government and felt they had nothing to lose in bringing forth an honest opinion. The warning responded to those who viewed *La Moda* as a vehicle for espousing damaging ideas and values:

> *La Moda* is not a hostile plan countering the customs of present-day Buenos
> Aires, as some have ventured to believe. Daughter herself of *porteña* ideas,
> she does not leave the pages open to all attacks, but instead focuses on the old
> age and tendencies of those fashions that are unworthy to belong to Buenos
> Aires anymore. Young Buenos Aires has lifted herself over the old Buenos
> Aires. All the editors, editing, ideas, and observations belong to our country:
> Why, then, are you offended by its shots? We are all the same people we
> criticize. It is not a foreigner. It is our society criticizing itself. (no. 18: 1)

The revolutionary tone of this article exposed readers to the strategies
employed to seduce them into accepting the precepts of liberal, independent thought. *La Moda*, its editors state, 'has followed and will
continue to follow similar forms. It is a disgrace required by the still
immature condition of our society' (no. 18: 1). According to the warning,
the editors of *La Moda* had manipulated the magazine's subject matter
only because of the infantilism predominant in Argentine society.

By 1841 the majority of the Generation of 1837 was living in exile in
Chile and Uruguay. In his autobiography, Juan Bautista Alberdi would
recall removing his scarlet insignia (required of all citizens in Argentina)
a mile from the shore of Buenos Aires as he made his way to neighbouring
Montevideo.

Fashion in Exile

In Uruguay, many of the members of the Generation of 1837 who had
written for *La Moda* settled into the ranks of other magazines and
newspapers. Andrés Lamas and Miguel Cané, the Uruguayan and Argentine editors of *El Iniciador* respectively, opened the doors to Alberdi and
other newly arrived exiles of the young generation, believing that their
participation in the magazine would revitalize the philosophical climate
of the River Plate region. *El Iniciador*, published from 15 April 1838 to
1 January 1839, had a short but productive run. In their desire to initiate
a path to progress and enlightenment, the editors' pens became swift
metaphorical swords directed against the residues of Spanish colonialism
and the tyranny of Rosas.

In this climate, fashion writing remained the genre of choice for
intellectuals of the Generation of 1837, despite the fact that its writers no
longer suffered under the arm of Federal censorship. Through the rhetoric
of fashion, the writer could question the role of the individual in the
context of democratic change. As Gilles Lipovetsky points out, the
emergence of and importance attributed to fashion is as indicative of the

rise of nationalist sentiments just as it is a reflection on the possibility for movement and change in a given society. In the pages of *El Iniciador*, Alberdi would write that emerging nations should prioritize the education of their citizens and the formation of customs that best suited the common goals of the young generation. 'Liberty as well as despotism lives in our customs', he writes in 'Sociability'. 'Whoever says customs, means ideas, beliefs, habits, uses' (no. 12: 253). For Alberdi, a custom served national interests only when it served its community by placing all on the path to equality and democracy.

Others theorized that the creation of national customs would help counteract the tendency among emerging nations to adhere to the traditions left by Spain. Manuel Irigoyen reminded the readers of *El Iniciador* that the war for independence had been only a step in a larger chain of events leading to national sovereignty. Great nations, he believed, did not depend culturally on others, but instead rested on the foundations of their own customs and ideas. The new republics would Americanize themselves only if they implemented new colours, proportions and forms. This task, as all could imagine, posed the greatest challenge to the region. In an essay entitled, 'War, the Gallows and the Dagger', Tejedor called for the belligerence of men so that the region might break its unending cycle of despotism – whether Spanish or Federal in nature. He explains, 'Ideas are not the wardrobe of humanity if they are shed without pain' (vol. 2; no. 2: 37). This metaphor resounded in other articles published in *El Iniciador*. If one could disrobe the body politic, then it might be reconstituted with the shield of democratic virtue.

Miguel Cané would use fashion as a metaphor in his writings to reflect both on the current state and on the future of national culture. Referring to the antiquated dress and manners of colonial times as 'cruel monuments', he sought to eliminate the relics of Spanish domination from the continent. In the first issue of *El Iniciador*, he evaluates the history of cultural stagnation in the region. Because the Spanish empire had permeated all aspects of daily life, one felt the force of its effects even if not registering them visually. He writes,

> Two chains connected us to Spain. One chain was physical, visible, and ominous. The other chain was no less ominous and no less weighted. It was invisible and intangible, like those incomprehensible gases that subtly penetrate all. It appeared in our legislation, our letters, our customs, our manners, and it imprinted on everything the seal of slavery, which in turn denied our absolute emancipation . . .
>
> The same goes for those ridiculous, exotic customs that we conserve with the respectful devotion of an antiquarian who guards his useless trinkets. Let

us try to show the antiquarian this embarrassing anachronism: American society, intelligent, republican, plebeian, religious, cannot be the old, rude, slavish, fanatical society of the days of the colonies . . . (no. 1, pp. 1–2)

The challenge of a young republic lies in creating fashionable dress and ideas that assumed the unique characteristics of its people, while retaining the dynamic and innovative spirit of a new republic. Cané would develop this idea in future articles. He writes, 'From the fashions of a people, one can ascertain the movement of spirit in the same way that one judges the level of culture of a man by looking at his state of dress. Fashion is the most flexible side of society, and because of this, it is perfected daily' (no. 3: 53). While his essay certainly spoke to all Latin American republics, it primarily targeted the Rosas government by rendering it obsolete. 'What will it take for us to *not* be what we are?' Cané asks. He replies, 'To march with the times, with fashion', a comment that also restated the premise of *La Moda*, the fashion magazine published a few months earlier in Buenos Aires (no. 3: 54). For Cané, a society could be timely and progress-minded only if it opened itself to the dynamics of change.

To expand on his ideas linking fashion to nation-building, Cané published a treatise in *El Iniciador* entitled 'Fashions'. His treatise employed fashion in a metaphorical sense to discuss political and philosophical currents that would help tailor the modern nation. 'Our century is a dressmaker because it is a century of creating movement, novelties, progress', Cané writes (no. 3: 53). Cané believed that the excess of luxury was not unlike the excess of liberty: could one really have too much, especially if one contrasted these options with the excess of misery and tyranny? With fashionable clothes and ideas, the emerging nations of the River Plate region could open themselves to constant enlightenment, distancing them from the darkness of ignorance that had pervaded Spanish-dominated America. The fatherland could elevate itself, he concluded, if the citizens of a new republic asserted themselves and instituted the fashionable precepts of a democratic political system.

Even from the margins of exile, prominent members of the Generation of 1837 continued to express their fashionable ideas and political goals for the emerging nations of the region. Through the unlikely medium of fashion writing, intellectuals such as Alberdi and Cané generated new philosophical currents that addressed national sovereignty and the ongoing renovation of the political arena through the unlikely medium of the fashion column. In one treatise on fashion, Cané would lay out the following scenario:

Fashion is the primary and most active of all agents of progress. There are no retrograde fashions, because all fashion is a learning process, a new edition, always more and more perfect, even if it is the same one thing. Its most beautiful attribute is its ability to die as do the circles formed by a stone that is dropped on the serene face of gentle waters. (no. 3: 53)

Continuing with the genre of fashion writing, Cané deposed the vestiges of Spanish colonialism and pondered the similar despotic tendencies of Federalist rule. If fashion and revolutionary politics were at the heart of the nation-building process, then one might expect to assume a proactive role in renewing nationalist sentiments and remaining open to the winds of change.

The Feminine Aesthetic

In April of 1852, two months after the Unitarian opposition finally defeated Rosas, a newly formed Buenos Aires newspaper produced an unusually audacious banner; it read 'Liberty, no licentiousness; equality between both sexes'. Just below, between the two refrains 'Being a flower – one can live without odor' and 'Being a woman – one cannot live without love', there appeared an engraving of the cloaked and blinded female figure of Justice. The newspaper was *La Camelia*, dedicated to the issues concerning the 'beautiful sex', and it would have a life of thirteen issues (from April 11, 1852 to June 20, 1852). Though its editors remained anonymous throughout publication, Janet Greenberg identifies them as Rosa Guerra and Juana Manso (Greenberg 1990: 192). Through fashion writing, the female editors of *La Camelia* would press their status as women, and more important, as citizens of the new republic. The magazine would touch subjects as diverse as the art of editing a magazine, education reform, and most importantly, the interrelationship between fashion and politics.

In the premiere issue, the *editoras* greeted their readers and colleagues in a way that placed them on an equal footing with their male colleagues who edited fashion magazines. They write:

What a bold enterprise it is when one throws herself into writing in a city that is so enlightened and when so many talents dedicate their pens to newspaper editing. Confident in the gallantry of our colleagues, we dare to present ourselves among them. We regret, however, that modesty inhibits us from extending to them a firm hug and the kiss of peace. Even though one famous woman writer says that *Genius has no sex*, we who lack their ability do not wish to overstep the limits that genius imposes on us. Instead, we extend to our male colleagues a strong, friendly, and fraternal handshake.

The weakness of our sex allows us to take refuge in the shadow of the *strong*, and so without any more preambles, we beg of our colleagues that they view our work with added indulgence. (no. 1: 1)

By characterizing their endeavour as a fearful and audacious one in an already enlightened city, the editors complimented their male colleagues while paving the way for an alternative, but equally significant, point of view. Although 'genius had no sex', *La Camelia*'s editors would not go beyond the limits established by their contemporaries. Such a modest introduction to their readership, like a peace treaty amidst a potential storm, still managed to open a forum for the discussion of issues that affected these women of Buenos Aires.

By entering a male-dominated public sphere, the editors became public owners of their discourse and thus were able to challenge existing institutional structures that had barred women from the Argentine cultural consciousness. In her appropriation of Habermas' theory of public and private spheres, Rita Felski formulates a *partial* public sphere, or a counter-public sphere, one made up of those marginalized by society. She writes,

> The logic of the feminist counter-sphere must thus be understood as ultimately rational, in a Habermasian sense, that is, not in terms of any appeal to substantive idea of a transcendental disembodied reason, but in the procedural sense of engendering processes of discursive argumentation and critique which seek to contest the basis of existing norms and values by raising alternative validity claims. (Felski 1989: 12)

Felski's analysis works especially well in light of nineteenth-century Latin America fashion writing. Through the channels of the fashion column and magazine, women's values and ideas of morality were disseminated to the public. The idea that the editors of *La Camelia* created an oppositional discursive space might seem to contradict their initial outline of intentions. However, they did contest existing norms and values in the way they chose to define (or not to define) their editorial participants.

La Camelia's three anonymous editors carefully disguised their identities in writing, defining themselves only through negation: 'Being neither girls nor pretty, we are neither old nor ugly.' One might hypothesize that this camouflage served as a means of protecting their private lives, now before the public eye. By defining themselves in the above context, the editors created an opening in a society that otherwise would have placed limitations on a woman's political involvement. Covered in the shroud of anonymity, the *editoras* were able to insert themselves as authoritative sources of information and challenge contemporary political attitudes. Francine Masiello writes:

> In refusing to specify physical attributes, the editors excluded themselves from circulating discourses on fashion, in which beauty and youth determined individual merits and condemned women to the judgment of others. (Masiello 1989: 276)

Without a name to judge, the reading public would have to take issue with the validity of the newspaper's claims, and not base its opinion on the reputation or the appearance of these women writers.

The editors were fully aware of the freedoms and pitfalls that accompanied anonymity, in part because of the controversy that had surrounded the use of female pseudonyms in fashion magazines like *La Moda*. Several male intellectuals of the Generation of 1837 had assumed female pseudonyms as a protective measure when mixing fashion and politics. Because of this practice, one might argue that women's fashion writing may have been read with the same seriousness as if men had produced it. With the added security of pseudonyms, the editorial participants of *La Camelia* managed to overcome 'the contradiction between self-protection and self-expression'. As Sigrid Weigel writes, 'Disguise in the form of literature gives protection as well as the chance to overstep the boundaries of the real and to postulate utopias' (Weigel 1985: 67).

While the *editoras* consciously withheld descriptions of their own appearance, they did not hesitate to present their ideas and criticism of idealized feminine fashion. Appropriating much of the vocabulary from the previously male-dominated discourse of fashion, *La Camelia* featured a regular column called 'Fashions'. In several of these columns, the editors re-examined the emergence of negative tendencies in the history of fashion. Initially at the forefront were reports of the changes brought about by the defeat of Rosas in 1852. *La Camelia* characterized fashion under Rosas as dauntingly oppressive, with little life and few colors. Immediately following the storm of tyranny, the women's fashion magazine appeared to have liberated women from a most sombre lifestyle, presenting them with numerous choices in style.

Old traditions and public spectacles that had flourished before the Federalist regime, such as the masquerade ball, regained popularity in the magazine's pages. An article entitled 'Masks' poked fun at the neurosis that forced every tyrant to outlaw entertaining forms of disguise:

This diversion was so feared by Rosas, for he believed that behind every mask lurched an enemy and within each domino, a dagger. Detested by every tyrant, this diversion has been put into practice again without any hint of disorder. May our youth continue as it has, with the decorum proper of enlightenment that will always be applauded by the beautiful sex. We women, although weak, constitute an organ of this enlightenment. We will not tire of repeating to all, 'Order and liberty! Down with licentiousness, for it leads to anarchy!' (no. 2: 2)

Because the masked ball had encountered none of the chaos one anticipated under Rosas, the author drew a parallel to the Nation's newly found stability and liberty. 'Masks' called on Argentine women to play an important part in the creation and subsequent institution of national customs. Though popularly deemed the 'weaker sex', the article argued that women constituted the moral backbone of society and, therefore, should play a role in the tailoring of the nation's leisure time. The current state of fashion and leisurely activities as described in the 'Fashions' column could easily have read as a barometer of national peace and order.

The editors of *La Camelia* promoted the concept of change inherent to the fashion system as a force that would allow the nation to rejuvenate itself continuously. Change, as the members of the Generation of 1837 had suggested, was necessary for all types of prosperity to materialize, whether industrial, economic or political. *La Camelia* would associate moral prosperity with fashion when it described the ideal Latin American woman. For its editors, fashion writing was a means towards acquiring a youthful yet moral perspective, a way of becoming the 'female friend of the new generation' (no. 1: 3). The editors provided the following explanation of the role of the fashion column in their first issue:

Do not believe that we plan to detail here all the puerility that we call Fashion – by no means. Although we are women and therefore lovers of all fashions, we are also sensible enough to overlook frivolities, especially when fashion plates abound. Our article has a moral tendency, because we very well know that Mrs. *Morality* is the beloved sister of *Liberty* and the enemy of little Miss *Licentiousness*. During the long period that, happily, has ended, Mrs. Morality was replaced by *Prostitution*. It is very just to see that, once she was thrown back into the dung from which she never should have left, Mrs. Morality could return from her exile and extend her charitable influence to all segments of society. (no. 1: 3)

For these *editoras*, Rosas had represented a barbaric turn towards moral indecency. Their call for a return to the spirit of independence, with the idea that freedom be bound by moral limits, elevated the status of women without denigrating her intelligence. To further the discussion on dressing intelligently, *La Camelia* explored those instances in history when women found themselves 'slaves to fashion' for reasons not of their own making. Several articles parodied the obsessive nature of those women who chose to sequester themselves with imprudent, yet incredibly uncomfortable, fashions. One article described the hairstyles worn by women during the reign of Louis XV, criticizing the women of the time for having forced artificial structures into their hair and displayed ridiculous thematic scenes. In one instance, 'Some Subscribers' wrote the magazine to denounce the imprudent dresses that were transforming the fashionable women of Buenos Aires into street sweepers. They especially railed against the use of extravagant petticoats, which, at their current size, seemed to take on an entire room. They write:

> It is the most uncomfortable feeling to have to run into posts and sweep the sidewalks of our narrow streets. It so happens that even in the stores with the most spacious counters and four or five young attendants, petticoats fill the space with their seven or eight yards of material. (no. 6: 3)

While the petticoat granted women fashion presence, it also required them to purchase inordinate amounts of material that did little more than sequester the figures of its wearers. 'In the end,' these subscribers concluded, 'we expect from the beautiful Argentine woman more prudence, more domestic economy, and less emission of petticoats.' Through fashion writing, women criticized the dysfunctional aspects of elite fashions, while at the same time identifying the potentially contradictory desire for sartorial pleasures. Like their predecessors of *La Moda*, these writers reminded readers of the need to alter European fashions so that they could wear them comfortably in a Latin American climate.

Through the act of assigning political function to garments and through the re-examination of the history of morality, gender and dress, we see that fashion writing proved a most effective tool in the tailoring of the nation. In early to mid-nineteenth century Argentina, fashion writing safely imported the political ideas of revolutionary Europe to Latin America, while it simultaneously criticized the arrogance and pomposity of those readers who mindlessly obeyed the dictates of fashion. As the intellectuals of the Generation of 1837 forged a national identity for the emerging nation, they relied on a protocol of unveiling in which the threads of ideology were woven through seemingly innocuous descriptions of clothing. As we have seen, the fashion description of *La Moda* did not need morally loaded phrases to communicate its political message. Often the message was latent, embedded in the choice of function and value assigned to the garment, a signification that one received but did not read (Barthes 1967: 231–2). Through the added security of female pseudonyms, many of these authors posed as writing women. The fashion system, or so it seemed, allowed for a woman to wear her politics on her sleeve. Such a strategy did not go unnoticed by women of the post-Rosas period. Taking up paper, pen and ink, the pioneer women of *La Camelia* surveyed the freedoms of the moment and spoke for themselves.

Acknowledgments

I am most grateful to the J. William Fulbright Foreign Scholarship Board, the US Information Agency, the Biblioteca Nacional of Argentina, the Department of Spanish and Portuguese at the University of California at Berkeley and the College of Arts and Letters at Old Dominion University for their support of my research.

Notes

1. The decree mandating the use of the crimson insignia went into effect on February 3, 1832. The decree can be found in Pedro de Angelis' *Recopilación de leyes y decretos promulgados en Buenos Aires desde el 25 de Mayo de 1810 hasta fin de Diciembre de 1835* (Buenos Aires: Imprenta del Estado, 1836).
2. I borrow the concept of an imagined political community from Benedict Anderson (1991), for whom the state is an imaginary idea(l) commonly shared by citizens and their governing bodies.
3. All translations in this article are mine, unless otherwise noted.
4. Alberdi's articles for *La Moda*, while mostly critical of the Rosas regime, can also be viewed as supportive. Félix Weinberg believes that the admiration displayed for Rosas was a ruse on Alberdi's part, in fact designed to attract Rosas to the precepts of the young generation (Weinberg 1977: 97–110).
5. In 1837, Alberdi elaborated on these ideas in his essay 'Fragmento' (Fragment). He writes, 'We should cleanse our spirit of all false colors, of all borrowed clothing, of all imitation, of all servility. Let us govern

ourselves, think, write and proceed in all things, not through imitation of any other people on earth, no matter what people's prestige, but exclusively according to the demands of the general laws of the human spirit and the individual laws of our national condition' (Alberdi 1886(1837): 111–12).

6. For more on the fashionable *peinetón*, see my earlier work on 'La moda como metonimia [Fashion as Metonymy]' (*Folios* 35:6, 1999, 3–11).

5

'The Epidemic of Purple, White and Green': Fashion and the Suffragette Movement in Britain 1908–14

Wendy Parkins

In her humorous pamphlet entitled 'Infection: A Warning to Anti-Suffragists and Anti-Militants',[1] the suffragette Rose Lamartine Yates outlined how the current fashion for and proliferation of commodities in the WSPU colours of purple, white and green spread the 'infection' of militancy. These colours had been officially adopted by the WSPU (the Women's Social and Political Union, the largest militant suffrage organisation in Britain under the leadership of the Pankhursts) in 1908 shortly before their first spectacular London procession and had quickly taken on a life of their own in Edwardian culture.[2] By 1909, Emmeline Pethick Lawrence, who had devised the colour scheme, could write: 'The colours have now become to those who belong to this Movement a new language of which the words are so simple that their meaning can be understood by the most uninstructed and most idle of passers-by in the street' (1909: 13). Yates recounts the 'recent experiences of a friend', a fashion-conscious and socially active anti-suffragist, who continually encounters the militant colours in a variety of shops and social gatherings and whose husband even dresses in the colours ('I'm not old-fashioned, I hope, I like to wear what other fellows are wearing'). When the husband is informed that his colours do not merely represent the season's fashions but stand for the militant suffrage movement, he blames his wife's ignorance: 'I'm not in favour of such folly; why didn't you tell me this before I decked myself out in these colours?' 'My dear, I didn't know', the wife replies, 'Percy, if these colours are so popular, perhaps there's something in the movement after all . . . We mustn't be old-fashioned, must we? Suppose we go to a meeting, or read the paper, and find out if it is all "noisy folly" as you say.' The couple are thus converted to the cause. Yates concludes:

Anti-suffragists! Anti-militants! remain at home. Beware of

Cakes,	Tea shops,
Places of Amusement,	Train journeys,
Drapers' shops,	Leather goods, sunshades,
Hosiers,	gloves, frocks,
Tailors,	Hatters,
London pavements,	Printers,

and, above all, private and public 'At Homes'!

All are likely to spread the epidemic of purple, white and green, and you never know how it may end with you!

Yates's fanciful account of the imbrication of the domestic, the commercial and the fashionable with the political undercuts the supposedly clear distinction between the public and the private realms on which the modern body politic was based. Social practices associated with metropolitan modernity around the turn of the twentieth century were already unsettling the discursive distinction between public and private which had played such an important part in the construction of Victorian ideology.[3] As Virginia Woolf noted in *Three Guineas*, from a woman's perspective the public and private domains are inextricably linked: 'It is from this [public] world that the private house . . . has derived its creeds, its laws, its clothes and carpets, its beef and mutton' (1992: 176). The rise of department stores, public transport and public facilities for women in city centres had in fact been transforming the lives of middle-class women and unsettling conventional notions of the bourgeois public sphere from the mid-nineteenth century onwards. By the close of the nineteenth century, women's presence in the newly available public spaces of cities was rendering obsolete a view of women as entirely ensconced in domesticity and of consumption as a thoroughly private, apolitical activity. Rita Felski has described a 'feminization of the public sphere' (1995: 90) taking place at this time, with a 'new prominence of icons of femininity in the public domain, and a concomitant emphasis on sensuousness, luxury, and emotional gratification as features of modern life' (1995: 90). Shopping was primarily a feminine leisure activity and the department store could be seen as a paradigm of a new kind of urban public space identified as 'distinctively feminine', associated with sensuality and the commercialization of desire rather than 'an ideal of political community and rational debate' (Felski 1995: 68). As both Rachel Bowlby and Elizabeth Wilson have argued, shopping offered women a relative degree of emancipation, not least in opening up new areas of the city previously out of bound to unescorted 'ladies' (Bowlby 1985: 22; Wilson 1985: 150).

In the case of middle-class women, new practices of consumption were an important means by which women were able to meet and observe one another in public, to perceive themselves, that is, as in some sense part of a public both addressed and constituted by advertising and department stores. Roger Fulford has even gone so far as to suggest that the tea shop – that venue available to women to rest from their shopping and meet unchaperoned with female friends – 'was an integral part of the women's liberation movement' because of the importance of women having a safe, social space to meet with other women (1957: 103). While institutions such as advertising and department stores interpellated women as part of a *consuming* public, not a political one, women's address as public subjects in any sense marked a significant cultural shift.

Changing social practices associated with shopping, fashion and advertising had, then, already resulted in a reconfiguring of the public realm before the advent of the suffragette movement which was to actively deploy practices associated with modern consumption to reconstitute the political. The suffragettes seized tactical opportunities for political protest from the everyday practices of modern life with which they were familiar in instances of what Michel de Certeau has called '[t]he tactics of consumption, the ingenious ways in which the weak make use of the strong' (1984: xvii). Street-corner speaking, newspaper selling, pavement chalking, sandwich-board advertising and even window breaking were all tactics derived from everyday urban experience which were deployed by women in a political context in the suffragette campaign. It was the suffragette deployment of fashionable dress and display, however, that offered the most profound destabilization of a binary opposition between the private sphere as the realm of consumption and the public sphere as the realm of politics. The suffragette practice of dressing in the latest fashions and the WSPU colours, and of patronizing and advertising certain stores, would show that a consuming public was not necessarily fundamentally opposed to the notion of a political public, as Yates' article humorously demonstrated. Through the use of fashion and specific colours the suffragettes forged a public identity for themselves in the public spaces of the city and introduced themselves and their cause into the sphere of political communication.

Within a traditional formulation of the public sphere as outlined in the introduction of this book, the suffragette campaign can be seen as by definition disruptive, as outside the legitimate domain of politics and public affairs in which participation was limited to men. Over the six years of the active campaign of militancy, suffragettes engaged in a broad range of forms of protest in their struggle to gain the vote for women, from the extremes of arson, window-breaking and hunger-striking to the more conventional forms of marches, public meetings and deputations. While suffragettes sought to claim the entitlements of modern democratic citizenship, their motto 'Deeds not Words' denoted their determination to take creative, dangerous or illegal action in order to achieve them. As such, suffragettes practiced what Holloway Sparks has termed 'dissident citizenship', which she describes as

> the practices of marginalized citizens who publicly contest prevailing arrange-
> ments of power by means of oppositional democratic practices that augment
> or replace institutionalized channels of democratic opposition when those
> channels are inadequate or unavailable . . . Dissident citizenship, in other
> words, encompasses the often creative oppositional practices of citizens who,
> either by choice or (much more commonly) by forced exclusion from the
> institutionalized means of opposition, contest current arrangements of power
> from the margins of the polity. (1997: 75)

Of course, the performance of dissident citizenship ran the risk of being classified as simply illegitimate, of proving that women were in fact not fit to be citizens because they did not follow the rules, and this charge was levelled at the suffragettes throughout their campaign. When on trial for their protests, suffragettes were treated merely as recalcitrant individuals rather than as political dissidents (see A. Young 1988: 285). They were not recognized as members of a public sphere nor as legitimate participants in public debate. What this notion of dissident citizenship insists on, however, is a recognition that discursive contestation and dissent are at the heart of citizenship, along with deliberation (Sparks 1997: 87). As Chantal Mouffe has argued, politics is 'about the constitution of the political community, not something that takes place inside the political community' (1992: 30). Suffragette protest was precisely concerned with disputing the constitution of the political domain: who could participate in it as well as what forms of participation would be considered legitimate. Suffragettes effectively challenged the boundaries of the political by throwing open to question what would count as public and what as private.[4] The wearing of the WSPU colours of purple, white and green, for instance – which became so popular that department stores like Selfridge's even devoted whole window displays to these colours – allowed women to construct practices of conventional femininity as political and to understand themselves as political subjects whether in the home, shopping, or protesting on the streets. In this way, apparently fixed demarcations between politics, fashion and consumption were unsettled and reconfigured by suffragettes.

In the performance of practices associated with fashion, suffragettes not only contested the current construction of the political domain but offered a new construction of the political subject. Suffragette protest was significantly enabled by its rearticulation of conventional practices associated with gender identity in relation to fashion (see Butler 1993: 2, 15). Public speaking and stone throwing, for instance, were both conventions of political practice with a long history (although with differing claims to legitimacy) but the reiteration of these conventions by fashionably-dressed 'ladies' profoundly altered the protest's conventional meaning. 'Ladies' speaking in places such as Trafalgar Square, a public space already politicized through its association with previous protest movements (such as the labour movement), identified themselves as public, political subjects who claimed a right to be heard in the political domain. In the process, they hailed other women to identify themselves as public subjects with a shared potentiality for feminist agency. The daring publicity of such moments of suffragette protest may also be thought of as acts of 'diva citizenship' which, according to Lauren Berlant, are moments of risk when a 'person stages a dramatic coup in a public sphere in which she does not have privilege' (1997: 223).

Fashioning the Public Subject

The suffragettes were not the first to mobilize practices of display for political purposes. As Lisa Tickner (1988: 55–7, 62–3) has noted, the influence of labour tradition and earlier suffrage campaigns on suffragette practices such as banner making, street oratory and Hyde Park gatherings was clear. But symbolic forms of political practice comprised a tradition of radical protest at least as far back as the French Revolution (Hunt 1984: 52; see also Introduction) and it is to that period that one really needs to look to find a precedent for the significance of dress, colour and accessories as a critical form of intervention in the political domain.[5] During the French revolutionary period, a wide range of commodities, especially items of dress, 'constituted a field of political struggle' by signalling the user or wearer's political affiliation and beliefs (Hunt 1984: 53). In a similar way, during the suffragette campaign, fashion and commodities were sites for the declaration of a political allegiance and the contestation of existing political arrangements. The Museum of London's Suffragette Collection contains many examples of suffragette commodities including stationery, card games, jewellery, badges, buttons, ties, scarves, handkerchiefs, tablecloths and tea sets, which testify to the 'infectious' spread, in

Yates's terms, of political symbolism far beyond the parameters of a traditional political public sphere (see Atkinson 1992).

The significance of fashionable dress in the suffragette movement was demonstrated firstly by the WSPU newspaper *Votes for Women* which almost from its inception in 1907 had featured fashion articles and advertising explicitly linked with the political campaign. In August, 1908, *Votes for Women* offered the following portrait of the suffragette:

> The Suffragette of to-day is dainty and precise in her dress; indeed, she has a feeling that, for the honour of the cause she represents, she must 'live up to' her highest ideals in all respects. *Dress with her, therefore, is at all times a matter of importance*, whether she is to appear on a public platform, a procession, or merely in house or street about her ordinary vocations. (30 July 1908: 348, emphasis added)

Fashionable dress was not a trivial distraction from the campaign but on the contrary an expression of a woman's commitment to the cause and an integral part of her identification and performance as a suffragette. Dress in fact was a distinguishing link across distinct sites (street *or* house *or* platform) which helped to establish the continuity of her performance as a suffragette. This point was not lost on businesses who advertised in *Votes for Women*: a full-page advertisement that appeared in May 1909, made this 'linkage' of fashion and politics startlingly explicit by representing fashionably dressed women as chained together (*VFW* 7 May 1909: 648; Figure 5.1). It may seem somewhat extraordinary for a respectable store like Derry and Toms of Kensington to represent their latest fashions through recourse to one of the daring forms of suffragette protest: the chains (which in the advertisement figuratively chain the women to the store) are a reference to a couple of notable incidents early in the campaign where suffragettes chained themselves in protest to sites symbolic of state authority. On 17 January 1908, Edith New and Olivia Smith had chained themselves to railings outside 10 Downing Street in order to create a diversion so that Flora Drummond could enter the house and attempt to 'crash' a Cabinet Council meeting (she was apprehended in the passageway Raeburn 1973: 47–8). On October, 28, 1908, Muriel Matters and Helen Fox, members of the Women's Freedom League,[6] had chained themselves to the grille of the Ladies' Gallery in the House of Commons (Raeburn 1973: 75).[7] The advertisement's juxtaposition of signifiers of protest and fashion, its linkage of chains and lace garnitures as feminine accessories, testifies both to the influence of suffragette deployment of fashion, and to the size of the potential market the advertisement addressed.

As Lisa Tickner has noted, 'Commercial manufacturers and retailers, from dressmakers to florists, were quick to advertize their wares in the purple, white and green. They may have been politically sympathetic, but they were also commercially astute' (1988: 93). The politicization of dress was a significant means by which the suffragette campaign undermined the demarcation between the political and domestic domains and mobilized a conventional femininity – 'dainty and precise' – for feminist protest, which could potentially politicize any context, including the symbolic space of the department-store advertisement.

'Behold the present-day Suffragette', proclaimed a *Votes for Women* column in 1911, 'pondering fashions side by side with political problems, for she is an essentially up-to-date being, and the sales are upon us' (July 7, 1911: 659). The juxtaposition of modernity, fashion and consumption with a radical political campaign could seem to associate problematically the stereotype of the irrational and insatiable female consumer with the suffragette as political subject (see Felski 1995: 62–5). Like the suffragette in popular representations,[8] the figure of the consuming woman was a site of great cultural anxiety around the turn of the twentieth century, arousing fears that women would evade social control (Felski 1995: 65). In texts sympathetic to the cause, the suffragette as consuming woman, or as the woman of fashion, existed alongside representations of the suffragette as martyr, demonstrating the discursive complexity of the suffragette subject: she could be both pleasure seeking or self denying, as the occasion demanded. Ethel Smyth's (1933: 197) portrait of Emmeline Pankhurst, for instance, represented the WSPU leader as variously long suffering and fashion conscious:

> she adored shopping, especially if connected with pretty clothes, her own costumes being the last word of neatness, daintiness, and good taste. No more irresistible magnet to Mrs. Pankhurst than a sale; no severer trial to people who loathe gazing into shop windows than to walk down Regent Street with her any day.

In a letter to Smyth after a life-threatening hunger strike, Pankhurst recorded her amusement at press accounts that stressed her appearance in prison and her interest in clothes, adding:

> It really is a pretty frock and it was a shame to be in it night after night in Holloway. Imagine the horror of the wardresses at seeing a nice velvet dress treated in that way! I think the authorities got a fright about me this time but they will find there is still a lot of life in me. (cited in Smyth 1933: 228)

Figure 5.1. Derry and Tom's advertisement, published in *Votes for Women* (May 7, 1909: 648).

Hunger striking in 'a nice velvet dress' is an image that neatly captures the apparent contradictions of the suffragette campaign. To read the suffragettes' conventionally feminine appearance as somehow at odds with their campaign is to miss the point. The suffragettes' conformity to middle-class prescriptions of fashionable femininity was a contestation of the construction of the female subject – as decorative but apolitical – through subversive repetition of practices which were seen to constitute femininity. As Judith Butler (1990: 147) has argued:

> The critical task for feminism is . . . to locate strategies of subversive repetition enabled by [constructions of the gendered subject], to affirm the local possibilities of intervention through participating in precisely those practices of repetition that constitute identity, and therefore present the immanent possibility of contesting them.

Repeating those practices of dress that constituted a woman's (classed) identity could, effectively, challenge contemporary definitions of citizenship by an emphasis on particularity. Traditional formulations of citizenship in the bourgeois public sphere were informed by what Michael Warner (1992: 382) has described as 'rhetorics of disincorporation', a rhetorical move by which citizens were simultaneously conceived as disembodied subjects yet citizenship was limited to certain kinds of bodies (those of white male property owners). Within this formulation, the particularities of the body were defined as outside the domain of public and political deliberation (see I. Young 1987: 67) and women were thus always already configured as illegitimate participants in the political domain (see Landes 1995: 98). The suffragette emphasis on a fashionable femininity drew attention to female specificity as grounds for inclusion rather than exclusion from the political domain: it insisted that women be political subjects *because of* their sexual difference not *in spite of* it.

This suffragette claim for inclusion while insisting on their sexual specificity was notably deployed in the mass processions staged at intervals throughout the campaign. The first of these processions, held in London on 21 June 1908, and known as the Great Hyde Park Meeting or Woman's Sunday, saw an estimated 30,000 women march in ranked formations with purple, white and green predominating. As described by Emmeline Pethick Lawrence:

> A quarter of a square mile of Hyde Park was set aside for the demonstration. Sixty-four trains were chartered to bring supporters from the provinces . . . [E]verything went like clockwork . . . great crowds accompanied the seven

processions which, starting from north, south, east and west, passed through the London streets under seven hundred floating banners accompanied by forty bands. (1938: 183–4)[9]

Banners, bunting, regalia and ribbons striped in the three colours had all been specially made for the event by a company specializing in such work (S. Pankhurst 1931: 284). After the spectacle, *Votes for Women* attested that:

> A prominent feature of the great Demonstration in Hyde Park was the fact that white dresses predominated, thus enhancing the value of the colours on banners and badges, and any one with an artist's eye must have enjoyed the spectacular effect of the seven processions, white, purple, and green, against the green of the park trees, and with the blue of a summer sky above. (30 July 1908: 348)

The repeated encouragements prior to the spectacle to wear the WSPU colours or adopt a certain style of dress sought to actively produce a shared identity for the participants and offered the women a new kind of identification: the opportunity to recognize themselves as political subjects as they constituted *en masse* a political public. The repetition of practices of dress conventionally thought to constitute Edwardian feminine identity – such as white summer dresses – challenged contemporary definitions of citizenship, marking an attempt to shift the terms of political discourse from the reproduction of universal reason (Eagleton 1984: 16) to a recognition of difference. Accounts such as Jessie Stephenson's description of her ensemble for the march implied the significance of the performance of fashion for a suffragette's self-representation:

> My milliner and dressmaker took endless pains with my attire. A white lacey muslin dress, white shoes and stockings and gloves and, like an order, across the breast, the broad band in purple, white and green emblazoned 'Votes for Women', a white shady hat trimmed with white May – also two grand [medallions] – one 'Chief-Marshall' and the other 'Speaker' – all very grand. (n.d.: 127)

In effect, the juxtaposition of the quasi-military sash in the WSPU colours and the Edwardian muslin dress signified the construction of a new kind of political subject, the woman-citizen. Women in white summer dresses and picture hats demanding political recognition served to question the very nature of political subjectivity itself.[10]

It could be argued that the role played by suffragette spectacles in forging a link between militant action and appearance was not a subversive one at all. After all, anti-suffragette caricatures, evidenced in postcards and cartoons of the time, also maintained that a suffragette was identifiable by a particular kind of body and appearance and it has been suggested that one reason that the WSPU urged its members to always look their best was to counteract this stereotype of the mannish spinster (Hamilton 1935: 75–6; Tickner 1988: 160–6). But more than an image was at stake. The constitutive experience of suffragette spectacles – thousands of women marching through London streets in formation – not only constituted a new kind of public (comprised of female political subjects) and articulated a political demand (for enfranchisement), it also constituted the suffragette subject as an embodied political agent. As Foucault has argued, particular subjects are constituted in and through particular discursive practices (1987: 10; 1977: 200). Practices of performance and display are inextricably bound up with the construction of subjectivity, with 'self-fashioning', to use Stephen Greenblatt's term (1980). Mobilizing certain practices of dress not only fostered a shared suffragette identity but performed a certain kind of subjectivity. Whether hunger striking in a velvet gown or wearing a white dress and sash for a procession, dress enabled the suffragette's self-formation as a defiant, dissenting subject.

For many suffragettes on many occasions, then, fashion was a form of agency: it enabled and abetted their protest. Many autobiographical anecdotes of suffragette protest begin by detailing the choice or purchase of an outfit. More than a framing device or a humorous digression, these accounts become part of the performance of dissent which begins with the assumption of a certain identity in order to perform protest. This identity did not mark the suffragette's subordination – somehow implicit in her embrace of feminine fashion – so much as empower her to undertake the action. Suffragette dressing up was neither an unwitting assent to the manipulations of consumer culture nor an unthinking adherence to middle-class conventionality. The critical potential of suffragette dress came from its challenge to the cultural intelligibility of women's fashionably dressed bodies as docile and ornamental. The dissenting body, dressed in a Liberty dress and a hat from Derry and Tom's, was a defiant display which challenged onlookers to look again.

'Politics and Millinery'

One particular item of Edwardian fashion, repeatedly mentioned in suffragette texts, was especially significant for its capacity to subvert the binary opposition between the ornamental and the political. Millinery figured prominently in descriptions of suffragette dress, despite the fact that, to twenty-first century eyes at least, a hat could easily be seen as a cumbersome impediment to a subversive political practice. Hats, of course, offered another opportunity for the prominent display of suffragette colours and retailers like Derry and Toms did not neglect to urge women to signal their allegiance to the cause through their headgear (see Figure 5.2). As the advertisement in Figure 5.2 attests, hats 'could be made up in the Distinguishing Colours of any Organisation'.[11] The relationship between shop and consumer was, in this case, a mutually advantageous one: Derry and Toms could appeal to a particular market, keen to equip themselves for the upcoming procession (on 17 June 1911), while the suffragette cause gained free advertising in the form of window displays devoted to suffragette colours ('we shall be exhibiting in one of our windows hats and toques made in the colours of the various organisations in connection with the Woman Suffrage movement').

Hats were not only important accoutrements for the massed processions, of course. Stephenson introduces the account of her first major participation in the suffragette campaign with an anecdote about buying a suitable hat. A hat, it would seem, was an essential component of her campaigning:

> One should always buy a hat when one is looking ill – if it suits you then it always will. The hat question before I went to Jarrow [to campaign in a by-election] worried me fearfully because I could not give it adequate attention. One day in Regent Street I suddenly felt quite ugly enough to buy my hat. I saw a very fetching fuschia-rose one in the window. These coloured hats hadn't been worn much then. I went inside and put it on and looked so delicious in it I could not believe it was me! (n.d.: 60)

Several days later in Jarrow, Stephenson continues:

> I happened to be wearing this self-same chapeau. But I didn't feel delicious in it as I couldn't get out of being dragged on to the platform at a meeting . . .

> Someone in the crowd said – jerking his hand towards the platform –
> 'Could she speak, please?'
> 'She – which she?' Mrs. Pankhurst asked, rather amused.
> 'The one in the red hat, please.'
> 'Yes, yes, the one in the red hat,' they all cried out. (n.d.: 61–2)

Figure 5.2. Derry and Tom's advertisement, published in *Votes for Women* (June 9, 1911: 604).

Stephenson, however, refused the invitation to speak, a refusal she subsequently regrets: 'Looking back, I see at every turn how foolish I was . . . The hat knew its job' (n.d.: 62). Stephenson's humorous ascription of agency to the hat itself shows that hats could create unique opportunities for political intervention. The wearing of a hat was in this case tactical: even the purchase of the fuchsia hat had provided Stephenson with an opportunity to tell the shop assistant about the cause (n.d.: 60).

A *Votes for Women* article by Evelyn Sharp entitled 'Politics and Millinery' further illustrated the unique juxtaposition of fashion and politics within the suffragette movement. Describing the WSPU Women's Exhibition held in May 1909 – a fundraiser on a grand-scale where stalls were stocked both with items made by suffragettes and donated from leading retailers – Sharp turned her attention to the hat stall: 'I suppose that nowhere outside the Women's Exhibition would hats be bought to the tune of complaints against the existing Government', Sharp writes, 'The combination of politics and millinery, though unusual, certainly added zest to the millinery, I thought' (*VFW* 21 May 1909: 688). As in Stephenson's narrative, hat purchases were transacted with an eye to future campaigning:

> the buyer asked anxiously, if it would do for Sunday in Hyde Park.
> 'Oh yes,' answered the seller, confidently. 'I'm sure nothing would make it come off.'
> This might puzzle some people who associate Sunday in Hyde Park with a band and a church parade; but nobody within hearing was puzzled. We all knew what it meant to stand on a lorry on a windy day, and most of us had listened in public to the lady [buying the hat]. (688)[12]

The anxiety expressed here about the hat's stability also hints at the cultural meanings of an un-hatted woman. Mainstream press photographs of suffragettes frequently depicted hatless suffragettes with long hair trailing, obviously dislodged from hair pins (see, for example, Mackenzie 1975: 55, 166, 196). The impression thus created of a dishevelled suffragette, slatternly and unladylike, was probably not accidental, given the general antagonism of the press to the suffragette cause. Unkempt hair signified an uncontrolled femininity, or worse still a failed femininity, and the symbolic significance of suffragette hair was chillingly represented in violent incidents that occurred at Welsh eisteddfods in September 1912. On one occasion, male spectators, responding to an implicit incitement from Lloyd George's speech, attacked protesting suffragettes with unusual savagery and there were reports of men parading with locks of suffragette hair pinned to their coats or hats.[13] Removing suffragettes' hats and pulling down their hair seems to have been a deliberate form of assault in these situations, intended to humiliate and insult the women, as Kitty Marion's account implied (n.d.: 223–4).

The hat was an item invested with cultural significance, then, bound up with a socially approved form of femininity based on *silent* display but in Sharp's article for the suffragette newspaper a hat was also an adjunct to a political performance of the body – a (hatted) woman speaking dissent while standing on a lorry – which becomes a site of intersubjective identification ('We all knew what it meant'). Sandra Stanley Holton has accounted for the suffragette interest in fashion as due to the militant 'appeal to male chivalry', which she argued character-ized suffragette conceptions of male-female relations (1990: 20-1). In suffragette texts, however, the emphasis was always on fashion as a practice that communicated with other women: it was a practice directed towards women, although men targetted signifiers of fashion in their attacks on suffragettes.

The pleasure taken in the appearance of other women was sometimes singled out in suffragette texts as a source of inspiration or encouragement for the author. Lady Constance Lytton (1914: 205) 'specially remem-ber[ed]' one young woman who 'wore a big hat and looked as remote as it is possible to look from stone throwing'. In this case, Lytton's pleasure derived from the contrast between the woman who appeared passively beautiful but was actually a stone-throwing (and hunger-striking) suffra-gette. The observing suffragette on one level enjoyed the conventional display of beauty as an aesthetic experience and on another level derived a covert pleasure from knowing the actions that belied the appearance of passivity. The appearance of suffragettes could thus offer their comrades complex pleasures from the clash of cultural meanings created by the apparent contradiction between their appearance, their political affiliation and their performance of protest. The story Margaret Haig (Viscountess Rhondda) told of her Aunt Janetta, another unlikely suffragette, illustrates well both the pleasures and the contradictions of a hat-buying suffragette. 'Aunt Janetta', who was a 'beautiful woman . . . with soft curly hair and a very gentle and spiritual face – the face of a saint – and she dressed well', intended to participate in the mass window-breaking campaign instigated by suffragettes in March, 1912, in London's West End shopping districts (Rhondda 1933: 162).[14] She chose as her target the windows of D. H. Evans on Oxford Street and, equipped with a hammer, smashed the first pane:

[Aunt Janetta] told one of her daughters afterwards that it had been almost impossible to strike that blow. The great plate-glass window looked so beautiful and well made that she could not bear to destroy it. However, she did it all the same, and then moved on to the next, and the next. Crash, crash went the hammer . . . Finally the policeman came up and arrested her.

She was let out on bail, and promptly went back to D. H. Evans to buy herself a hat there and thus make up to the firm for any inconvenience to which her action might have put them, for she was a most scrupulous woman. 'It was I,' she explained pleasantly to the shop assistant, 'who broke your windows yesterday,' and could not understand why that young woman from then on regarded her with suspicion. (Rhondda 1933: 162–3)

On this occasion, the hat was bought *after* the militant act, not before, but the juxtaposition of shopping and vandalism, matched by the contrasts of Aunt Janetta herself – fashionable but saintly, timorous but determined – aptly signified how suffragette protest could disrupt the boundaries of public and private by insisting on women's political agency and how a suffragette's appearance could seem to embody her dissident citizenship.

Such narratives could, however, be interpreted by those unsympathetic to the cause as a sign of suffragette vanity and excessive femininity. In her memoirs, Cicely Hamilton (1935: 75), recanting her involvement in the suffragette movement, stressed the WSPU's obsession with feminine fashion:

A curious characteristic of the militant suffrage movement was the importance it attached to dress and appearance, and its insistence on the feminine note . . . all suggestion of the masculine was carefully avoided, and the outfit of a militant setting forth to smash windows would probably include a picture-hat.

Hamilton had also attacked suffragette politics in her earlier novel *William: An Englishman* through the representation of a central character, Griselda Watkins, who was

almost ostentatiously gracious and womanly; it was the policy of her particular branch of the suffrage movement to repress manifestations of the masculine type in its members and encourage fluffiness of garb and appeal of manner. Griselda, who had a natural weakness for cheap finery, was a warm adherent of the policy, *went out window-smashing in a picture-hat* and cultivated ladylike charm. (1920: 20, emphasis added)

Griselda's inauthentic hyper-femininity (she was naturally inclined to be unnatural) was metonymic of the illegitimate politics of the suffragette movement to which Griselda belonged. The image repeated in both passages, of a suffragette smashing windows in a picture hat, marks a troubling contradiction which Hamilton cannot reconcile with 'legitimate' political practice. Hamilton's criticisms of the suffragettes' departure from a legitimate politics of the authentic public sphere was shared by other disenchanted suffragettes like Teresa Billington-Greig, who was an early defector from the WSPU,[15] and Sylvia Pankhurst. In *The Suffragette Movement: An Intimate Account of Persons and Ideals*, Pankhurst indexically linked her mother and older sister's interest in fashion (which she did not share [1931: 98]) with what she depicted as their self-aggrandizing leadership style. Like the fictional Griselda, Christabel ultimately lacks serious political purpose in her sister's account, a kind of 'tragic flaw' evident from childhood through Christabel's snobbishness and love of fine clothes (1931: 98).

Mary Richardson, one of the most active 'guerrilla' suffragettes, also presented a suffragette femininity of excess (as distinct from an excessive femininity) in which the picture hat was a crucial signifier – but to very different purposes than in Hamilton's case. Setting the scene before the protest which became known as Black Friday because of the extreme violence meted out to suffragettes,[16] Richardson (1953: 8) wrote:

> If you would see us as we were on that Friday, picture the Caxton Hall crowded with seated women wearing the large hats which most of us wore in those days and which were held on our heads with hat-pins thrust through thick, long hair. That was also how the women on the platform were dressed, in big picture hats and in the long, flouncy skirts which were then fashionable. But, even so early in the movement, we militants wore flat-heeled shoes.

Richardson's description of a femininity of excess (*large* hats, *thick* hair, *flouncy* skirts) as constitutive of suffragette protest is counterposed with the final image of the flat-heeled shoes, deliberately drawing attention to the apparent contrast between fashion and utility, femininity and politics. The flat-heeled shoes were metonymic of the way that suffragette deployment of fashionable femininity disrupted the cultural intelligibility of ladies of fashion.[17] Theirs was fashion with a purpose; even carrying a fan to a bishop's garden party could be tactical: 'A closed fan can be a very good weapon of defence', Richardson confided (1953: 59).

Guerrilla Fashion and Cross Dressing

The cultural intelligibility of the suffragettes' bodies was, then, open to interpretation; the disparity of meanings between the appearance and the actions of those bodies activated a clash of meanings within an agonistic public sphere, which effectively contested what would constitute the political and who could legitimately participate in it. Whether the fashionable suffragette was celebrated or denigrated, the well-dressed woman who raised a hammer to smash a Bond Street window was seen as performing a moment of cultural rupture, performing gender 'wrong' in Butler's terms (1990: 140). Performing certain actions and dressing in certain ways – more specifically, dressing in certain ways in order to perform certain actions – signalled the subversive possibilities afforded by the repetition of practices constitutive of feminine identity. Butler has also argued that the forms of protest which have the greatest efficacy are those that, while drawing on conventions of previous protest cultures, are not immediately legible, 'the ones that challenge our practices of reading, that make us uncertain about how to read, or make us think that we have to renegotiate the way in which we read public signs' (1996: 122). The variety of suffragette practices of dress and display instigated such a process of negotiating the meanings of feminine appearance and women's status within the body politic.

In the more extreme and covert forms of protest of the later part of the campaign, fashion could also be usefully deployed by suffragettes who relied on each other's knowledge of fashion and dress codes (and, concomitantly, on the ignorance of police and other masculine authorities of the same). Pleasure could be derived through a shared knowledge of fashion – its possibilities, its limitations – which suffragettes saw as their unique feminine provenance. Mary Richardson (1953: 162–3) records Annie Kenney's description to her of one notable incident of protest:

> 'Well, here's the story,' Annie began. 'Mrs. G.C., dressed like a fashion plate, stepped out of her car at the side gate that leads to [Westminster] Abbey. She entered with superb dignity and mingled with the sightseers who were there . . . Well, she stood round admiring the architecture until the tourists had moved off; and then she took a tiny bomb from her muff, tossed it with rather poor aim in the direction of the Coronation Chair – and the Stone of Scone has lost one of its corners. With an air of quiet self-possession she left the chapel and the Abbey and approached the gate. Here she was greeted by a polite policeman who offered to call her car. She smiled agreeably, tipped the bobbie handsomely and drove off quite unruffled.' Annie began laughing again . . . and I laughed with Annie to think of the elegant Mrs. G.C. voluntarily becoming a criminal.
>
> 'Well, it isn't surprising, perhaps, Polly,' Annie said. 'It just shows what fine clothes and an elegant appearance will do.' She leaned over and put her hand on my arm. Her blue eyes twinkled and she said, 'I think you and I had better put on some smart togs before we tackle our next job.'

This story of the elegant bomber with her 'tiny bomb', like Mrs. Pankhurst's delight at the wardresses' outrage over her 'nice velvet dress', served to lift the flagging morale of hardened campaigners like Kenney and Richardson. Their exchange of 'frivolous' fashion gossip confounds the demarcation between the 'serious' (political protest) and the trivial, and complements Mrs G. C.'s defiance in deploying conventional femininity to elude arrest. The prevalence of narratives of fashionable protest – and the unapologetic pleasure derived from them by other suffragettes – suggests the importance of this self-representation for suffragettes who thus recognized in each other the signs of dissident citizenship.

As the story of Mrs G. C. shows, dressing up often gave suffragettes a certain urban anonymity, allowing them to be what de Certeau (1984: 93) has called 'ordinary practitioners of the city', blending into the urban street scene both before and after the incident and providing an effective means of evading arrest. In the 1912 window-smashing raids in the West End Richardson recorded that those suffragettes who 'went quietly away, as if they had been out for a morning's shopping, escaped capture' (1953: 40). Fashion as a suffragette tactic was not, however, limited to middle or upper-class suffragettes, nor was it limited to the high fashion of the time. A wide variety of dress styles and accoutrements of fashion were put to various uses by many suffragettes to attract or evade attention. Dressing up (in historical costumes, prison uniforms or national/regional dress), cross-dressing to enter a male bastion, or disguising themselves to avoid police, the suffragettes demonstrated a skilful manipulation of dress and costume codes, which problematized notions of authentic identities – derived from class, gender, or regional background. Such dress practices again demonstrated the impact of modern cultural practices, associated with theatre, advertising and window-display, on suffragette activities. The ingenuity of suffragette deployment of the resources of modernity was made explicit by Kenney who wrote: 'We were like one of the big stores, if one thing did not suit (and the audiences soon told us) we would take them into another department' (1924: 148).

Kenney was herself a good example of the strategic deployment of forms of dress in the campaign. At times, Kenney, the former Lancashire mill-girl, would appear at suffragette events dressed in the traditional costume of the mill worker, complete with shawl and clogs (S. Pankhurst 1931: 256), at others 'in a frock of pale lettuce-green silk[18] . . . more like an aristocrat from the West End than an Oldham factory girl', as fellow working-class suffragette Hannah Mitchell admiringly described her (1977: 159). Kenney's autobiography represented such events as tactical appropriations of costume, as performances for political purposes. Of a deputation in March 1907, in which factory women from the north participated, Kenney (1924: 113–14) wrote:

> The idea was to get Lancashire and Yorkshire factory women to come down to London in clogs and shawls and march on Parliament. We are all interested in the thing we do not possess! Mystery is always attractive. The West End is attracted by the customs of the East End, and the East End by the West End . . . So clogs and shawls would attract not only the public but Parliamentarians, who, like all people, look forward to a change.

The wearing of a particular costume is here a consciously communicative act, grounding the women's enactment of political contestation. Kenney's ability to dress in either shawl or silk as the occasion demanded signified her social mobility as a suffragette.

The most famous incident of cross-class dressing was Lady Constance Lytton's masquerade as a working-class woman named Jane Warton, in order to prove that prison authorities treated working-class suffragettes much more harshly than their upper-class comrades. In *Prisons and Prisoners*, Lytton (1914: 239–41) offered a detailed account (including photograph) of the process of assuming the clothes and identity of 'Jane Warton':

> I accomplished my disguise in Manchester, going to a different shop for every part of it, for safety's sake. I had noticed several times while I was in prison that prisoners of unprepossessing appearance obtained least favour, so I was determined to put ugliness to the test. I had my hair cut short and parted, in early Victorian fashion, in smooth bands down the side of my face . . . A tweed hat, a long green cloth coat, which I purchased for 8s. 6d., a woollen scarf and woollen gloves, a white silk neck-kerchief, a pair of pince-nez spectacles, a purse, a net-bag to contain some of my papers, and my costume was complete . . . Before leaving Manchester I realized that my ugly disguise was a success. I was an object of the greatest derision to street-boys, and shop-girls could hardly keep their countenances while serving me.

Lytton's carefully considered adoption of disguise was effective in concealing her true identity from prison officials long enough to be assaulted and repeatedly forcibly fed and, on her release, the incident received attention from the press and the Home Office (Lytton 1914: 307–10; S. Pankhurst 1931: 331–2).

The aristocrat forcibly fed when dressed as a working-class woman or the working-class suffragette in a Liberty silk gown precisely challenged conventional practices of 'reading' femininity and dissent. But disguise was also another means by which suffragettes deployed the conventional association between women and 'dress sense' to their tactical advantage. To avoid detectives waiting to arrest her outside a suffragette meeting, for instance, Kenney took some elaborate precautions:

> I was to be dressed up as an old lady, with a rustling silk skirt, a silk blouse, elastic-sided boots, a cape, an old-fashioned bonnet, and a grey wig. I was to be very old. To complete my outfit I had to wear glasses and carry an ebony stick . . . Something, however, had still to be done to fill my face out a little. Two plums were found and I put one in each cheek. It was perfect, but not a word could I utter. (Kenney 1924: 235)

Kenney's inability to speak in her disguise did not, however, render her incommunicative. Her disguise effectively communicated a playful defiance which could inspire other suffragettes to similarly unconventional practices.

Women's facility with and knowledge of dress was repeatedly deployed by suffragettes against their male opponents, such as when disguise on a mass scale was adopted after the 1 March window-smashing raid in 1912. When Richardson went to Bow Street police-station to gain information on the arrested women she was puzzled to find forty-nine detained suffragettes changing clothes:

> Apparently it was the custom for a constable to offer the court a detailed description of an offender if she had refused to give her name. It was therefore essential in such a case that a full description of the wearing apparel of the offender be recorded for purposes of identification. I realized why there had been that wild scramble to exchange clothes in the room upstairs. I knew the fun would start. It did, and quickly. A tall, very young constable read from a tiny notebook, 'The woman I took into custody refused her name, your worship. She was wearing a blue coat, a red hat with a veil attached . . . '
>
> At this point the magistrate checked him. 'You say a blue coat and a red hat, constable? I see no woman in the dock answering your description.'
>
> An uneasy silence followed. The constable flushed crimson; then he picked out the first of the smiling women in the dock. She was dressed in a brown coat and a brown hat with no veil of any sort.
>
> The magistrate puffed and blew for a moment; then, with a bored air, he said, 'Case dismissed.'
>
> . . . Incredible as it might seem, on that afternoon fully half of our women escaped punishment at Bow Street because of a constable's failure to identify his prisoner properly. (1953: 41–2)

During the period of the so-called Cat and Mouse Act, a law by which hunger-striking suffragettes were released on licence from prison to recover before returning to their sentences, disguise was also used effectively to allow licenced prisoners to avoid re-apprehension. Emmeline Pankhurst, for instance, evaded arrest when police watching the house she was occupying followed a cab bearing a 'veiled lady' believed to be Pankhurst while the WSPU leader escaped in another vehicle (E. Pankhurst 1979: 317–18). Marion also evaded re-arrest by similar means:

> On Saturday afternoon two friends called, one like me in general appearance but dressed differently to my usual tailor-made style. She removed her coat, hat and veil which I put on while she donned the hat and coat in which the detectives had lately seen me . . . [M]y 'double', leaning heavily on someone else's arm went out surrounded by others bidding her farewell, and entered a waiting taxi, which was promptly boarded by the two detectives as it drove off . . . A sentinel at the gate gave the signal 'coast clear' when the other caller and I walked out, turned left . . . boarded a bus and were lost in London's traffic. (Marion n.d.: 250)

Sometimes, a change of hat alone was enough to conceal a suffragette's identity from police. When Christabel Pankhurst fled the country to avoid trial in 1912 she merely substituted a plain straw hat for her customary millinery excess and thus escaped detection (S. Pankhurst 1931: 374).

Cross-gender dressing was also effected on occasion and, like the suffragette deployment of fashionable dress, it carried varying significations in different contexts. Tactical use of cross dressing included Lilian Lenton dressing in a schoolboy's suit to avoid arrest (Street 1960: 9) and Jessie Kenney disguising herself as a telegraph boy in order to gain entry to 10 Downing Street and protest personally to the Prime Minister (she almost succeeded) (Atkinson 1996: 35). Elements of cross dressing with a military inflection were adopted by several prominent suffragettes. 'General' Flora Drummond, for instance, was well-known for riding at the head of suffragette processions 'with an officer's cap and epaulettes' (S. Pankhurst 1931: 266). Drummond's masculine-military profile reflected her organizational role in the WSPU and her indefatigable service to the movement. Vera Holme, 'Jack' to her friends, was Mrs Pankhurst's chauffeur who also affected a masculine-inflected military dress style, wearing 'a striking uniform in the colours with a smart peaked cap decorated with her Royal Automobile Club badge for efficiency' (*VFW*, 20 August 1909: 1094). Holme's role as chauffeur unsettled both gender and class conventions: as a woman driver who dined with the hosts and not with the servants, she symbolically represented the freedom from both conventional feminine appearance and behaviour potentially available to suffragettes.[19]

Perhaps the most notable example of a suffragette who adopted a military dress-style was Mary Leigh, a suffragette known for her daring protests and self-effacing nature. The military bearing often emphasized in descriptions of Leigh was due in part to Leigh's role as drum major of the WSPU drum-and-fife band, formed in 1909. It may be difficult now to see a uniformed band as a form of feminist protest but the drum-and-fife band was of great symbolic significance to suffragettes and non-suffragettes alike. Mainstream press accounts of the band's first appearance stressed that this was the final marker of men's superfluity (cited in *Votes for Women*, 21 May 1909: 693) and expressed suspicion that women were actually capable of such a performance: 'So great was the surprise at seeing women thus equipped and thus able to march with military precision that some onlookers questioned whether they were not boys in disguise' (Yeoman vol. 2: 9). An all-woman band, drilled to military precision and wearing uniforms in the WSPU colours, provided suffragettes with a visual representation of a collective feminist agency. Photographs of Leigh in her drum major uniform – holding the silver mace, staring defiantly at the camera and saluting – which appeared in *Votes for Women* and were sold as postcards, offered a powerful singular embodiment of this agency. Leigh as suffragette soldier was also consistent with the WSPU's recurrent representation of the campaign in terms of warfare, from appropriating Joan of Arc as a kind of patron saint to explicitly designating the later campaign of property destruction as 'Guerrilla Warfare'.[20] The body of Leigh in such photographs and descriptions – its dress, comportment, gesture and morphology – reiterated meanings associated with military discourse (duty, courage, strength) in order to signify commitment to the cause: the salute offered a corporeal metaphor for the motivation behind all the diverse forms of protest associated with the suffragettes. The connotation of blind obedience and devotion to duty at the expense of the individual which the military salute evokes was, however, confounded by Leigh's own history in the movement. There is ongoing debate about the extent to which guerrillas like Leigh operated on their own initiative without the leadership's knowledge or approval and Leigh's drum major photographs, far from denoting passive obedience, could have signified to contemporary viewers the need for ongoing resistance, for contestation even within the movement itself.[21] Suffragettes like Leigh, and to a lesser extent Drummond and Holme, contested the constitution of the political domain by the disjuncture they embodied between the dissenting female subject and the liberal political subject, construed as rational, deliberative and, by implication, masculine. Adopting a military dress style in order to perform acts of dissent, these women enacted dissident citizenship and represented an alternative embodiment of the suffragette subject that co-existed with the fashionable suffragette and again attested to the discursive complexity of suffragette subjectivity.

Conclusion

George Dangerfield also recognized suffragette fashion as a meaningful dimension of the campaign but for him it represented the illegitimacy of the movement. In *The Strange Death of Liberal England*, he wrote:

> The female wardrobe, with its endless combinations of colours and varieties of material, with its infinite suggestions of new social relationships, offers itself as a convenient short cut into history; but is the history thus arrived at by any chance true history? (1961: 143)

Pondering 'two preposterous contrivances', the high starched collars and straw hats worn by some women during the suffragette period, Dangerfield asked rhetorically: 'what are they, after all, but the fugitive and casual symbols of acute psychological dyspepsia?' (1961: 143, 148). Dangerfield understood fashion as symptom: the suffragette conveyed her latent masculinity by wearing masculine-influenced items of clothing. For Dangerfield, then, fashion provides access not to 'true' history, understood as concerned with the domain of public life, but to the secret, pathological history of the self, testifying to the suffragette's aberrant psychology and gender misidentification. Contra Dangerfield, I have argued that fashion was a form of feminist agency centred on the suffragette body: it enabled the woman to act, enhanced the performance of her protest and powerfully communicated to other women. Instead of seeing suffragette fashion as a psychologization or trivialization of politics, it should rather be seen as a component of feminist agency, which deliberately drew attention to the suffragette body in order to contest the legitimacy of the masculine political subject. The display of the fashionable suffragette body engaged in explicitly political actions offered a subversive repetition of conven-tional practices associated with modern femininity and thus challenged normative definitions of citizenship and political agency as the provenance of men. The suffragette performance of fashion, which stressed the female specificity of the protestors laying claim to citizenship, challenged the normativity of liberalism's claims such as universality and consensus and insisted on difference and dissent as vital to the conception of modern citizenship.

Acknowledgement

I would like to thank the Centre for Research for Women, Western Australia, for their generous assistance which enabled the inclusion of illustrations in this chapter.

Notes

1. 'Infection' was originally published in *The Suffragist* in October 1909, but subsequently reprinted as a pamphlet.
2. See *Votes for Women* (hereafter *VFW)* 18 June 1908: 249. The colour scheme was devised by Emmeline Pethick Lawrence and she provided an account of its significance in 'The Women's Exhibition 1909 Programme'. Another account of the colours also appeared in *Votes for Women*, 30 July 1908: 343.
3. This is not to hypostasize Victorian ideology which was itself an unstable construction, subject to contestation and reaffirmation throughout the Victorian period, as Mary Poovey (1988) has notably argued.
4. On the political as a domain where the constitution of public and private are debated and contested, see Fraser (1992a: 129).
5. On this point see also Richard Wrigley's essay in this volume.
6. The Women's Freedom League (WFL), a rival suffragette organization, was formed as a breakaway from the WSPU in 1907 (Raeburn 1973: 40).
7. Unable to unchain the women, authorities finally removed the protestors still attached to pieces of the wrought-iron grille which were wrenched out of the surrounding stonework. The fact that the Ladies' Gallery was screened off by a grille was a significant aspect of this episode of suffragette protest. Debate ensued as to whether the grille should be replaced and a Select Parliamentary Committee decided that in future women (accompanied by men) should be admitted to the open gallery previously reserved for men only (Raeburn 1973: 75).

8. See Tickner (1988) for extensive examples of popular representations of suffragettes in cartoons and postcards as unwomanly, unbecoming and ridiculous.

9. Figures vary, but it has been estimated that the crowds numbered over 250,000. See Tickner (1988: 96).

10. While white summer dresses were seen by the WSPU as unostentatious and therefore highly suitable for the processions, Tickner questions the affordability of such dresses for all participants (1988: 294 n. 125). Stephenson's description, however, is not without a hint of playfulness; as a legal secretary her means were limited and her account of her work for the cause is always shadowed by worries over losing her job as a result of her WSPU involvement.

11. While the WSPU's purple, white and green were the most widely used and recognized colours, other suffrage organizations also adopted colours to distinguish their members. The WFL chose green, white and gold; the constitutional suffragists, represented by the NUWSS (National Union of Women's Suffrage Societies) chose red, white and green. The smaller, often professionally based organizations also adopted colours, such as the Actresses' Franchise League, which used pink and green. (If one was a member of both the WSPU and the Actresses' Franchise League, one would then have a choice of colours to wear!) Shifting allegiances over the course of the movement also led to variations of colours: when Emmeline and Frederick Pethick Lawrence broke away from the WSPU in 1912 and formed the Votes for Women Fellowship they adopted purple, white and red as their colours. Another defector from the WSPU, Sylvia Pankhurst, used purple, white, green and red as the colours for her East London Federation. For a fuller account of suffrage colours, see Tickner 1988: 265.

12. See photographs of Emmeline Pankhurst on the Hat Stall at the Women's Exhibition (Atkinson 1996: 91). See also Kaplan and Stowell's discussion of a 1908 play which explored suffrage themes called *Tilda's New Hat* (1994: 167–8).

13. Responding to suffragette interruptions during his speech at Wrexham, Lloyd George stated: 'I remember little eisteddfodau at which prizes were given for . . . the best hazel walking sticks. One of those sticks, by the way would be rather a good thing to have just now' (cited in *VFW*, 13 September 1912: 802). *Votes for Women*, quoting from mainstream newspapers, reported, 'Each of the women was smacked on the face, each one lost her hat, each one had bunches of hair torn ruthlessly from the roots' (13 September 1912: 802). Marion

reported, 'My hair was torn down, handfuls grabbed from every side, and pulled up by the roots' (802). Another unnamed suffragette reported 'We were torn apart, our tight-fitting caps were wrenched off, our hair savagely clutched and pulled down and used as a means of torture' (*VFW*, 27 September 1912: 835).

14. Sylvia Pankhurst described the raid on 1 March 1912 as follows: 'In Piccadilly, Regent Street, Oxford Street, Bond Street, Coventry Street and their neighbourhood, in Whitehall, Parliament Street, Trafalgar Square, Cockspur Street and the Strand, as well as in districts so far away as Chelsea, well-dressed women suddenly produced strong hammers from innocent-looking bags and parcels, and fell to smashing the shop windows . . . Damage amounting to thousands of pounds was effected in a few moments . . . In fashionable Bond Street few windows remained' (1931: 373–4). The following Monday, 4 March a second raid targeted Knightsbridge, Brompton Road and Kensington High Street (1931: 374). Hundreds of suffragettes were arrested.

15. Billington-Greig was one of the founders of the WFL, after splitting from the WSPU in 1907. See her 1911 account, *The Militant Suffragette Movement* (reprinted in McPhee and FitzGerald [1987]), for a critique of the movement based on a binary opposition between legitimate political protest and 'advertisement'.

16. Black Friday was a deputation to the House of Commons held 18 November 1910, in which hundreds of suffragettes were assaulted and injured by police and male bystanders alike. See Murray and Brailsford (1911) for detailed statements of injuries.

17. High-heeled shoes could also, however, be co-opted to suffragette purposes. When Stephenson lacked a stone to smash a window, a fellow suffragette offered her 'magnificently-heeled' shoe which served the purpose admirably (154; see also the account of this incident in *VFW* , 2 December 1910: 142).

18. A gift to Kenney from Emmeline Pethick Lawrence (Kenney 1924: 106).

19. Holme related an anecdote to Antonia Raeburn of driving Christabel Pankhurst to dinner at Lady Sybil Smith's home: 'Lady Sybil heard that the chauffeur had come and she thought I was an ordinary chauffeur. I had gone past the fanlight in the front door when Lady Sybil's chauffeur came up and thinking I was a chauffeur too, he caught me by the arm: "Like to bring the bugger round to the yard, mate?" "No – er!" I said, "I think not." Just at that moment Lady Sybil came out in her white dress and said: "Come in, Miss Holme, and have some dinner." Her chauffeur nearly went dotty. I must say the chauffeurs

were always frightfully nice to me and the maids used to get into the most frightful state of joy thinking a man was coming when they saw me' (Raeburn 1973: 95).

20. On this point, see Cheryl Jorgensen-Earp (1997).
21. See Parkins (2000). Leigh, always a commited pacifist, was clearly untroubled by the military connotations of her WSPU uniform: until at least the mid 1960s she wore it to the annual Labour Day marches in London (Mitchell Collection).

6

Scouts, Guides, and the Fashioning of Empire, 1919–39

Tammy M. Proctor

The Boy Scout movement officially came of age in 1929 at Arrowe Park near Liverpool. This celebration of the twenty-first birthday of Scouting in Britain was a two-week long world jamboree, which coincided with the anniversary of the founding of Scouting in 1908. This literal and symbolic growth to maturity for the movement was an event that brought together 30,000 Scouts from more than forty foreign countries and thirty-three British colonies. Organized as a self-sufficient world, the camp resembled a small city when it was completed in late July, and as the *Daily Mirror* recorded on 22 July, 'there will be no need for any scout to go outside the boundaries of the camp for anything he needs' (TC/259, Scout Association [SA] London; *Annual Report* 1930: 21). Despite torrential downpours and mud, curious onlookers flocked to this self-contained camp, especially on the August Bank Holiday, when an estimated 56,000 visitors entered the jamboree. Total attendance excluding uniformed Scouts and Girl Guides well exceeded a quarter million people, making the jamboree a huge emotional and financial success for the organization. The Scouts themselves seemed a bit dazzled by the crowds, as the *Yorkshire Post* reported on 6 August: 'It has intrigued the Scouts all day that they were a spectacle at which people had come to gaze.' Indeed the jamboree had become a national pageant, and the press followed the events of the jamboree closely, but also offered commentary on the symbolic meaning for Britain and its empire of this gathering. As *The Times* noted on 1 August 1929:

> The Canadians marched in effective green and yellow jumpers; the Brazilian Sea Scouts wore sky blue; and there was not a white face in the troop from Ceylon. England marched behind the flag of St. George, and close to our own contingent were the Indian Scouts in brilliant turbans . . . race succeeded race until after 45 minutes the Scouts had given . . . fresh concrete evidence

that their territory is boundless and their cause the cause of friendliness and mutual aid capable of world-wide interpretation.

Noting the uniformed ranks, but outlining the flamboyant and obvious differences in clothing and in skin, the press and spectators were treated to a youth marching in the name of internationalism and friendship. Yet, in many ways the jamboree spectacle reflected the power of nationalism, giving lie both to the stated internationalist and pacifist aspirations of the events. The variety of flags, uniforms and languages illustrated the unusual sight of global youth for every Scout and visitor, and each contingent carried flags and wore national costumes or uniforms. Camps were placed according to countries, and Scouts visited each other in national and regional contingents. *The Times* again commented on the exotic variations in the otherwise unified and uniformed display of young men two days later when the boys marched for inspection by the Prince of Wales: 'contingent after contingent swept by, each, though a section of the corporate body, displaying its individual nationality by something distinctive in uniform, by the manner of saluting, by display of national dress, or in some other way.'

Figure 6.1. Jamaican Scouts at the 1929 Jamboree in Birkenhead (Liverpool).

Figure 6.2. Three Algerian Scouts.

The jamboree reflected the contradictions inherent in the act of uniforming youth from around the world and echoed the ambiguous teachings of the Scout movement itself. Uniforms functioned as a unifying symbol in the international Scout and Guide organizations, apparently erasing difference and hiding 'otherness', yet also reflecting the differences of nationality, age, race, religion, class and gender that were important ways of ranking youth in the movements. Uniforms established a standard of 'civility' and 'smartness' that youth in each new country had to strive to imitate, while simultaneously inscribing difference on the young bodies. As recent scholarship has demonstrated, 'Britain sought with increasing desperation to preserve the fiction of a unified Imperial nationality, to symbolize to the world the continuing unity of an Empire which in reality was crumbling' (Thane 1998: 42). Organizations such as the Scouts and Guides reflected some of these same concerns with nationalism and imperial unity, but the movements were also pulled toward a new ideological project of internationalism that had emerged by the 1920s.

This chapter uses the uniforming of Scouts and Guides as a way of interrogating inter-war notions of imperialism, internationalism and goodwill that these youth movements tried to articulate. By examining the Guide and Scout movements' concerted expansion worldwide after the Great War, we explore how British notions of difference undermined and complicated the uniformity the movements thought they were creating. Further, uniformed youth organizations such as the Scouts and Guides demonstrate the 'ubiquitous' gendering of national and imperial citizenship in Britain in the 1920s and 1930s (Melman 1998: 14).

Although movements had developed in countries outside of Britain prior to the First World War, the most sustained and organized expansion of Scouting and Guiding came in the 1920s with the creation of international departments in the organizations. With all of this activity and growth, British Scout and Guide officials saw the need for organized global associations that would allow collaboration between national Scout organizations while fostering a spirit of cooperation and education between boys. In truth, British leaders worried that unless a British-led coalition existed, the movement could stray from the intentions and mission of the founder. Concerned with this idea of uncontrolled development of programmes in other countries, British and American leaders felt the need to provide leadership for fledgling movements, especially in non-white and non-English speaking regions. These same leaders saw an opportunity to create a post-war atmosphere that encouraged cooperation among those of European ancestry around the world – whether in the US, Britain, Australia or South Africa.

The Guides began the process when Olave Baden-Powell, Robert's young wife, founded two new entities in February 1919: the Guide International Council and the Imperial Council, 'for the purpose of carrying assistance and inspiration to those countries newer and consequently smaller and less experienced in the world of Boy Scouting and Girl Guiding'. The International Council was dominated by US and British personnel from the beginning, with its headquarters and financial backing coming from London and its first organizing meeting in Oxford in 1920, while the Imperial Council was run by a single woman, Mrs Fisher-Rowe (Girl Guides Association [GA], *Annual Report* 1919: 21; Hoover, 14 May 1926; *The WAGGGS* 1938: 2; Kerr 1932: 167). These early sections functioned for a few years, but at the 1926 World Conference at Camp Edith Macy in the US, Guide and Girl Scout leaders decided to create a more substantial international organization, to accommodate the expanding movement. The World Association of Girl Guides and Girl Scouts (WAGGGS) was formed at the World Conference in Hungary in 1928, with twenty-eight founder member countries, and the Imperial Council became the Overseas Association, the new name stressing the close alliance between colonies and metropole. The WAGGGS consisted of a World Bureau in London and a World Committee made up of nine elected members from various countries. The British woman chosen to direct this vast world organization was Dame Katharine Furse, former head of the Volunteer Aid Detachment and the Women's Royal Naval Service during the war (Kerr 1936: 388–90).

Like the Guides, the Scouts planned an international organization at their first international gathering, held at Olympia in 1920. At this meeting, Baden-Powell was proclaimed World Chief Scout, and a unanimous vote heralded the formation of an International Bureau and Committee. The former International Commissioner for British Scouting, Hubert Martin, was chosen as the first director, and the International Bureau was established in London with funds from an American donor, F. Peabody. As with the Guide organization, biennial international conferences were held beginning with the Paris Conference of 1922 (*The History and Organization of World Scouting* n.d.: 2; Lund 1971: 1–3; Wilson 1959: 44–5).

With the international expansion and consolidation of the 1920s, Scout and Guide leaders sought to prove that the 'fundamental needs of young people are much the same all over the world' (*WAGGGS Information* 1938: 11). Baden-Powell apparently hoped to create a truly popular movement, albeit one that would allow white elites to train others to meet the responsibilities of their particular station in life. Non-whites were admitted to the movements to be trained to fulfill their potential within the constraints of their birth. To realize these goals within international Scouting and Guiding, leaders realized that they would have to come up with a flexible programme that would help them avoid the potential problems that they would face. The movements had some success in their development of programmes that could be adapted to meet the needs of different countries, but the issues of religion, race and gender remained obstacles throughout the inter-war period.

By the 1920s, significant uniformed youth movements existed through-out the world, many organized by nationalist groups or other political movements, such as fascists, National Socialists, and communists. All of these organizations looked to youth as a viable and vital force for the future, and most of them used uniforms as social and political tools to ensure conformity and loyalty (de Grazia 1992; Kahane 1997; Mosse, 1985; Peukert, 1987; Whitney 1994; Laqueur 1962; Rempel 1989; Stachura 1975; Stachura 1981; Weaver 1992; Hirsch 1997). In addition to uniforming youth (Proctor 1998), these organizations shared with the international Scout and Guide movements an interest in mass rallies and spectacles, parading their aspirations on the backs of the young. Scouting and Guiding, British organizations begun by Robert Baden-Powell in 1908 and 1910 respectively, sought to transcend the goals of these other youth groups both in Britain and abroad by moving onto the international scene in the 1920s and 1930s, using the language of goodwill and cooperation. Officially, the Guides and Scouts attempted to downplay nationalism in favour of a rhetoric of world citizenship. As Baden-Powell said in a speech in the US in the 1930s:

If the World War did no other good, indeed it did mostly harm, it did, I think, open our eyes to the fact that patriotism is only a narrow patriotism if it confines itself to getting to the top of one's own country – we want to look beyond that. It wants to look beyond that and see how we can help in the world to bring about peace, and that is a special responsibility for great nations . . . (B-P Collection [946-986] Reel 8, Boy Scouts of America [BSA]).

The movements hoped to create a feeling of collaboration among nations in Europe and to foster a cooperative spirit in the Empire. In particular, Baden-Powell and his organizations looked to the US for the construction of a British/American alliance to 'peacefully penetrate' countries and instil Anglo-American values. This goal echoed imperial constructions of the civilizing mission, imbuing the modern notion of the world citizen with an older idea of the White Man's Burden. In the nineteenth century British imperialism had been justified by theories of white racial superiority, and imperialism was constructed as a duty and a destiny for white men, in particular. Fed by emerging ideas of Social Darwinism, imperial apologists developed a reinvigorated and powerful myth of a 'white' community who would lead the colonized 'upward' and 'forward' (MacDonald 1994: 4, 53–4; Tidrick 1990: 49–50; McClintock 1995; Kennedy 1996). As anthropologist Ann Stoler has found, colonial authority was based on this notion of a homogenous colonizing community, which shared class backgrounds, racial attitudes and a common culture, even though this homogeneity was an illusion (Stoler 1989). This myth also reflected the gendered nature of colonialism, creating a complex nexus that functioned to mold both the colonies and the metropole. The international brotherhood/sisterhood emerged amidst this period in the 1920s when these older myths of imperial identity co-existed with a new articulation of empire in post-First World War Britain. Scouts and Guides tried to reconcile these two impulses as they expanded into the empire and the world.

Echoing a move in Britain to define who was British (Thane 1998: 29–45), Guides and Scouts in the inter-war period could reconcile their conceptions of exclusion with their stated inclusive policies by erecting boundaries within countries. Girls could scout, but in different uniforms and with an independent organization. Non-whites could be Scouts, but in separate divisions. Catholics could be Guides in Ireland, but in closed companies. Modifications and accommodations determined the character of Guide and Scout companies. Concerned with gender and racial segregation yet drawn to the language of international cooperation espoused by agencies such as the League of Nations, Scouting and Guiding used their newly founded World Associations and the funds from US/European associations to create a movement with a multi-national membership that became the largest youth organization in the world. By the 1980s, the Scout and Guide movements had a combined world membership of more than twenty million extending across the globe (Thompson 1990: 33; *75 Years of Scouting* 1982: 55).

Uniforms accompanied the Scouts and Guides in their imperial and international expansion, functioning both as a symbol of the power and unity of the movements but also as an attractive draw for youth. In his study of consumption and ritual, Grant McCracken notes the fluid cultural meanings reflected in clothing. As McCracken usefully explains, clothing establishes social distance by signaling status and rank, yet it also can be used to represent collective principles or ideals (McCracken 1988: 59–61). Uniforms are designed for a purpose, but they also have a history that is both hidden and apparent (Enloe 2000: 261). In short, clothing expresses multiple meanings for both wearers and viewers, simultaneously empowering an individual or group with a sense of identity and dividing people according to status. The ambiguity of clothing seems less obvious with a uniformed movement, whose members are presumably dressed alike, but the fact of uniformity meant that any deviations in style, colour, or function are highlighted even more. In addition, complicated under-coding goes on with uniforms, so that uninitiated outsiders might not recognize the subtle cues of difference, while the insiders note and experience every deviation, signaling placement in the hierarchy of the organization (Davis 1992: 7–10). The institutionalized contradictions inherent in the process of uniforming youth actually strengthened the movements allowing Scouts and Guides to 'foster solidarity without consensus', a powerful function of ritual (Kertzer 1988: 69).

Uniforms had delineated the various sections of the Scout and Guide movements since the early days of the organizations. Beyond reflecting national and regional identification, uniforms were transformed to reflect rites of passage as Scouts and Guides aged. Brownies (aged eight to ten) and Cubs (aged nine to eleven) gave way to Guides (aged eleven to fifteen) and Scouts (aged twelve to sixteen), who in turn became Rangers (over sixteen) and Rovers (over sixteen). In other words, children became adolescents, and adolescents were transformed into young adults. Each age level had different uniforms, badges, and accessories. Often the age indicator was as subtle as a different colour of badge or tie or hat.

Uniforms also marked the separate sex structure of the organizations. The skirts and shorts of the two organizations point to the important role of uniform in maintaining the gender distinctions vital to Scouting and Guiding's ideologies. Initially, British Guides wore long skirts and neat hair braids, with boots, heavy tunic tops, and wide-brimmed hats. Early skirts were designed to be wide and full, allowing girls greater movement and freedom in their outdoor pursuits. In the 1920s and 1930s, Guide skirts shortened to knee length, but girls continued to be respectable with heavy, dark stockings. Skirts still forced girls to remember their feminine roles and to keep their tomboyish inclinations in check (Davin 1996: 70–81). They could and did attach knives, haversacks, and other backwoods paraphernalia to their belts, but they were not encouraged to adopt trousers or Scout attire. In addition, Guide uniforms were dark blue because khaki was considered too military for girls (Grayzel 1997; Hillman 1999).

The Scout shorts served a similar function for boys and men. Scouts wore shorts, long socks, khaki shirts and wide brimmed hats. The shorts, adopted by both men and boys early in the movement, set the Scouts apart from other youth movements and from soldiers, and they reflected Scouting's imperial beginnings. The boys' uniform borrowed from one Baden-Powell had designed for the South African Constabulary at the turn of the century, imbuing the movement with a serious purpose. In addition the uniforms signalled the creation of 'boyish men' (since adult leaders wore shorts) and 'manly boys' ready for imperial adventure (Phillips 1997: 87). In short, the ambiguity of girlhood and boyhood as expressed in the Scouts and Guides created a space for experimentation for both adults and children in the movements, but also sought to teach the fundamental tenets of masculinity and femininity in a safe, yet fun, setting.

Complicating this problem of how to train both boys and girls in their assigned gender roles was the international expansion, which provided new cultural contexts and challenges. In addition to a variety of religious, racial and cultural hurdles, Britain had fundamental disagreements with the US about the gendering of the organizations. From the founding of the Girl Scouts of the USA in 1912 by Juliette Gordon Low, British and American Scout and Guide leaders found themselves in an argument over the nature of the girls' movement. The Girl Scouts totally disregarded British Guiding's carefully drawn boundaries between boys and girls. American girls called themselves 'scouts', and just like the boys, they wore khaki uniforms and modelled their programme after the outline in *Scouting for Boys*. After a series of battles in Britain to create a separate and appropriate girls' movement of a different name, it seemed that the American Girl Scout movement could only cause uncomfortable questions about the nature of British Guiding. British leaders continually pressed the Girl Scouts to adopt the name 'Guides', arguing that only confusion could result, but Helen Storrow, Vice-President of the Girl Scouts of the USA, made the American position on the question of naming clear in a 1920 report:

> Our name, Girl Scouts, is very dear to us, and seems to us the logical name. The terms scout and scouting apply to girls and their activities as appropriately as to boys, and represent the same law and ideals. The idea that we are trying to make boys out of the girls is soon dissipated when the girls show their increased usefulness at home, and demonstrate womanly activities at their rallies. The suggestion to change the name met with determined opposition from both our girls and their officers, and we shall in all probability remain scouts. I wish most heartily we might share the same name. Would the Guides consider changing? I wish they would (Girl Scouts of the USA [GSUSA]).

After ten years of emphasizing that Girl Scouts did not exist in Britain, Guide leaders were as unlikely to change their name as the Americans were to embrace the Guide name and emblem. However, real problems arose in the 1920s as the World Association began to recognize official movements in new countries. Apparently, Girl Scout and Girl Guide organizations existed side by side in some places, and in other cases, Guide and Scout organizers squabbled over the naming of the new organization. The British and American leaders became quite territorial in the matter of new organizations, and correspondence between the two countries reflected a continuing tension over how to name the girls' movement.

Siam was one such country of contention when in 1921 girls began to organize a sister movement to Boy Scouting. Olave Baden-Powell wrote to the Girl Scout leaders in the United States, urging the Americans to allow her leaders to 'guide' Siam in its development. She pointed out that strong Guide organizations existed in neighbouring Malaya, Hong Kong, and Burma, and she also noted that a Guide organizer had already been dispatched to the area. After a delicate reference to the fact that Guide and Scout work are the same 'except in name', Baden-Powell launched into her real objections.

Baden-Powell pointed to problems in Palestine and India with Girl Scouts wrecking local Guide movements and causing confusion about the 'true' nature of Guiding. Above all, she worried that Girl Scouting was equated with masculine pursuits, especially in non-Western countries:

> It is not the name IN AMERICA that matters, but the misinterpretation that is ALWAYS put upon it in other countries. It so obviously shows that it is to all intents and purposes the same thing for the girls as 'scouting' is for boys, and good as we know that to be in a strange, and especially an Eastern, land, it goes against the movement . . . (Baden-Powell 1921, GSUSA).

In short, she believed that Girl Scouting would be considered the same movement as Boy Scouting and that parents would envision co-ed activities, which she thought would be counterproductive. As she noted in her letter, 'pushing Western ideas onto Eastern peoples needs care and tact', implying that the British had a better understanding of such processes than the Americans:

> We have to reckon, in promoting this quite modern and Western idea, with Caste, Creeds of all kinds, Climate, Languages, Customs, Racial feelings and National feelings, as well as Politics and it really is most important that where it is being pushed it must be done by the right people in the right way (Baden-Powell 1921, GSUSA).

Of course, underlying Baden-Powell's surface objections to the name was the desire for British headquarters to control new movements springing up, but her comments also illustrate the continuing importance of the gendered nature of the movements in Britain and abroad. Perhaps this concern was best expressed by Boy Scout leaders, who felt compelled to comment on the question of girls. At the Boy Scout International Conference in Paris in 1922, a resolution was passed to request that Guides stop using the name 'Scout' or 'Eclaireuse', echoing the strong disapproval many boys' organizations felt over what they saw as girls aping boys. As Hubert Martin pointed out in a memo to Robert Baden-Powell, 'It is one of her [a woman's] jobs in life to guide – not to Scout, which is the man's job.' He continued:

> But my personal anxiety about many Guide companies is the danger that they, through wrong leadership, will produce a race of tomboys, than which there is nothing more objectionable . . . It seems to me that the use of the term 'Girl Scout' is a big question of principle and that the persistence of its use is symptomatic of the tom-boy, aping the man, instead of concentrating on woman's most important sphere – the home . . .

Martin really touched on the heart of the issue: had girls become too masculine? Were they losing their femininity and their domestic skills? As he wrote in his report, 'The tendency amongst the girls of today is to neglect their own sphere, the home, and try to ape the man – hence the collar and tie, the "Eton crop" etc. etc.' (Martin 1926, GSUSA). As with many of the tensions confronting the Scout and Guide movements in the inter-war period, international expansion also brought to the fore old anxieties about the teaching and reinforcing of appropriate notions of femininity and masculinity.

Uniforms, which functioned so well as an indicator of sexual identity in Britain, were problematic in the Empire. Many Guide and Girl Scout groups adopted khaki uniforms and imperial-style pith helmets or straw hats merely because the dark blue material and heavy felt hats of the Guides were uncomfortable in tropical climates. Eventually in some places a compromise was reached; in Trinidad and Tobago, Guides traded their khaki blouses for light blue blouses, and gave up their khaki 'cricketer' hats for panamas (Girl Guides Association of Trinidad and Tobago 1974: 35). In New Zealand, girl peace scouts were forced to give up their khaki and their 'fearsome emblems such as curlews, moreporks, and peewits', in exchange for membership in the World Association. After 1923, the girls toed the Guiding line in navy blue dresses and 'reluctantly changed their emblems from their more adventurous ones to violets, snowdrops, etc.' (*Thirty Years of Guiding in New Zealand* 1953: 7, 9).

The Scouts also struggled to reconcile notions of masculinity and imperialism during their international expansion. Non-European boys living in the empire were often depicted as both effeminate (therefore unmanly) and sexually dangerous (therefore unScoutlike); so how was the Scout movement to inculcate appropriate masculinity and Scout conduct in these boys? Although clothing could inspire subaltern peoples to excellence, many British leaders felt that no amount of Scouting or uniforming could create 'true men' from imperial subjects. As Michael Budd usefully noted, 'Baden-Powell's belief that other races could excel physically and remain degenerate demonstrated how the body could be read as a kind of clothing that covered more profound failings' (Budd 1997: 81). For decades, British males had been justifying their power and forming their identity around the idea that they were manly and males in the colonies were effeminate, and the concept that each could be Scouts on equal footing was hard to accept (Sinha 1995). Was it possible to uniform British and African bodies in the same way? Concerns about the proper way of inculcating masculinity and femininity led to divisive policies regarding race and potential 'racial mixing'.

The Scout and Guide white global community was continually threatened and compromised by the large numbers of non-white youth who wanted a part in the movements. Officially, the two movements maintained a non-discrimination policy that prohibited exclusion of youth because of race or colour, but in reality that policy was problematic. In Bermuda, Guides were designated 'white only' until 1930, and in the Bahamas, non-white Guides were prohibited throughout the inter-war period. South Africa maintained separate branches for 'Bantu', 'Indian', and 'white' Scouts and Guides until well into the 1930s, never really solving the difficulties of racial exclusion (Proctor 2000). Even in countries that had mixed organizations, non-white groups were often subject to 'special', or simplified activities and rules. Once again, uniforms became a way of distinguishing between different races and ethnicities within some countries, reinforcing the exclusionary policies that the two movements claimed to have abandoned.

Examples of the attitudes of British officials toward some countries with non-white or multi-racial memberships are the journals, reports and correspondence of Olave Baden-Powell. In candid notes, Baden-Powell writes of the difficulties of adapting the British Guide programme for people in other countries. She expends a terrible amount of energy on the issue of developing 'appropriate' companies in the Empire, trying whenever possible to establish British local control.

In St Helena, a small island off the coast of southern Africa, the Guides and Scouts were run by a 'native' clergyman, L. C. Walcott, and his English wife. Baden-Powell could not fault Mrs Walcott's abilities, calling her the 'prop and stay' of St Helena Guiding and 'perfectly splendid'. However, she considered her unsuitable as a Guide leader in many ways, describing her as 'a very pathetic person', because of her marriage. A Guide leader seconded this opinion in a letter to Olave Baden-Powell regarding Walcott in 1936, 'She has, of course, grave limitations, one of which is the fact that she is married to a native' (Baden-Powell 1930, GA). Baden-Powell did not question either of the Walcotts' abilities as leaders or their enthusiasm for the movement; instead she worried about the dangers of mixed-race marriage. What kind of example might the Walcotts set for susceptible youngsters?

When called upon to inspect the Scouts and Guides of St. Helena in 1936, Baden-Powell himself gave them middling marks. He noted how hard the group was trying despite a lack of money, but he cannot resist commenting on race:

Figure 6.3. Olave Baden-Powell with an international contingent of campers at the First World Camp at Foxlease (UK) in 1924.

Scouts, all more or less coloured, well turned out in uniform with bamboo staves but mostly without shoes or stockings, clothing being very expensive and the people very poor. Nice intelligent looking boys . . . Walcott, keen, well meaning . . . coloured Scoutmaster (Baden-Powell 1935-36, TC/10 – SA).

The poverty of many African groups, such as the ones described in St Helena, combined with untrained leaders and lack of materials (badges, uniform accessories, handbooks) meant that the tone and practicalities of their versions of Guiding and Scouting sometimes looked quite different. Mission-associated Scout and Guide groups often used make-shift materials and uniforms, which displeased international officials concerned with reputation and uniformity. Olave Baden-Powell reflected on the problems of these inappropriate members of the association in 1930:

Guides in these four places [Gambia, Gold Coast, Sierra Leone, Nigeria] are all African natives, as there are no white children living there – excepting perhaps one or two exceptions...It is to my mind quite an open question whether we are justified in going on with guides in these places as it is really almost a travesty of what WE would call Guiding. The mentality of those people is so very different from the European, and they are so VERY far behind in development, and it is really hard that we in these days bring Western Twentieth Century civilization to them and expect them to jump straight from a civilization of SEVERL [sic] hundred years back direct into what we have now here to-day! (Baden-Powell 1930, GA)

As Baden-Powell goes on to point out, the problem from her perspective is that the girls in these areas have organized themselves into Guide companies. If the World Association was to have any hope of controlling the growth of world Guiding, then it was going to have to accept and help develop these organizations in the colonies lest they go it alone. And youth in the colonies did want to be Guides and Scouts. They got copies of official literature and began Scouting in their schools and at home, forming their own pseudo-Scout organizations if they could not find sponsorship. What attracted youth from the empire to these movements?

Youth of the empire were attracted to Scouting and Guiding for the same reasons that young people in Britain and the US wanted to join: adventure, travel, international connections, and a sense of belonging. Adventure, as Richard Phillips has recently noted, has broad appeal because of its 'transformative capacity' (Phillips 1997: 165). Boys and girls from a whole host of countries recognized that in the game of scouting they could find a space for their own imaginative and real adventures. Sometimes in their attempts to 'scout', youth could be ingenious and courageous. For instance, one British official visiting South Africa spoke of seeing 'native' boys using mining pit props (as Scout staves) in an attempt to be 'true' Scouts: 'The pathetic faces of those little black boys trying to look like Scouts almost moved my wife to tears, especially in view of the fact that she heard that the police had, two or three days before, locked them up for the night for carrying staves without permission' (*Berrow's Worcester Journal*, 23 March 1929, TC/243 – SA) Just as poor boys (and girls) in Britain had marched with broomsticks for staves, Africans, too, wanted this symbol of Scouting for themselves.

In British colonies, race was a special concern because of the growth of nationalist movements. Colonial authorities were often ambivalent toward missionaries, who often as not created revolutionaries rather than docile workers in their mission schools, but officials also treated youth movements with some suspicion, figuring that they could perform a similar function (Allman 1994; Ross 1986). 'Belge' Wilson, Deputy Commissioner of Police and Scoutmaster of a mixed troop of Anglo-Indian youth in Calcutta, remembered struggling mightily for the admittance of Indian boys into the Boy Scouts Association after the First World

War. Wilson noted that there was a Government of India Act forbidding the movement on the grounds that 'Scouting might train them to be revolutionaries.' Finally, in 1921, the various official and unofficial Scout groups in India were amalgamated into one association, which the government sanctioned. Janice Brownfoot found a similar reluctance in Malaya to accept Guiding at first. Colonial officials seemed to see the movement as subversive at first but later embraced the Guides by the late 1920s (Wilson 1959: 19–20; Brownfoot 1990: 64). This concern by imperial officials is interesting, given that parents often worried that youth were being incorporated and assimilated into British organizations.

Lakshmi Mazumdar, daughter of a middle-class Bengali family, wanted to join the Girl Guides upon meeting her first British person in 1922, an official from the Guide Association. Her parents disapproved because 'our family had a tradition of fighting against the British' and 'never liked that we should have any connection with the British community'. Mazumdar continued in her desire to join the Guides, but at her investiture her father asked once more, 'do you want to give your allegiance to the British king?' Mazumdar told her father that she 'shared his views about Independence and all that', but she still wanted to join the Guides at school and 'have friends' (Mazumdar).

Despite these familial and national tensions, boys and girls in the colonies continued to organize themselves into unofficial and official Scout and Guide groups, obtaining the uniforms and literature in any way that they could. Of particular interest seemed to be the organizations' hats, large Stetsons, and the merit badges, earned through tests. In Natal, for example, so-called 'Indian' Scouts refused to associate with the Scouts of India by wearing pagri [turbans], instead they were 'most anxious to wear the [British] Scout hat' (Walton 1936, TC/10-SA). Often British officials thought it easier to enforce and protect the uniform code by making the clothing available than to deal with 'unofficial' and sloppy uses of it. Olave Baden-Powell noted problems in many areas she visited with the uniformity of non-British groups, some of whom pinned on badges rather than sewing them or who were otherwise correctly uniformed except for shoes. In one case she urged a company in Southern Rhodesia to abandon the khaki uniforms they had obtained (which were too much like the boys) and to embrace the 'official' blue uniforms of the Guides, hoping to 'coerce them into coming into line' (Baden-Powell 1930, GA).

In addition to problems of race among countries in the empire and world, Scouts and Guides also faced the issue of internal divisions within nations. One of the trickiest of these situations, which was also tied closely to gender and race, was the problem of competing religious traditions. From the organizations' beginnings in Britain, uniforms and tests were modified slightly to accommodate differences among youth, and the movements emphasized religiosity rather than religion. Scouting and Guiding promoted themselves as movements tolerant of all religious beliefs in order to attract a variety of Christians, and much resistance had been overcome by emphasizing individual spirituality and nature reverence. For example, at regional and divisional camps, separate ceremonies were held for Protestant and Catholic youth. While British Catholic Girl Guides prayed to 'Our Blessed and Immaculate Mother, who is the Guide of all Guides', a Protestant girl wrote of being 'inspired I am sure with the Guide spirit, which being interpreted is God's spirit' (*The Catholic Women's Outlook* 1925: 45 – GA; de Beaumont 1920, GA). Even Britain's Jewish population, leaders believed, could be easily included in religious celebrations because they believed in the same God as the Christians. With the expansion of the movements outside of Britain, however, the inclusion of non-Christians and non-Jews became an issue, and leaders worried about world camps combining Hindus, Muslims, Buddhists and Catholics. At a conference held in London's East End in 1930 on the issue of Scouting and the Churches, a rector from Spitalfields, Revd Colin Carr, voiced the objection that many Christians in the movement shared. He accused Scouting of carrying 'comparative religion' too far, and he called this policy 'anti-Christian'. Carr continued, saying, 'we cannot put our hearts into a movement which inculcates into boys at the most impressionable age that it does not really matter whether they follow Jesus Christ, Buddha or Mahomet' (*Verbatim Report* 1930: 19–21, TC/229-SA).

Baden-Powell maintained a predictable stance on the issue, saying any religion was better than none at all. He continually spoke of the 'realisation of God in Nature', as more important than a dispute over particular beliefs and practices. To one earlier complaint, he answered:

So far as having an Arab and Hindu at our 'Scouts Own' at Gillwell, we could easily have driven them away by keeping the service to a strictly Christian line. We preferred to take the wider view of recognizing our brother Scouts as being also sons of the same Father with ourselves. They were broad minded enough to listen to our Scriptures; it was not very much for us in return to listen to a chapter from the Koran. You probably know the Koran yourself and will agree that it contains very fine ideas and inspiring words, and I am positive we did ourselves no spiritual harm but good from what we heard that day (Baden-Powell 1921, TC/25-SA).

Baden-Powell here suggests not only that strictly Christian services be sensitive to non-Christians but also that other religious traditions be welcome in mixed gatherings. He asks for a tolerant and open approach to religious practice.

Although challenges occurred throughout the 1920s, by the early 1930s, individual religious expression was the order of the day, and prayers, sermons and publications carefully reflected the inclusion of non-Christians. In adult training notebooks, trainers were adjured to 'inculcate reverence, whatever form of religion the boy professes'. They were also taught to use nature to teach the kind of interdenominational spirituality that Scouting and Guiding espoused: 'Not nature study as a form of worship or substitute for religion, but step towards gaining humility and reverence.' Prayers also reflected the religious policy with vague references to deities: 'Do Thou raise our thoughts and purify our aspirations; Strengthen our wills on the side of what is right and good, and against what is wrong and evil' ('Scouting and Religion', 203, 212–14, TC/124-SA). Abroad, the importance of this religious policy cannot be underestimated, as members who would have been excluded from many international social organizations because of their non-Christian beliefs were welcomed to worship as they pleased. Scouts and Guides provided separate worship facilities at camps, events, and training, and they encouraged generic prayers for peace in mixed gatherings. In addition, the Scouts and Guides were lenient with the rules in individual countries.

One way in which the Guides and Scouts dealt with the issues of religious non-conformity was through the use of distinctive badges and uniforms. For instance, in Malaya, a large multiracial and mixed-religion national Guide movement arose in the 1920s, led at first by white missionaries. As Janice Brownfoot has demonstrated, Guiding achieved success in the Muslim community because of its non-sectarian pronouncements and because Malay Guides were allowed to design their own uniforms. The khaki uniform was modified by Malay Guide Ibu Zain to meet restrictions on Muslim girls that required them to cover their limbs (Mladejovska 1938: 38–9; Brownfoot 1990: 61–4). Likewise, girls at a mission school in Poona (India) were allowed to wear saris rather than the khaki uniforms other Girl Scouts and Guides wore in that country ('Anonymous report on Guiding in Jubbulpore', GA). Both of these examples illustrate ways in which a small change in uniform could smooth a difficult situation.

More complicated problems arose in the global Scout and Guide communities over the accommodation of religious beliefs and the solution of disputes in areas with more than one dominant religion. Policy was to require affiliation of different divisions under the aegis of one national organization, but this could sometime be difficult in countries where different religious groups had separate movements. For instance, in France, four groups existed side by side: the Scouts and the Guides (Catholic) and the Eclaireurs/Eclaireuses (Protestant), and each had separate rules, leadership, and uniforms. In Malta, where Guiding began in 1918, 'Trouble arose between the Maltese Roman Catholics, and the English Protestants, and they had a "crisis" every few weeks.' Eventually, two divisions were formed that reflected the religious divisions, but also the racial divisions in Malta (Baden-Powell 1930, GA). In these cases, it was difficult to know which division 'officially' to recognize.

In addition to questions of recognition, Scout and Guide officials were called upon to deal with regional and local disputes within countries over religion. In the Caribbean, one Guide leader wrote, 'we are all mixed up, our greatest difficulty being class and degrees of colour.' She illustrated her difficulties by listing the six companies in Trinidad and Tobago:

Co. 1 – middle class black co with equally divided religion; leader Anglican
Co. 2 – middle class white co, 2/3 Roman Catholic; leaders Anglican
Co. 3 – high class black and few white Anglican
Co. 4 – very poor black co, 1/3 Roman Catholic; Roman Catholic leader
Co. 5 – poor black Anglican co, with 2 Scotch Church leaders
Co. 6 – poor black Anglican co, with Roman Catholic leader (Lake 1925, GA)

For the leader in Trinidad and Tobago, class and race were more important distinctions than religion, when deciding how to divide the companies. On nearby St Lucia, the opposite was true, as nuns protested when a Protestant leader tried to take over a Catholic Guide company (Vinter 1925, GA). This problem arose in many countries with non-homogenous populations, especially in the US, the Caribbean, and British/ French colonies (Perry 1993a, 1993b). In countries such as Ireland and Canada, distinctions between Catholics and Protestants were of paramount importance because of the political resonance of religious identities. Religion was tied to culture, politics and language, and separate Scout and Guide groups were the rule. For example, in Canada, the Guides in Quebec formed a separate branch with different uniforms and badges, which one official historian claimed were 'more suitable to Roman Catholic French Canadian thinking and culture' (Gloin 1974: 103). The Quebec Guides even renamed their branch for younger girls, calling them Jeannettes rather than using their English-speaking neighbour's name,

'Brownies'. Although the Quebec Guides agreed to a loose affiliation with the English-speaking Guides in 1938, the two organizations did not merge until the 1960s, and they still bear the dual name, Girl Guides of Canada/Guides du Canada.

Yet Scouting and Guiding could often unite youth of different religious backgrounds, or at least the organizations could promote education and understanding. In India various organizations formed and were loosely affiliated nationally. As Olave Baden-Powell reported of her Indian tour in 1930: 'Guiding is perhaps the ONE platform upon which all kinds can meet – Mohammedans, Hindus, Brahmins, Parsees, Buddhists, Christians and Jews' (Baden-Powell 1930, GA). In Malaya, too, Brownfoot notes the social change that Guiding inspired, citing the All-Malayan Camp of 1931, which included patrols of Malays, Chinese, Eurasians, Japanese, Sri Lankans, Indians, British, and Australians. She argues that Guiding allowed girls to cross ethnic, cultural and religious lines (Brownfoot 1990: 65). The international organizations aimed to create international cooperation and did all that they could to create exceptions for those who needed to change the promise or the uniform or the activities in order to be loyal to their countries, religious beliefs or families. This flexibility was one of the reasons for the successful expansion and longevity of the international movements. And while it is true that Scouting and Guiding brought youth together for international exchanges and friendships, uniform modifications ensured that religious boundaries continued to be a fundamental division among Scouts and Guides.

The expansion of Guiding and Scouting internationally was a great boost for the movements in Britain, and it won them acclaim from educators, government officials, social organizations, and even the League of Nations. As a book for the Boy Scouts of America noted in 1929:

> Like Joseph's coat, the nations of the earth have many colors . . . [yet] The Scout Uniform is outside evidence of inside aims and ideals . . . Details of color, custom, and costume mark the different nations of the earth, but in Scouting they are all alike. . . What a contribution this to international peace, international love, international understanding! When the future lawmakers of the earth are clad in the visible or invisible Uniform of the Scouts, the world will have entered into the fulfilment of the dream of its surest seers and its safest prophets. (Reimer 1929: 128–9)

However, the extension of the Scout and Guide programme into other countries produced problems both abroad and at home, as contradictions appeared in the ideologies and activities of the organizations. Practically, this meant that the organizations had to accommodate different races, religions, languages, and nations in its new global brotherhood/sisterhood while in the process of defining the meaning of the international movements (Proctor 2000). The difficulties of uniforming these differences remained both a solution and an insuperable problem for the Guides and Scouts, partly because it uncomfortably reminded British leaders of the limitations of their all-embracing international vision. Uniforms were necessary to project an image of unity and brotherhood/sisterhood in the Empire and world, but also needed to function as a means of maintaining gender and racial boundaries.

In many ways, the 1929 coming-of-age jamboree demonstrates well the spectacular ambitions of the organizations and the problems of fashioning the empire, and ultimately the world, into Scouts and Guides. Throughout the two-week jamboree, the media highlighted the 'Scouty' world, which contained much of what Britain hoped to be in the late 1920s. As nationalist movements in the Empire and economic problems at home led Britons to question imperial power, the Jamboree showed a practical Commonwealth, while also functioning as an old-style imperial pageant, complete with royal splendour and the parade of imperial subjects (Cannadine 1983). The jamboree presented a whole empire and indeed a whole world brought together by British diplomacy and goodwill, reflecting a new discourse on empire that was emerging in the 1920s. Britons were encouraged to view the empire not so much as a sign of national power, but as a vast market held together with cooperation and mutuality rather than exploitation and aggression. Baden-Powell explicitly tied the Scouts into the project of rearticulating the imperial project in the last edition of *Scouting for Boys* he wrote:

> Empire is not a Jingo term meaning that we want to spread ourselves aggressively over vast territories in rivalry with others – it stands rather for team work of free young British nations growing up in different parts of the world in friendly comradeship of mutual goodwill and co-operation (Baden-Powell 1942: 255).

In short, the Scouts and Guides both reflected and helped shape a phenomenon that the British Empire experienced in the interwar period: the simultaneous rearticulation of empire as a goodwill enterprise and the perpetuation of older notions of British imperial privilege. The movements fashioned for themselves a youthful empire, clothed in 'goodwill' intentions yet armored with the weapons of racial and gender segregation.

7

Peeking Under the Black Shirt: Italian Fascism's Disembodied Bodies

Simonetta Falasca-Zamponi

On 30 October 1922, at the end of a staged march on Rome that the fascists had organized to unsettle the Italian government, Mussolini met with the king, Vittorio Emanuele III, to discuss his new role as Prime Minister. Wearing a black shirt, he told the King: 'Please accept my apologies if I am forced to introduce myself while still wearing a black shirt. I just came from the battle which was luckily bloodless' (Salvatorelli and Mira 1952: 153). While seemingly expressing contrition over his attire at court, Mussolini's reference to the black shirt during his first encounter with the symbolic figure of state power actually initiated a battle of symbols that lasted Mussolini's entire career, first, as Prime Minister and, then, as Duce and dictator of Italy. Loaded with multiple meanings, Mussolini's pronouncement and attire in the presence of the King conveyed more than a polite apology. It presented Mussolini as the hero of Italian peace in a high-risk situation of civil war; it established him as a fighter, the valiant and courageous protagonist of a battle that was 'luckily bloodless'; and it also showed that Mussolini did not waste any time in taking up the responsibility of leading the country. He rushed to the king to accept his appointment and preside over Italy's fate. That is why, as his apologies suggested, he did not have any time for changing his clothes.

The rich symbolic value Mussolini entrusted to the black shirt in his linguistic exchange with the King might not be evident until we investigate the behind-the-scene events leading to Mussolini's visit to the monarch. Contrary to appearance, Mussolini had reached the 'battle' zones he mentions in his utterance only after the King phoned him to come to Rome and accept his nomination as Prime Minister.[1] Until then, Mussolini had been stationed at his headquarters in Milan, waiting for events to develop. Once on the train to Rome, Mussolini stopped at some of the locations around the capital to visit his faithful who had convened there to march on Rome. But the overall situation was much less dramatic than Mussolini's words to the King suggested. In reality, the battle was minimal because the march never took place; the King had summoned Mussolini before any conflict broke out. (It is doubtful, in any case, whether Mussolini's troops would have ever overcome the royal army.) As Mussolini visited a hotel prior to seeing Vittorio Emanuele, he could certainly have changed his clothes before the royal meeting, if he wished to. Instead, Mussolini opted for having the black shirt on, and emphasized its importance while apologizing for it.

Why did the black shirt find itself at the centre of a symbolic battle that, launched on that October day, characterized Mussolini's regime for more than twenty years? Why did Mussolini entrust a piece of clothing with such semantic power? What kind of symbolic weight was the black shirt supposed to carry for Mussolini and, as we will see, for all of fascism? This chapter will consider the odd fate of the black shirt in Italian fascism as a starting point for laying out the symbolic and aesthetic relationship Mussolini's regime established with the clothed bodies of its subjects, but also, and especially, the unclothed ones. Through the literal stripping of the fascist's attire, that will parallel the theoretical unveiling of fascism's core 'philosophical' creed, this chapter will argue that the enormous attention the regime gave to the fashion of its fascist members expressed a radical programme of intervention in the body politic that envisaged an almost apocalyptic disappearance of 'real' natural bodies. Indeed, I claim, one cannot probe the role of the black shirt and the importance the regime assigned to it without at the same time exploring and assessing the regime's troubled attitude towards the body. It is only by examining the black shirt with reference to the materiality of the human senses that fascism's construction and definition of citizenship becomes fully intelligible; it is only by unearthing the connection between the body natural and the body politic that the regime's whole totalitarian project emerges. Thus, and in a sense paradoxically, this chapter argues that in order to understand fascism's fashioning of the body politic and its crucial role in the regime's self-construction and representation, we need to undress the fascist body, we need to look underneath the black shirt where the human senses reside.

'The Cowl does Make the Monk', or Aesthetics versus Ideology

In 1914 Giacomo Balla, one of the central participants of the Futurist artistic movement, proposed the creation of a Futurist suit. Described as anti-neutral in a manifesto issued on 11 September the suit, with the colours of the Italian flag – red, white and green – was supposed to counter the notorious lassitude of Italians and instead incite them to an active life of high energy.[2] The Futurist suit represented a sign of the new, a solicitation to fantasy and imagination in daily life. As such, it was supposed to liberate Italians from the 'slavery of the body', the 'denial of muscular life', but, also, from 'fearful indecision', 'pessimism' and 'inertia'. The suit was aggressive, dynamic, joyful, against neutral colours and, one could add, manly. At the outbreak of the First World War, when Italy was stalled in a neutral position, the poet Cangiullo, in one of the pro-war rallies organized by the Futurists in Rome, wore the 'anti-neutral' suit designed by Balla. As the manifesto explained, the colours red, white and green expressed an active war stance.

In a typical Futurist mode, Cangiullo combined political activism with the artistic aim of transforming the lived environment. For him, as well as Balla, art was supposed to enter and inform the profane daily life and thus lose its sacred aura, as Walter Benjamin (1968) would later write. This was, after all, Futurism's innovative programme: to abolish the line between art and daily life, and to encourage an art in action that would bring forth the renewal of social existence and even the 'reconstruction of the universe'.[3] The Futurists pursued the reintegration of art into life through several avenues, fashion being only one of them. Through a new conception of clothing, as well as music, literature and food, the old bourgeois world with its means–ends rationality and attachment to the past would be overturned by a cultural revolution in which beauty and dynamism would reign supreme.

The Futurists, whose leader Filippo Tommaso Marinetti later joined Mussolini when he founded the fascist movement in 1919, foreshadowed fascism's own impatience with, and revolt against, the bourgeois world – a world both Futurists and fascists saw as characterized by comfortable life, inaction, conformism and philistinism. The Futurists were especially effective in combining a cultural critique with a political one. For them, the bourgeoisie's failure to be modern, its passatism, depended on a conservative mentality and a decadent life style that deprived it of the ability to govern, and also rendered it dangerously weak, 'feminine'. Thus they advocated the coming of 'new men' who could turn Italy's destiny around and rejuvenate the national spirit.

Disaffected with a traditional politics that privileged stasis and stagnation, fascism was embedded in the malaise that involved Marinetti and his acolytes. Like the Futurists and other cultural movements of the time, fascism, especially after it established itself securely as a regime, conceived of politics as affecting the whole way of life and not merely policy making. Italians' lives had to be changed, their 'ways of eating, dressing, working and sleeping' needed to be transformed, Mussolini declared in a speech to doctors (1934–9, vol. 8: 21). Just as, according to the Futurists' proclamation in the manifesto of clothing, wearing an anti-neutral suit would turn a peaceful 'dead' person into a colourful active warrior, so Mussolini increasingly identified style with (political) substance. In part sharing the Futurists' aestheticized vision of politics, Mussolini emphasized form (intended as appearance, effects, orderly arrangement) in his political intervention. He thought of himself as an artist politician who could create the world anew and would be able to produce a work of art, a beautiful harmonious whole out of Italy and the Italians. In line with the times' negative judgment of the crowd, identified with emotions and lack of logic, that is with women, Mussolini conceived the 'masses' as material to be forged and shaped, an object to be molded. Through the artistic manipulation of the mass-matter, its homogenization into a unitary whole, the end-result of a fascist masterpiece would be achieved.

As a political avant-garde, according to its own self-definition, fascism followed the artistic avant-garde in its pursuit of a renewed world (a reformed Italy) through intervention in daily life. The regime's increasing attention to daily habits and gestures in the 1930s was conceived as a necessary step towards the transformation of Italians into new fascist 'men'. A peculiar stance in which external look was made to overlap with substantive changes, appearance with content, style with spirit, emerged during the campaign for the reform of customs launched by the regime in 1932. The identification of fascist qualities with ways of behaving or looking became tightly entwined at the same time that the connection between ways of looking and behaving was drawn. Fascist fashion, and in particular the black shirt, became the focus of scrutiny under the regime's gaze.

The central stage the black shirt came to occupy during the reform campaign was the logical consequence of the shirt's history, implied in the episode of Mussolini's encounter with the king in 1922. On that important October day, despite the implication that the black shirt was not the proper attire in which to meet Vittorio Emanuele, Mussolini made a point in wearing the shirt because he invested it with a high symbolic value. The black shirt, Mussolini first and foremost wanted to communicate, was a uniform of combat, and fascism, through its leader, aggressively put itself at the reins of Italy's future during a threatened March on Rome. Mussolini wished to emphasize fascism's violent character, whether fictive, as in the case of the march, or real. According to his political vision, violence, as 'history's wheel', was a dynamic means to bring about change. This is the reason why he had named his movement Fasces of Combat, as he told the people of Trieste on 20 September 1920: 'Struggle is at the origin of everything . . . the day when there is no fight would be a day of sadness, it will be the end, the ruin . . . We call our Fasces Fasces of Combat, and the word combat does not leave any doubt' (1951–63, vol. 15: 221). Subscribing to a philosophy of life that glorified violence as the engine of history, the fascist movement saw in permanent struggle the source of new moral values and new energy. In view of what many considered Italy's decay in the hands of a bourgeois political class that shied away from struggle, the fascists along with other youths, including the Futurists, invoked violence and war as necessary to regenerate Italian society. Mussolini claimed that only permanent struggle through the destruction of materialism, utilitarianism, liberalism and parliamentarism could save the world from barbarism and degeneration.

But why was the black shirt supposed to promote the identification of violence with fascism? Historically, violence had indeed marked the origins of the black shirt. In the early stages of the fascist movement, members of the squads who engaged in violent attacks against socialist and leftist organizations wore black shirts, and they metonymically came to be called Black Shirts. For those who wore it, the black shirt signified

Figure 7.1. Early version of the black shirt.

absolute revolt against traditional, conformist politics identified with suits and top hats. It showed fascism's distance from the legalistic practices of compromises and parliamentary debates. It stood for action and combat. When Mussolini wore the black shirt in the presence of the king on the occasion of his nomination as Prime Minister, the black shirt was brandished as a reminder of fascism's revolutionary character, of what being 'fascist' meant (a contrast to the legal way in which the appointment took place). And even when Mussolini later dismantled the squads in 1923, the black shirt symbolically remained a fascist outfit, a sign of fascism's historical exordium, of its fundamentally revolutionary character. Thus, despite the dissolution of *squadrismo*, on the one hand, the appellation of Black Shirts extended to all fascists, and Mussolini continued to address his followers as such for the duration of his regime. On the other hand, the shirt did not merely remain a relic for museum exhibits celebrating the fascist revolution. Rather, it was supposed to be worn by all participants in the numerous fascist organizations, including women and children's groups. The shirt was part and parcel of the regime's life and identity, and one of the ten fascist commandments stated: 'He who is not ready to sacrifice body and soul to Italy and to serve Mussolini without question is unworthy to wear the black shirt, symbol of Fascism' (see Seldes 1935: 408).

During the 1920s fascism continued to sacralize the shirt. Mussolini proclaimed that the black shirt should not be worn every day, and those who wore it improperly were supposed to be arrested (1934–9 vol. 4: 352). As he specified on another occasion: 'The black shirt is not the ordinary shirt, and is not a uniform either. It is a combat outfit and can only be worn by those who harbor a pure soul in their heart' (1934–9, vol. 5: 110–11). The black shirt had a sacred value that should not be spoiled by mundane usage, Mussolini suggested, despite the fact that he himself wore the shirt on random occasions. Whereas in the 1920s the shirt was highly acclaimed and little regulated, the 1930s campaign for the reform of customs, as mentioned earlier, initiated a new path. In 1932 for the first time the statute of the Fascist Party included an article that stated: 'The black shirt constitutes the fascist uniform and must be worn only when prescribed.'[4] Prescriptions were soon issued, and over the years they multiplied and varied according to situations and occasions. University professors were supposed to wear black shirts on graduation days (Borgese 1937: 304); rectors and deans were ordered to dress in black shirts during important university ceremonies (Koon 1985: 66); in 1943 elementary school teachers were obliged to dress in the Party uniform during school hours (Koon 1985: 65). Alternatively, on 5 July 1938, journalists and photographers covering news of ceremonies presided over by the Duce were told to dress in a black shirt (ACF – AS, B. 70, 5 July); on 13 September 1937, an injunction ordered Party members not to wear decorations on their uniforms at the special exhibit of the Revolution (Gravelli 1940: 99).

Rules were also issued on details and accessories complementing the black shirt. In the summer of 1933, an injunction permitted youth to wear the black shirt without the tie but absolutely forbade rolling up the sleeves (ACF – PNF: 369). Later that summer, a fluttering tie was not permitted (Gravelli 1940: 68). The following year an injunction forbade wearing the black shirt with a starched collar (Gravelli 1940: 68). Continuously and relentlessly, the Fascist Party cleansed the misuse of the shirt, as in purification rituals. And when injunctions failed to be followed, the Party secretary Starace would launch serious accusations, as he did in 1936: 'We still register on the part of some members of the party a tendential reluctance to wear the fascist uniform in events and meetings. These attitudes, emanating from a bourgeois spirit that is absolutely in contrast with the fascist mentality, and with the present time, need to be severely corrected' (ACS – PNF: 370, no. 577). Attachment to the old and typical, which constituted what motivated Italians to resist rules, infuriated Starace, as it was a sign of a 'conservative mentality, which is typically bourgeois and thus not fascist' (ACS – PNF: 370, no. 577). One could not wear a black shirt and then behave like a bourgeois. That was a contradiction in terms, and unacceptable, as far as the party was concerned.

In the 1930s, during the years of the regime's stabilization, the wearing of the shirt became regulated and detailed to unprecedented levels. From being the 'combat outfit' of the squads in the early years of the fascist movement, the black shirt had expanded to cover the entire body politic under Mussolini's dictatorship. The shirt had become a sign of fascist faith and obedience to the regime, and also a tool to make Italians into fascists, 'citizen-soldiers', 'new men'. The shirt did not merely represent fascism; it represented Italy, fascist Italy. Along with other daily practices that affected the individual body, the regime asked the shirt to play a performative and not a purely symbolic role: the black shirt was supposed to change people, their attitude and character. Failure to wear the shirt denoted little fascist spirit, as Starace continuously reminded party members.

The case of the black shirt exemplified fascism's extreme belief in the power of aesthetics over ideology, that is, to put it simply, the belief that in order for the regime to prevail and dominate politically, one did not need doctrinal teaching, but rather proficiency in wearing the black shirt, for example. Within fascism's vision, symbols had become reality, or better they were taken for reality, they came to be identified with reality. Thus, the reform of customs advocated the Roman salute over the handshake and imposed the Roman goose step on the troops as signs of fascist character. The tight observance of aesthetic rules signified one's identity as 'fascist'. The cowl did make the monk, we could say especially with reference to the shirt.[5]

In her pioneering book on fashion, Elizabeth Wilson (1985) claims that dress can be generally said to play symbolic, communicative and aesthetic roles. In the case of the fascist regime's black shirt, it is my conclusion that the aesthetic role took the place of the symbolic – an aesthetics that did not deal with personal identity, however, but rather with a political (fascist) one. Fascist identity was being mediated by the fashioned body. Under Mussolini, dressing had become a political act, as the whole private/public divide was being reconceived and redeployed by the regime. The body beneath the dress underwent a similar fate, when fascism connected the aesthetics of the body (politic) to its aestheticized vision of imperialism and expansion. Biological bodies became the private property of the fascist state, as the fashioned body was being turned into a fighting one.

The Body as Warrior, or What has become of Private and Public?

Mussolini's aesthetic political project envisaged the 'reshaping' of Italians into a new generation of citizen-soldiers who would guarantee the fascistization of the country and the creation of a new fascist order. Since activity and movement were key words in Mussolini's conception of a country's vitality, the 'new men' fascism invoked were supposed to be dynamic, intrepid and willing to embrace risk as life's rule. At the same time, they also had to be disciplined and ready to sacrifice themselves for the wellbeing of the nation. Citizen-soldiers, following the party's dictum, needed to 'believe, obey, fight'. Fighting was indeed crucial to fascism's self-definition, and violence critically marked fascism's identity, especially at the level of rhetoric and self-representation. Within this context, it is not surprising that war became the outcome of fascism's fascination with violence. Although the regime engaged in an actual armed conflict only during its later years in power, when it attacked Ethiopia in 1935, colonial desires and visions of a new Roman empire were paramount in fascism's ideology, and visible since the early years of the movement. Expansion and the conquest of new lands underlay fascism's political project, and allowed the regime to discharge violence onto other soils, while keeping peaceful relations at home. In this way the beauty of the totality that Mussolini pursued was maintained, without renouncing the role of violence as 'history's wheel'.

As the spectre of war loomed behind the regime's policies and decisions, the battle for demographic growth which the regime launched in the second half of the 1920s added momentum to the regime's violent vision. In this 'battle' population growth signified power and Italy's ability to compete in the international arena. Population expansion, as experts and politicians debated, created a nation's might: birth decline was a presage of disaster. 'All nations and all empires have felt the grip of decadence when they have seen their birth numbers go down . . . The destiny of Nations is tied to their demographic power . . . If we diminish, gentlemen, we do not build an Empire, we become a colony!' (Mussolini 1934–9, vol. 6: 44–7). Thus Mussolini addressed fascist members during a famous speech delivered on Ascension day (26 May 1927), well before any military campaigns were undertaken. A nation's vitality depended on its size, Mussolini declared. At a time of declining fertility rate, the urgency of the matter, to him, was undeniable.

With the launching of the demographic campaign, the regime began to count bodies, as it counted on them to expand and grow stronger. Anxiety over infertility, and the belief in the power of numbers, led to the adoption of a range of measures promoting marriage and child-bearing. Women were penalized for abortions; chastised for thin waists; rewarded for multiple births. Men, on the other hand, were taxed if bachelors (see Horn 1994). Lack of children became a sign of weakness and sickness, both physical and moral. It denoted the absence of biological 'virility', but at the same time, and especially, it imperiled the nation's might. The regime continuously drew connections between warriorlike attributes, which supposedly corresponded to 'virility', and visions of demographic growth and fertility. Metaphorically, 'virility' as the means and expression of supremacy depended on biological fecundity, but biologically fecundity too was contingent upon virile attributes. Ultimately, biological virility produced soldiers for the army and enlarged the nation's power and 'virility'. Not surprisingly, when Italy conquered Ethiopia in 1936 Mussolini described the occasion as a test for the Italian army's 'virility' (1934–9, vol. 10: 31, speech of 15 December 1936). In a highly masculine interpretation of violence, war coincided with 'virility' and came to be opposed to the feminine theatrics of parliamentary debates and liberal politics, that is with the peaceful way in which the bourgeois class had been running state affairs thus far, according to the fascists. War, as a virile discharge, ultimately granted life.

The 'virility' the regime expected of Italians was not, however, foreseen in individualized terms. In this sense, fascism's 'new men' differed from the unique, heroic types the Futurists invoked. Instead, the regime foresaw virility as a synthetic essence of the whole infused by the leader, the outcome of a homogenized group of people: the 'masses' turned into citizen-soldiers through the work of the Duce. Within this vision, only the politician could transform the female 'masses' into warriors. Only as a whole, and under the guidance of the leader, did the 'masses' show virility. As Mussolini put it in the 1935 speech that preceded the invasion of Ethiopia: 'Twenty million men: only one heart, only one will, only one decision' (1934–9, vol. 9: 218; speech of 2 October 1935). Or, as he told Italians on another occasion: 'Each of you must consider himself a soldier: a soldier also when you are not wearing the uniform, a soldier also when you work, in the office, in factories, in yards or in the fields: a soldier tied to all the rest of the army, a molecule that feels and beats with the entire organism' (1934–9, vol. 5: 164; speech of 28 October 1925). A homogeneous virile army of ready-to-fight soldiers was what Mussolini required for fascist Italy to exist. Individual bodies needed to disappear within fascism's body politic.

The regime's identification of war with de-individualization illuminates the role fascism assigned to wearing the black shirt in civilian life. In its function as uniform, the black shirt reaffirmed the necessary unity fascism required of Italians and erased people's differences; by making individuals visually indistinguishable, the shirt assigned Italians their fascist identity and made of them a warriorlike body. At another level, one could also argue that the black shirt worked to stage and dramatize fascism's fantasy of a manly world. For fascism's was definitely a masculine world, at least in ideal terms. It was not by a mere slip of the tongue that Mussolini in his preparatory speech for the invasion of Ethiopia (quoted above) had mentioned 'twenty million men'. The citizen-soldiers fascism envisioned, the 'new men' as warriors, were all gendered masculine and of fighting age. The 24 million Italians who did not participate in the army found themselves excluded from fascism's dream of virile conquests. Incidentally, starting in 1932, fascist women, while still required to wear them, changed the colour of their shirts from black to white. Was it just a coincidence?

Fascism's relationship with women was indeed quite idiosyncratic, as demonstrated by Mussolini's own vision of the masses as female and his negative judgment of them. On the one hand, the regime needed women as procreators of the virile army, producers of (fighting) bodies that would expand Italy's territorial horizons. On the other hand, fascism fundamentally mistrusted the feminine gender. Mussolini, for example, although he never openly stated whether he considered women inferior to men, believed that women and men were not equal. 'Let's confirm that she is different' he once declared. 'I am rather pessimistic. I believe, for example, that a woman does not have a large power of synthesis, and is thus unfit for great spiritual creations' (1934–9, vol. 5: 61; speech of 15 May 1925). In Mussolini's argot, 'spiritual creation' equalled art – that is politics.

Should one then conclude that women in fascist Italy were relegated to the so-called private sphere (see De Grazia 1992), whereas men participated in public life? One must answer in the negative, because, in fact, the whole private/public was reinvented and reformulated by the regime and used to reframe all citizens' participation in politics (see Weintraub and Kumar (eds) 1997). Fascism did not consider the private sphere innocuous or unpolitical; instead, it pushed political intervention deep into people's intimate life. Reproduction, the private sphere par excellence, for example, was targeted by the regime with laws and regulations that fulfilled fascism's aim to grow numerically. The whole field of reproduction was 'reconfigured as a national duty', whereas contraception and abortion came to be defined by the new 1930s penal code as 'crimes against the integrity and health of the stock' (Horn 1994: 66, 80). According to this definition, people's choices on reproductive matters ran the risk of undermining the whole social body; collective imperatives – the health of the whole – depended on the health of its constituent parts.[6]

Because what is private is normally connected to individual choices and escapes rules of uniformity, the regime was highly concerned with the general domain of personal life, as it clearly displayed in its campaign for the reform of customs. In this crusade, ways of dressing, but also of behaving and speaking, underwent extreme scrutiny under the regime's gaze since they were taken to signify people's fulfilled or unfulfilled fascistization. Even daily gestures needed to undergo state control, because failure to follow the rules proved one's inability to fit in the whole. Italians had to act as fascists and not as individuals, the regime's intervention in everyday practices relentlessly suggested.

What we witness with fascism, then, is the simultaneous process of depoliticizing the private while also re-politicizing it. On the one hand, the regime tried to neutralize the potential danger of a retreat to privacy that would let people tune out from the regime's demands, and foster opposition. On the other hand, the regime politicized Italians by turning all their actions into supporting acts for the regime's wellbeing. In what was a truly radical move, the regime suggested that individual needs under fascism were not merely relegated to the private sphere; rather issues of personal wellbeing were supposed to disappear. The private coincided with the public, and was in a sense phagocitated by it, annulled, annihilated. The notion of citizen-soldier clearly spelled out that Italians were primarily and exclusively fascism's pillars; they were 'public' servants.

The suppression of the private, or its politicization, surely provides yet another proof of fascism's suspension of people's rights. It shows the absolutist character of fascism's dictatorial rule, the radical manner in which Mussolini exercised power. At the same time, it also shows fascism's deep fear, and lucid understanding, of the power of the body natural. As the material site of desires, the senses, happiness, as the principal expression of one's right to satisfy personal needs, the body, I claim, lies at the centre of fascism's critical attack on the private. With its individualizing drive towards unlimited wants – its freewheeling claims to consumption – the body challenged fascism's totalitarian vision of an homogenized polity and required a radical response. That the regime was fully aware of this threat, that the body constituted the fundamental impulse that drove the regime to invade and colonize the private, can best be detected in fascism's critique of the bourgeois. The connection of 'bourgeois' with capitalism, and therefore with consumption, made of the trio an explosive combination that risked undermining the regime's ascetic ideals.

For, 'ideally', as I am going to discuss in the next section, the regime did not consider people's bodies as real. Mussolini's understanding of the 'masses' as a piece of marble, dead matter, and the regime's vision of the Italians' engulfment within the body of the dictator (whose body was normally described as metallic, immortal, endowed with superpowers, in sum not biologically dependent) conveyed fascism's uneasiness with the body, its denial. Subscribing to the myth of man's irreducibility to the yoke of the senses, fascism opposed mind to body, reason to emotion, active to passive, public to private, the cultural to the natural, man to woman (see Klinger 1995). Following the Western tradition of dualistic thought, fascism envisaged the rational, spiritual, cultural man – Mussolini – confronting the irrational, sensual, natural woman – the 'masses'. The latter constituted a danger, a threat, and needed to be neutralized by being molded and folded into the body politic headed by the duce-dictator. Yet this task was not easily accomplished, and the regime perceived as the biggest obstacle to this end the figure of the bourgeois, the 'man' of desires and needs, the consumer – the woman in disguise.

The Disappearance of the Subject, or Body versus Spirit

The uniformity within which fascism conceived Italians' participation in the regime was reflected and realized in the wearing of the black shirt. Anti-fashion, the black shirt stood for equality and sameness, rather than change; and even though the fabric and styles of the fascist uniform underwent some transformations over time (see Pericoli 1983), these changes still fared as secondary vis-à-vis what remained the uniform's essential characteristics of indistinctiveness and widespread use. The regime deeply mistrusted fashion. As a product of capitalism, and connected to consumption, fashion engendered forms of material pleasure that were counter to fascism's core beliefs. Morally preoccupied with social atomism and individualism, in fact, fascism had always defined itself as anti-materialist. It emphasized the spiritual essence of human existence, while invoking ideal values. It discredited rationalistic and utilitarian motives for fostering unlimited desires and private enjoyments. Ever since he became the leader of the Fasces of Combat, Mussolini presented fascism as a movement that, unlike liberalism, bolshevism and Catholicism, did not promise final contentment and did not 'trade in miraculous drugs to give "happiness" to humankind' (De Begnac 1950: 182). In contrast, Mussolini believed that the overcoming of 'primordial needs' would only undermine the individual's vitality and spirituality, and deprive life of its meaning; liberation from needs would only cause the pacification of drives and, therefore, the end of movement and the decline of civilization.

During his whole political career, 'economic happiness' became one of the main targets of Mussolini's fascist polemic against socialism's doctrines and liberalism's individualistic principles. In the 1932 *Doctrine of Fascism*, written in collaboration with the philosopher Giovanni Gentile, Mussolini asserted: 'Fascism denies the materialistic conception of "happiness" as possible . . ., it denies, that is, the equation well-being= happiness which would turn men into animals who only think about one thing: to be fed and fattened, reduced, that is, to vegetative life purely and simply' (1934–9, vol. 8: 79). Fascism did not tolerate the coupling of materialism, with its focus on bodily needs, and happiness, also because concern with one's own material well-being counteracted fascism's totalitarian goals, its ethics of discipline and sacrifice, its organic conception of the world:

> The world is not this material world that appears on the surface, in which man is one individual separated from all others and is governed by a natural

law which instinctively leads him to live a life of egoistic and temporary pleasure. The man of fascism is an individual who is nation and fatherland. It is moral law that links together individuals and generations in a tradition and a mission; that suppresses the instinct of an enclosed life revolving around pleasure to establish in duty a superior life free from limits of time and space. This is a life in which the individual through self-abnegation, the sacrifice of his particular interests, and death realizes that wholly spiritual existence in which his human value resides. (1934–9, vol. 8: 79)

Instincts, pleasure, interest and egoism were all bundled together in Mussolini's critique of private desires. The regime's pretence to a spiritualized world fundamentally entailed the repression of basic individual demands and personal needs, so much so that, in a supreme exaltation of the spirit, Mussolini envisaged the transfiguration of the individual, 'the man of fascism', into a self-abnegating particle of the nation – the whole. And he attacked people's materiality as the most destabilizing element for the triumph of the spirit, the core site of political rebellion. Mussolini clearly understood that the suppression of private desires, beginning with those directly emanating from the body, was necessary to eliminate conflicting demands in a totalitarian state that required the individual's subordination to the will of the *dux*. The presence of a private, personal sphere separated from the public universe of the fascist regime was naturally deemed a political threat. For fascism, individual desires needed to be public, that is, political. Consumption and material pleasure, instead, threatened to circulate those much maligned individualistic principles in a society that aspired to become totalitarian.

Fascism's critique of the 'bourgeois' inserted itself in this philosophical-political context. However, because the term 'bourgeois' is historically such a semiotically rich and overburdened term, the regime confronted many ambiguities and contradictions when launching its critique. Confusion about the economic, cultural and social connotations of 'bourgeois' daunted the fascists, who over the years tried to distinguish between the economic and moral dimensions of 'bourgeois'. On the one hand, the regime was aware that it needed to suppress individual desires if it intended to pursue its totalitarian vision. Within this context, the 'individualistic' bourgeois had to disappear. On the other hand, the regime realized that if it wanted to play a substantial role in the international arena it had to sustain individual entrepreneurship in industry and commerce. In this instance, the 'economic' bourgeois was needed. Faced with this considerable dilemma, the regime adopted different strategies to try and overcome what looked like insurmountably contradictory goals.

Since it relied on a system of capitalist production, fascist Italy needed to reconcile the idiosyncratic plans of condemning consumption while spurring a market economy, of attacking the bourgeoisie in the guise of the parasitic consumer while exalting it as an economic asset. The results of these acrobatic jumps were not always positive. Yet the regime never abandoned the moral-political side of the controversy over the bourgeois and consumption. It never gave up trying to limit the dangerous effects brought by a massive drive toward the exaltation of personal needs, the fulfilment of desire. And it never stopped expressing its contempt for the 'conservative' bourgeois whose life appeared as antithetical to the presumed spiritual and moral visions of a true fascist.

Fascism most often depicted the 'conservative' bourgeois as wearing suits and top hats and as focusing on ideals of personal wellbeing, the quiet life, and maintaining the status quo – all qualities that naturally went against the fascist characteristics of dynamism, discipline and self-sacrifice. The bourgeois was fat and lazy – a passive and vile parasite. When in the 1930s Starace launched the reform of customs to improve the Italians' fascist style, the campaign negatively labeled as 'bourgeois' several popular practices and daily habits. Resistance to wearing the black shirt, but also slowness in adopting new speaking and writing rules, an inability to perform straight Roman salutes and to give up the odious custom of shaking hands, were all condemned as 'old style', remnants of past times, in a word 'bourgeois'. In 1938, an Anti-Bourgeois exhibit organized by the Fascist Party magnified some of the bourgeois traits of moral inferiority through a series of caricatures that ridiculed typical bourgeois attitudes and mentality. Prolixity and sedentarism, lassitude and exhibitionism, were depicted as emanating from and reflecting the bourgeois way of living. The bourgeois was seen as following his own desires and wishes in the pursuit of material satisfaction and happiness: 'to be fed and fattened' as Mussolini put it.

The representational figure of the bourgeois came to bear the stigmata of fascism's negative understanding of the material, the body, and was turned into a symbolic locus of cultural contention, a discursive field for elaborating and negotiating strategies over the definition of the public/private divide, the relationship between the social and the individual, and the links between production, capitalism and consumption. For, indeed, I would argue, behind the regime's stereotypical image of the parasitic, leisured man, behind the representation of the decadent dandy with his false mannerisms and effeminate gestures, behind the figure of the materially satisfied and superficial bourgeois, lurked a more encompassing interlocutor for fascism: the 'egoistic' man, that is the hedonistic person, the autonomous subject, the consumer, in sum the liberal individual. Through the fictional image of the hedonistic bourgeois, fascism attacked autonomous reason and political freedom, while trying to define and delineate the characteristics that would turn the traditional Italian into the ideal fascist citizen, subordinate subject of a totalitarian state. Whereas citizenship defines the right to participate in the governance and shaping of one's own country, Mussolini's regime took citizenship to mean total identification with and subservience to the ends and goals of fascism. Fascism demanded participation and participation was based on belief. Total faith in, and obedience to, the regime were fundamental requirements for membership in the community. Citizenship was predicated upon blind faith in the dogma; only true believers could be included.

From this point of view, material satisfaction was synonymous with betrayal of the common good, national well-being, in other words, the opposite of citizenship. In order to be included as citizen, one needed to give up personal rights and private autonomy. As the regime proclaimed in its philosophical-political manifesto, fascism is 'a religious conception in which man is seen in his immanent relation with a superior law, with an objective Will that transcends the particular individual and elevates him to a conscious member of a spiritual society . . . Anti-individualistic, the fascist conception is for the state; and it is for the individual since he coincides with the state which is the universal conscience and will of man in his historical existence' (Mussolini 1934–9, vol. 8: 69).

Fascism's official philosopher and co-writer of the *Doctrine*, the neo-idealist Giovanni Gentile, affirmed in his theories that the realization of a spiritual society could only take place through the overcoming of individualism and individuals, that is through the action of the transcendental 'I' that denies nature (see Gentile 1912, 1913, 1916, 1917). For Gentile, nature and the individual represented negative alterity in the process of the Spirit's becoming. Empirical subjects, identified with materialism, were only instruments for the making of spiritual reality, objectivations of the transcendental subject, of its consciousness of itself to itself. Being that which is thought, empirical subjects were deprived of an autonomous conscience and negatively assigned to the realm of nature. Although they were crucial to the generating of the thinking thought, since the 'I'-God, who is but self-creation, creates itself through humans and the world, the perennial movement of the thinking thought's self-creation perpetually relegated empirical subjects to the negative realm of fact. For Gentile, '[a]ll is good that is act, all is bad that is fact' (Del Noce 1990: 39). Gentile's interpretation of reality gave absolute value to action, while completely disregarding the subject-object. The opposition between spirit and nature being explicit and paramount in his interpretation, Gentile's system ultimately foresaw the obliteration of the individual into a de-personalized, de-individualized whole – a desensitized body politic. De-materialization was necessary for the spirit to become. The transcendental subject could then just pursue his will to power as the only moral imperative guiding him in a world reduced to things – a position that closely resembles Mussolini's interpretation of the duce's role in fascism.

In his later writings Gentile's philosophical impatience with materialism turned into a political advocacy for the leader's supremacy – a leader whom he defined as 'living doctrine', a personality above all others, a universal will which irradiated spiritual values. Gentile identified fascism with Mussolini, posited the Duce at the centre of the state, and proceeded to deny individual autonomy in the name of a superior will that expressed the higher status of the state. For Gentile, fascism was the driving force towards the never-ending new, a spiritualizing movement that, based on faith and struggle, looked at historical reality as continuously becoming. In order for fascism to perform this task, however, the individual needed to be transfigured in the whole and absorbed by the state. The regime's higher goals, as defined by the spiritual leader, entailed the submergence of individual needs and wants, the cancellation of drives and desires, the overcoming of happiness as the material basis of pleasure. Within the conception of the world elaborated by Gentile, in sum, fascism required spiritual unity, a depersonalized, de-individualized whole, ultimately a desensitized body politic.

The radicality of Gentile's anti-materialist philosophy, and its dehumanizing implications, is not a far cry from fascism's own aesthetic-political fantasy of total control. Mussolini's anti-materialist vision paralleled Gentile's philosophical thought, as fascism envisaged the elimination of individuals' subjectivity along with their senses. Mussolini denied the sensual dimensions of the body as the presupposition for autonomous will. He thus foresaw the overcoming of not just an individual class or category, not just the bourgeois, but rather of all humans and their materiality, their 'natural' being. Through an assault on pleasure and hedonism, private desires and personal needs, fascism's redefinition of the political was imagined along the axis of the senses. Along this axis, fascism generated its own self-representation, its self-understanding as a spiritualized enterprise that purportedly actualized a superior moral existence.

Conclusions

The discussion of fascism's anti-materialism and its denial of the body concludes, and gives meaning to, this chapter's consideration of the black shirt's role in Mussolini's Italy. Throughout this chapter I have argued that fascism's focus on the black shirt, from Mussolini's first symbolic visit to the king to the idiosyncrasies of the campaign for the reform of customs, was not merely a curiosity, an index of the regime's capricious nature and irrational behaviour. The black shirt was at the centre of fascism's political project, a constitutive means for realizing the totalitarian whole that the regime pursued in its drive for military expansion. As a type of uniform, that therefore ensured uniformity and anonymity, the black shirt defied all the caprices of fashion and luring fantasies of self-expression that the nascent consumer culture was fostering, and that fascism feared. The black shirt made the individual wearing it a fascist, and steered the person away from the selfish self and toward the state. Personal identity was replaced by a fascist identity, as the regime rightly understood the radical potential of a consumerism that, with its focus on the individual, would lead people toward achieving personal fulfilment rather than sacrificing themselves for the fascist cause. A consumer ethic of lust and autonomy was antithetical to fascism's culture and vision; the black shirt ensured that all Italians fitted into fascism's ideal of a harmonious whole supervised by the Duce. Abnegation, not self-promotion, was required for fascism to thrive.

If the black shirt, by fashioning bodies, made them fascist, the dressed body, however, also presented fascism with a dilemma about the material needs and desires of the physical body, the body that consumes, the body that senses. As it is always untamed, unfinished, and somewhat dangerous in its materiality (Wilson 1985), the body became even more threatening in an era of consumer culture and for a regime that aspired to be totalitarian. How could the regime, then, control and contain the body's material drives and desires? The regime, of course, tried to pursue this goal by working to mould and discipline bodies. Fascism dictated body shape through the exemplary figure of the dictator; scorned the thin woman; imposed the Roman salute and goose-step. But the regime knew it could not make sure that the body's 'animal' nature would not at some point resurface and rebel.

Fascism's awareness of the body's instinctual basis constituted the springboard for Mussolini's and Gentile's radical anti-materialism and corollary pursuit of the subject's obliteration. Yet the direct link between fascism's totalitarian vision of a homogenized whole and its anti-materialist attack on the body has generally been ignored in analysis of fascism's anti-materialism. Although interpretations differ over the importance of Marxism versus other intellectual currents in influencing fascism's anti-materialist position, analyses have generally insisted on the relevance of spirit to fascism's self-definition and its elaboration of an original political culture. Fascism's self-proclaimed distance from materialism, it is argued, promoted its invocation of ethics and appeals to moral values, and made of fascism a revolutionary movement, a transformative force within the panorama of Italian politics (see Sternell, with Sznajder and Asheri 1994). What fascism tried to escape, what it positioned as the 'other' of spirit, has not been explored.

Figure 7.2. Fascism's body politic.

In this chapter I have claimed that fascism's spiritualism, philosophically based on a critique of materialism, reveals the dream of cancelling out empirical subjects in order to establish a depersonalized, de-individualized whole. The body, as the 'other' of the spirit, became the main site of fascism's intervention on the body politic, a pivotal locus for the regime's totalitarian project, the privileged place for creating a harmonious whole, a homogeneous fighting body of de-individualized people. Fascism's body politic rested on the elimination of the individual body, the obliteration of the subject, ultimately a desensitized, uniform and uniformed harmonic creation. Dress became one element in fascism's aesthetic-political design and totalitarian vision. The black shirt and other items would turn inchoate masses into 'new men', citizen-soldiers belonging both to the Italian nation and the fascist state. Fascism's vision of its citizenry was that of a disembodied whole phagocitated by the body of the dictator.

Whether the enforcement of the black shirt could achieve any result in this direction is quite a different matter. The regime's aesthetic aspirations in a sense triumphed over its realpolitik. Mussolini's artistic-political experiment turned out to be pretty much a failure, all things considered. This was partly due to the fact that fascism pursued conflicting goals: on the one hand, it wished to mould a citizenship, a 'fascist' public; on the other hand, it held a deeper desire to annul the other in a fantasy of total control and autotelic existence. Moreover, the regime could not stop the modern attractions of consumption, although it tried to counteract the inevitability of modernity by offering Italians a political spectacle centred on the star-like figure of the Duce (Falasca-Zamponi 1997). Ironically, or tragically, one might say, it was the body of the dictator that, with the material reality of his death, marked the end of the regime while dangling from a metal structure in Milan in 1945. His upper torso naked, Mussolini could not be spared the humiliation of the humiliated body fed as a spectacle to the Italian 'public'. Undressed, Mussolini's exposed body had become senseless, exposing the senseless nature of twenty years of fascist dictatorship.

Notes

1. On the fascist March on Rome, see Repaci (1972) and Falasca-Zamponi (1997).

2. For the manifesto, see Crispolti (1987).
3. See Balla's and Depero's 1915 manifesto 'Ricostruzione futurista dell'universo' in Crispolti (1987).
4. See article 3 of the Statute in Missori (1986): 379.
5. See Bottai, *Diario*, entry of 19 August 1938, which reports Mussolini's comment: 'The cowl does make the monk', cited in De Felice (1981): 102.
6. The rise of physiology at the end of the nineteenth century had generally favoured the circulation of organic metaphors in the West. The idea that the whole is more than the sum of its parts, and that an equilibrium among parts was necessary for the health of the whole was certainly not exclusive to fascist Italy. Yet, Mussolini's regime took to the extreme the idiosyncrasy of the relation between whole and parts, as more and more the idea that national interest was superior to any need of the population expanded, and war was taken to be a priority, fascism's *raison d'être*.

–8–

Camisas Nuevas: Style and Uniformity in the Falange Española 1933–43

Mary Vincent

At the founding meeting of the Falange Española on 29 October 1933, its leader, José Antonio Primo de Rivera, referred to his new fascist party as 'a way of being'. His 'poetic movement' was to have its own 'spirit of service and of sacrifice, the ascetic and military conception of life' (J. A. Primo de Rivera 1972: 56, 57). Such an emphasis on *estilo* or *modo de ser* ('style' or 'mode of being') was to characterize the Falange throughout its existence. Style came spontaneously from within and was summed up in words such as 'happiness', 'pride' and 'veracity'. It was also demonstrated visually in the daily actions and displays that made evident the 'permanent essences' of the Falange's *modo de ser* (Pemartín 1941: 35–8). When, in March 1934, the Falange – now merged with its precursor, the JONS, – held a rally in the Teatro Calderón in Valladolid, the 'electric atmosphere' of a hall filled with banners and insignia, Roman salutes and fascist shirts gave a graphic demonstration of exactly this style (Payne 1961: 55; Jato 1953: 92–3).

Such visual display was, however, notably absent from the meeting in Madrid's Teatro Comedia which set up the Falange. Both orators and audience wore suits, and this lack of uniforms, according to one participant, 'disappointed those attending' (Jato 1953: 59). José Antonio – who always had his suits tailored in London – even mentioned dress codes in his speech: 'yes we do wear ties; yes you can call us *señoritos*'. For educated men, the choice of a suit was not often questioned: Ramiro Ledesma Ramos, founder of the Madrid JONS, who repudiated all *señoritismo*, invariably wore one (J. A. Primo de Rivera 1972: 56; Preston 1999: 79; Payne 1999: 59; P. Primo de Rivera 1983: 84–5). However, both men would soon put their suits aside as José Antonio reinvented himself as Spain's most famous wearer of the Falange's proletarian blue shirt.

Shirted Men

This blue shirt was to become crucial to the party's identity. Yet, this clothing of the Falange – so dramatic in the visual evidence of the period – goes almost unmentioned in historical studies.[1] Adopting a shirt as party or militia uniform was, of course, a self-conscious homage to Italian fascism (Pemartín 1941: 44–5). It meant action: wearing that shirt was a deliberate identification with both the radical right and the youthful politics of street fighting. Uniforms were an intrinsic part of fascist identity, part and parcel of its new 'dialectics of fists and pistols' (J. A. Primo de Rivera 1972: 56). The 'new fascist man' did not wear a suit and tie, at least, not out of the office. In the 1930s, the blue shirts of the Falange belonged to a visual political language, one that both confused the visual and the behavioural and which conveyed visual messages through the aesthetics not only of appearance but also of display.

On the urban streets of Republican Spain, Falangist blue shirts jostled with the khaki shirts of their rivals in the JAP, the red kerchiefs of the socialist left and the red and black scarves of the anarchists.[2] But wearing your political identity on your sleeve (or round your neck) was not simply about the usefulness of distinguishing friends from enemies in street brawls. This new language of clothes spoke of both informality and organization. The shirts and kerchiefs – both easily obtainable, untailored, and deliberately proletarian – were youthful and unconstricting, allowing an apparent ease and speed of movement. They brought a new visibility in political mobilization: the cadres were on the streets, openly agitating, demanding to be seen.

The massed presence of young men in blue shirts suggested a collective, masculine definition of power (Mosse 1996). The shirts were a uniform, emblematic of the Falange's emphasis on discipline, hierarchy, and violence. They were adopted enthusiastically, with no hint of the recalcitrance displayed, for example, by anarchists, who customized their uniforms even when integrated into the Republican army.[3] For the Falange, a disciplined body of men had to be uniformed, albeit in a deliberately informal way. Although General Franco later combined the blue shirt with military dress, José Antonio rejected suggestions of a navy blue or military-style uniform (Jato 1953: 116). The original Falange had little truck with epaulettes, gold braid, or the other trimmings of conventional army life. What was important was spirit – the spirit of the barracks, the fellow-feeling of comrades, the experience of the trenches. The blue shirts were intrinsic to the Falange's 'trenchant, ardent and militant' style;

life, to those that wore them, was 'a militia' (J. A. Primo de Rivera 1972: 137).

Clothing young men in blue shirts was not simply about mobilization; it was also about militarization. Spain's neutrality in the First World War meant that there were no Spanish veterans with direct experience of the trenches or of demobilization. All Spain's wars had been fought by its army, usually in colonial settings. The uniforming of youth in the 1930s, while a clear indicator of the increasing militarization of Spanish society, was part of the intense political mobilization experienced under the Second Republic rather than a legacy of world war. On the right, this process of militarization was explicit; on the left, a deep-rooted distrust of the army led to the rejection of overt 'militarism'. But both left and right were preparing to fight.

The Falange's blue shirt was the foundation of an increasingly elaborate visual lexicon. Adopted after the incipient party had merged with the JONS, it replaced the imitative black shirts *jonsistas* had previously worn to demonstrate both their fascism and their modernity. Ledesma Ramos, for example, had provocatively combined a black shirt with a red tie to address a largely Marxist audience in Madrid in 1932. Those present rose to the bait and 'of course, it ended in fighting' (Jato 1953: 50). But ties, even red ones, were emblematic of the bourgeoisie and were rarely combined with the blue shirt until – in a gesture far more appropriate to Franco's party than to Primo de Rivera's – a black tie was imposed as a sign of respect for José Antonio, shot by a Republican firing-squad in Alicante gaol.

The shirts were a new style for a new generation. Blue represented the *mono* or overall, which was the characteristic weekday dress of the Spanish working man.[4] The shirt was thus recoloured in a nationalist idiom, though the quintessentially fascist (and foreign) Roman salute was retained. So too was the JONS's black and red flag, its theft of the anarchist colours a reminder of the syndical aspirations of the radical right. Unsurprisingly, however, it was the colour blue that became representative of the Falange; the underground escape routes established in Republican Madrid during the Civil War were, for example, called Auxilio Azul (Blue Aid), a counterpart to the Republican Socorro Rojo (Red Aid) (Suárez Fernández 1993: 51).

The colour of the shirts was 'precise and happy . . . but also clean and hard-working (*trabajador*), strong, without deceit or weakness, like other pale and indistinct colours'.[5] Although dark blue was 'a whole and proletarian colour', it was also, of course, the counterpoint to red.[6] Falangists were invariably known as 'blue shirts' and, to them, the garments were more than sign and symbol of comradeship. Under the Republic, wearing a blue shirt, particularly in public, was an act of political defiance. According to José Antonio, girls were fined for appearing in blue shirts, while street brawls started at the sight of them (Gallego Méndez 1983: 44–5). They could be worn as a badge of honour, even as a new identity. One woman, Laura Colmeiro, mortally wounded while carrying out 'an act of service' during the Civil War, asked for a blue shirt in which to die (Jato 1953: 289). Great care was taken that the shirts did not fall into the wrong hands – a concern that, like Colmeiro's manner of dying, gave the garments a quasi-liturgical status. During the early months of 1936 considerable numbers of shirts and armbands were sewn in secret by members of the Falange's Sección Femenina in preparation for the military coup planned for July. Where the coup failed, the shirts were burnt (P. Primo de Rivera 1983: 69, 75, 77; also Suárez Fernández 1993: 41, 51).

As a military rising turned into civil war, the Falange Española de las JONS experienced an enormous influx of new members, finally becoming a mass party. Under General Franco – who emerged as undisputed leader of the insurgent forces in the autumn of 1936 – the Falange was forcibly merged with the only other acceptable political movement on the right, the Traditionalists or Carlists. Members of the Falange Española y Tradicionalista de las JONS, still commonly known as *falangistas*, now combined the blue shirt of the Falange and the Carlist red beret. This forced merger was opposed, at least initially, by many pre-war members of the Falange. They soon came to call themselves *camisas viejas* (old shirts); those who came into the single party of Franco's incipient state were *camisas nuevas* (new shirts) (Ellwood 1990; Chueca 1983: 127–68). When, in 1941, Franco sent a military division to fight on Hitler's eastern front, it recruited heavily among *camisas viejas*. Known as the 'Blue Division' – again from the colour of the volunteers' shirts – this pro-Axis enterprise, later to be recycled as an anti-communist crusade (Alegre 1996), provided Franco with an outlet for recalcitrant Falangists. Initial enthusiasm was huge, but severe losses, difficult fighting conditions, and, of course, the Axis defeat brought many back disillusioned to a regime which was fast accommodating itself to the Atlanticist realities of an Allied victory. In bitter dissent, some of the returning veterans burnt their blue shirts.

This was the Falangist equivalent of Communists tearing up their party cards. Burning blue shirts was an act of sacrilege, a violent disavowal of an earlier identity as well as a comment on a regime which deployed 'an aesthetic style' created by the Falange, 'through posters, newspaper illustrations, magazines, calendars, uniforms, the stage management of ceremonies and film production'.[7] An important part of this aesthetic centred on the figure of José Antonio, whose name, face, clothes, and bearing were all incorporated into the iconography of the Franco regime. After his execution, Primo de Rivera became *el ausente* (the absent one). His name was painted on the outside of every parish church in Spain, heading memorial lists of Nationalist war dead, and was greeted with rousing choruses of *'¡Presente!'* when called out at Falangist rallies. In contrast, his body was carried from Alicante to El Escorial in silent procession, on the shoulders of blue-shirted pall-bearers, his coffin covered with a black velvet cloth embroidered by members of the Sección Femenina with a gold 'cross of the angels' (Suárez Fernández 1993: 114– 14; P. Primo de Rivera 1983: 225-31).

José Antonio's youth, good looks, and aristocratic background made him an exemplary subject for this kind of iconography. There was a pronounced romanticism, even an eroticism, about the idealized portraits of the young, dead blue-shirted leader that were popularized by both party and regime. The deliberate theatricality of the cult of *el ausente*, which, like much Falangist propaganda, depended on staged events, massed salutes and disciplined, uniformed cadres, contributed to both its impact and its artifice. But Falangist iconography could strike a more intimate note. *Cara al sol*, the party's 'song of war and love' which was first sung at the rally held in Madrid's Cine Europa on 2 February 1936 is one such instance.[8] As the first stanza makes clear, the song is sung to his girlfriend by a young man leaving for battle:

Cara al sol, con la camisa nueva	Face to the sun, in the new shirt
que tú bordaste en rojo ayer,	That you embroidered in red yesterday,
me hallará la muerte si me lleva	Death will find me if it takes me
y no te vuelvo a ver	and I don't see you again.

The effectiveness of the lyric owes much to its mixture of sex and death: every stanza speaks of longing – for death, for comradeship, for reunion, for the dawn. The intimacy is striking, particularly when compared to the stilted and vainglorious patriotic hymns which had served both the original JONS and the Falange's rivals in the JAP. *Cara al sol*, like the blue shirt, is one of the most recognizable and memorable cultural artefacts of Spanish fascism. Significantly, both put gender at the core of Falangist identity. As the much-quoted second line of the anthem reminds us, men may have worn the shirts, but women made them.

Uniformed Women

For the Falange, as for every other 'shirted' movement in inter-war Europe, putting men into uniforms reflected ideas of patriotic service, direct action, and youth. Many of those who joined the party under the Republic were very young: one 'martyr' was only fifteen when he died in a street fight in 1934 (Jato 1953: 95). Falangists' actions, as well as their masculine stance and dress, were designed to show off Spain's virile youth. Yet, while they were not founder members, the Falange also established a women's section (Sección Femenina: SF), led by José Antonio's sister, Pilar, though ultimately subordinated to the male leader. This was the only branch of the Spanish fascist party that would become larger and more developed than its Italian counterpart (Payne 1999: 477).

Yet, despite the post-war institutional success of the Sección Femenina, José Antonio had originally opposed women's entry into the Falange, given the violent nature of many party activities. Even as members, woman were excluded from street fighting. Yet, during the heady days between February and July 1936, women aided and abetted male violence, concealing guns in the lining of their coats or in the high boots that were then coming into fashion. Girlfriends, who made up a high proportion of the original members of the Sección Femenina, not only provided cover for street fights but were also used to ferry arms (Jato 1953: 94; Gallego Méndez 1983: 20, 25–6; Suárez Fernández 1993: 49).[9] Pilar Primo de Rivera was, however, to repudiate any more active role: 'the Sección Femenina never took part in street fights: the men of the Falange were too much men to involve us in those duties' (1983: 70).

Here is the crux of the difficulty fascists faced when mobilizing women. They faced the demands of patriotic service just as men did, both as auxiliaries to the violence that would renew the fatherland and as mothers of future generations. This gave women a visibility that, at least on the political right, they had never had before. Falangist women may not have fought, but they wore the blue shirt. Donning a garment designed for action, even for violence, clearly challenged perceived gender roles. Yet, as the words to *Cara al sol* indicated, fascism was founded on a clear sense of gender difference. Women were never envisaged as citizens in the same way as men. Their political role was trammelled while their social and cultural role was determined to a greater extent than that of men by other forces: the weight of traditional social norms, the heavy influence of Catholicism, and the demands of their role as domestic consumers (de Grazia 1992).

For men donning uniforms meant fighting and dying at the front. For women the blue shirt was redefined to mean service, an essential but auxiliary role. During the Civil War, Falangist women acted as nurses and staffed dining rooms and soup kitchens as well as sewing uniforms. Spain's first systematic welfare service, Auxilio Social, was established by the Sección Femenina during the war, becoming the vehicle for Spain's first ever mass mobilization of women. In Franco's new state, social service for women became the equivalent of military service for men.[10] Falangist women's original, and arguably most substantial, contribution to the war effort, however, explicitly concerned the production and care of clothes.

Great stress was put on both handiwork and the women's hands that carried it out.

> The men went to the front intoxicated with *Cara al sol* and the comrades [fem.] remained in all those places where their hands or their smiles were needed, to work, work, work . . . In the munitions stores and the arsenals, the Sección Femenina blackened their agile fingers with gunpowder and lead . . . In the hospitals they made bandages, sheets, compresses. And in their houses . . . they knitted balaclavas, scarves, gloves, socks, pullovers for comrades in the frozen trenches.[11]

All female Falangists were instructed to fashion clothes for the front, particularly winter ones, as well as the customary armbands, banners, and flags (Gallego Méndez 1983: 55). This was a military task: the organization of tens of thousands of volunteers was undoubtedly the party's most important contribution to the early war effort. Keeping Falangist militia units – which were not assimilated into the army until after 24 April 1937 – supplied with clothing and blankets had true military purpose, notwithstanding the gendered way in which it was carried out.

The importance of female labour in keeping soldiers warm, clothed, and uniformed was recognized immediately, in part because of the specific relationship women were presumed to have with clothes. When Pilar Primo de Rivera fled Republican Spain on a German gunboat she undertook 'those tasks more suited to women' by mending the sailors' clothes (P. Primo de Rivera 1983: 79). This relationship between women and clothes was not about fashion – that frivolous and often immoral bourgeois diversion – but about the military exigencies of supply. As the providers of clothes for their families, women were the obvious choice for such a duty, regardless of their status as non-combatants. Most garments were still made at home although, admittedly, the economic resources to buy clothes, wool, or cloth usually came from male earnings.

Women were thus the producers as well as the providers of clothing, a relationship that fitted easily into the autarkic discourse that characterized economic policy in the early years of Francoism (Richards 1998).

The association of women and clothing was hardly surprising. In Republican-held Madrid garment-making workshops also made a decisive contribution to the war economy; these were often set up by the anarcho-syndicalist trade union (CNT) or the Socialist Youth (JSU) to use female labour (Balbás, Cabezali, Calleja, Cuevas, Chicote, García-Nieto and Lamuedra 1988: 167–9, 176–8). Behind the Nationalist lines, however, women's productive relationship with clothes had a moral as well as an economic purpose – a conflation that characterized autarky. In Valladolid, for example, a 'soldiers' workshop' manufactured 378,970 garments, ranging from underwear to overcoats, in its first year of production, employing 1,856 seamstresses in order to do so. In an accurate reflection of both the Falange's and the Nationalist war effort's class base, a significant number of these women worked without pay (García González 1989: 182–7).[12] In Valladolid, Falangist families were well represented in the list of workers, but the association between social status and war-work was seen beyond the birthplace of Onésimo Redondo's JONS. In neighbouring Segovia, for example, village women remembered how the Falangist sewing-circle and soup-kitchen were run by 'girls with a [social] position' and 'ladies of good family' (Fontecha, Gibaja and Bernalte 1988: 208–9).

After unification with the Carlists in 1937, the Sección Femenina was charged with both the production and the storage of uniforms, setting up warehouses and employing 20,000 women in its workshops. Laundries were established to wash, mend, and care for soldiers' clothes. Hygiene was also crucial and the laundries maintained their own 'disinfection service' for soiled and infested garments. This became the archetypal Falangist war-work for women. Less specialized than nurses, laundresses shared in the heroism of the front without abandoning women's traditional duties or expertise. The first women to enter the roll of *Mutilados de Guerra* sustained her injuries in a *lavadero* on the Madrid front. Washing was also humble work; like many of the servants and washerwomen they employed in peacetime, Falangist laundresses had to wash in streams and rivers. Undertaking such duties in time of war thus typified feminine virtues; of all the work undertaken by the Sección Femenina, this was 'the most humble, the most silent [and] that which required the deepest and most lasting sacrifice'.[13]

Despite the adoption of the blue shirt, it was a source of pride to Falangists that 'our women have not worn trousers . . . Our women have renounced nothing of their feminine self '.[14] The shirt had somehow become devoid of its military significance simply by being put on a female body. Both during and after the war, the Sección Femenina was presented as the antithesis of the *mono*-clad Republican militiawomen, those 'overalled, loose-haired viragos' who 'became more horribly mannish [*hombrunas*]' day by day.[15] The notion of a biological female nature underpinned both the Falange's notions of gender and its sartorial vocabulary: the blue shirt held distinct meanings for men and for women whereas trousers were completely unacceptable for girls. It was a point of honour that none of the party's women died bearing arms, even though some were executed and others killed at the front. As the first issue of the Sección Femenina's post-war magazine put it, 'A rifle in the hands of a woman dishonours the gun, the poor, unhappy girl who carries it and the men who look at it.'[16]

The exclusion of women from armed service was part of an insistence on maintaining 'natural' gender roles that structured the entire Nationalist war effort. Reinforcing the association of men with guns and women with (knitting) needles was a powerful symbol of the 'order' that reigned in both the Nationalist war zone and Franco's new state. This 'order' was counterposed to the 'chaos' of the Republic: in one, a 'natural' gender order was accompanied and underpinned by Catholicism; in the other, anti-clericalism contributed to the perversions of free love (Albert 1989: 371–8; Albert 1998; Thomas:1990). Such pronounced dualism seemed to outweigh the blurring of masculine and feminine in the blue shirt. Indeed, the rigid reassertion of gender roles in Franco's new state, together with the intersection of religion and domesticity, has led many historians to categorize the Sección Femenina as traditional and backwards looking. Women were defined solely as mothers destined 'to live for home, husband and family'. Informed by traditional Catholic values, the postwar SF became 'an organization predicated on the social submissiveness of women . . . offering practical classes in cookery, needlework and other domestic skills' (Graham 1995: 198; Preston 1999: 130. Also Smith 1989: 474–7; Gallego Méndez 1983; Pastor 1984).

Franco's Falange was, of course, not the radical street-fighting militia it had been under the Republic. Now the party was a means of mobilizing Spaniards behind the *Caudillo*, an institutional support for an authoritarian and Catholic state. Nevertheless, several analysts have commented on the paradoxical nature of a movement that deployed activists who were single and economically self-sufficient while preaching the virtues and rewards of marriage and female subservience (Graham 1995: 193). The rhetoric of domesticity was employed even as the massed cadres of Spain's fascist womanhood marched through the streets, displayed their sporting accomplishments, and mobilized on behalf of the *Caudillo*. The visual appearance of the Sección Femenina conveyed conflicting messages. Claiming, as Stanley Payne has done, that the Sección Femenina's 'tone . . . remained relentlessly conservative' is to define that tone only in terms of discourse and rhetoric. The Falange's mobilization of women is thus separated off from Catholic traditionalism, which is taken to define the Sección in a way the politics of display did not (Payne 1999: 323, 477).

Although it has received little attention from historians, how Falangist women dressed was a testament not to tradition but to modernity. As the Sección Femenina fashioned itself in a blue shirt, uniforms (previously confined to fee-paying schools) became part of middle-class women's own visual vocabulary. Never before had masses of Spanish girls presented themselves as disciplined comrades, whose tightness of command enabled visual spectacles such as lying down in formation so their bodies made the national coat of arms (London 1996: 237). Such uniformed displays spoke of discipline, order and hierarchy and rendered invisible the unreliable ego of the individual. This collective refashioning laid aside the atomized 'self' of the old liberal order, so reviled by both fascism and Catholicism.

Uniforms were also part of José Antonio's famous assertion that Falangists were 'half monks and half soldiers'; the blue shirts reminded their wearers that 'their life must be brave, austere and disciplined'.[17] Subsequent theorists argued that, as both militia and 'military order', the Falange had both uniform and habit; as a uniform the blue shirt was a reminder of 'our military basis', as a habit of 'our religious essence' (Pemartín 1941: 43–4). But, unlike religious habits, uniforms were self-consciously modern. With the corresponding deportment, both might represent the abnegation of the self, and 'the control of the will',[18] but they differed radically in visual appearance. Suggesting that the one garment served both purposes lacked sartorial credibility. In the case of women, in particular, photographic evidence testifies to the sharp contrast between the uniform and the full religious habit, which, complete with medieval wimple, was worn up to the mid 1960s. With the exception of nurses, members of the Sección Femenina went bareheaded indoors. Their mid-calf length skirts were hardly comparable to the voluminous folds and layers that covered the body of the nun. And they also, of course, wore men's shirts. The Falangist militiaman, standing upright, his blue shirt uncovered even by a jacket, struck a much more sexual pose than any monk.

Curiously, perhaps, the most modern profession wore the most tradi-tional clothes. These were the Falangist nurses – one of the party's most important contributions to the war. The dissemination of new knowledge about medicine, hygiene and science was a key component of numerous post-war campaigns, many of them characterized by the rhetoric of natalism, which, like that of autarky, had become almost definitional in European fascism.[19] In keeping with the demands of clinical care and scientific standards, Falangist nurses dressed entirely in white. This was a symbolic rather than a practical choice, embodying cleanliness and dedication. After all, keeping the uniforms white must have entailed much hard work. But the visual connotations of purity were important to a profession that was largely made up of unmarried women but which put aside feminine modesty in order to care for wounded men (Roberts 1994: 73–7). It was no coincidence that the nurses' starched white folds and rolled-up sleeves echoed the dress of the other main body of nursing staff on the Nationalist side, religious congregations. Nurses' veils, in particular, were reminiscent of the abbreviated habit that became familiar in the Catholic world after the Second Vatican Council (1958–65). Despite their front-line duties Falangist nurses never adopted army-style dress unlike, for example, British military nurses who went into khaki during the Second World War (Starns 1998: 95–7; Smith 1989: 374–5). Nor did they sport the customary Falangist dark blue except in the rather ceremonial nurses' cape. Rather, their uniform suggested clinical standards and a quasi-religious vocation.[20]

The nurses also wore aprons, which, paradoxically, came to represent the Sección Femenina's scientific endeavours. The full-skirted, bibbed white aprons, tied at the waist, suggested an understanding of the female body that was both maternal and erotic. The aprons accentuated both hips and bust, so presenting a highly feminized silhouette that almost countermanded the garments' domesticity. Aprons were humble items of clothing, associated with kitchens as well as hospitals. In the canteens of Auxilio Social:

> white aprons over their dark dresses, their badge of red yoke and arrows showing up plainly against the navy-blue of their blouses; they are ready to begin their work of serving.[21]

For those in danger of being splashed by blood or by cooking oil, aprons were practical items of clothing. As they were worn over other clothes, including the uniform, donning an apron indicated when a comrade was on active duty. Seamstresses wore them too; the white aprons in the Valladolid workshop, for example, 'gave a clear sense of uniformity' (García González 1989: 183). The aprons thus exemplified the egalitarianism of the Falange as well as the abnegation of its female comrades. Yet, borrowing servants' clothes could not disguise the clear class difference between those who served in the SF's canteens and those who had to eat in them. Recipes featured in Falangist magazines demanded ingredients many could never have tasted during the 'hungry 40s', such as chocolate, cream, and foie gras.[22]

There is a famous photograph of Sección Femenina members distributing the 'white bread of Franco' after the fall of Barcelona (Carr 1986: 166). Their white aprons stand out among the sepia tones of the picture, reinforcing the contrast between the victorious and the defeated. The women's neat, domestic appearance, their hands filled with bread, their hair tidied up off their faces, presented an image of order and plenty that was easily contrasted to the destitution of the 'liberated' city. The white aprons could, though, also be juxtaposed against other images of deprivation. They were routinely worn by those visiting the 'obscurest corners of the Peninsula' as health visitors and vaccination campaigners and, again, epitomized the contrast between young Falangists and countrywomen (Otero 1999: 205). The crisp, starched aprons stood out against the shapeless garments and dirty clothes of the rural poor. In this context, grooming and a well turned-out appearance meant not only authority and social status but also knowledge. The Falange was taking scientific method as well as political and religious conviction to the destitute and the dispossessed.

Many Sección Femenina aprons had the party's emblem, the yoke and arrows, embroidered in red on the bib. As these garments were invariably home-made, the emblem varied in size and stitch, though not in design or colour. The same motif appeared on the left-hand breast pocket of the blue shirt. Here, its colour alluded to the heart's blood and spirit, though red was also the colour of martyrdom. Inherited directly from the JONS, the yoke and arrows came from the shield of the Catholic monarchs, Ferdinand and Isabella ('symbol of the heroic virtues of the race'), where it symbolized the unity of Spain.[23] The Sección Femenina also adopted the letter Y as its emblem, after Isabella's spelling of her own name. To historians looking to emphasize the nostalgic, backwards-looking component of Spanish fascism, this choice of emblems has seemed highly significant (Preston 1999: 129). The desire to recapture the imperial glories of the past was undoubtedly a crucial element in the Falange's political thought, as was a yearning for political and religious unity. But the way in which the yoke and arrows design was used was not purely nostalgic.

Figure 8.1. Sección Feminina members sewing linen.

Fashion and the Falange

When, under the Republic, upper-class girls displayed Falangist insignia on their clothes, they were using them not only as political badges but also as fashion accessories (Gallego Méndez 1983: 44–5). Carmen Primo de Rivera, sister to Pilar and José Antonio, married in Burgos cathedral on 19 December 1938 with the yoke and arrows embroidered on her wedding dress. The bridegroom played his part in this 'solemn, Catholic and Falangist ceremony' wearing a blue shirt (P. Primo de Rivera 1983: 133; Suárez Fernández 1993: 78). In other cases the uniform itself was dressed up, typically by the addition of high-heeled court shoes, which were even occasionally, and implausibly, seen in posed photographs of nurses (Otero 1999: 18–21). Earrings, wristwatches, and hairstyles offered other opportunities for customizing the uniform. Such sartorial choices served, in part, to define the individual against the collective, so undermining the ideological purpose of the uniform (de Grazia 1996: 351–4). Even to Falangists, fashion was, after all, about display.

Male and female Falangists alike, however, assumed that men would primarily observe this display and women provide it. Unlike men, women were targeted as fashion consumers by advertisers and retailers in Spain as in the rest of the Western world. This trend, developed during the 1920s and 1930s continued into the post-war, with Falangist women's magazines bringing images of fashion, consumption and glamour directly into the home. Women were to be decorative, despite the discipline of uniforms. The first Sección Femenina delegate from the Galician province of Pontevedra had been a beauty queen, a life history that easily fitted José Antonio's desire for 'a happy, short-skirted Spain' (Payne 1961: 75; Suárez Fernández 1993: 34). The Falangist emphasis on joy (*alegría*) and on youth come together in this rather frivolous phrase. Under Franco, teaching manuals used by the SF in girls' schools outlined not only girls' enjoyment of clothes, but also their duty 'always to be well turned out: at home and in the street . . . alone or in company'.[24] Such an injunction suggests a greater concern with conventional respectability than with fascism. Certainly, bourgeois conventions featured largely in the post-war Falange, epitomized perhaps by the addition of a tie to the men's uniform. But José Antonio's initial reluctance to mobilize women at all suggests that bourgeois manners always interacted with more radical imperatives.

A loss of radical edge has also been linked to the aging of the originally youthful Falange. However, a prohibition on married women holding positions of command and the stipulated age for social service kept the women's section relatively young. And while young women were often just as shackled by middle-class convention, they were perhaps more aware of their position as fashion consumers and more willing to experiment with different looks. Outside the parade ground, some of these styles were highly traditional. One of the war dead, María Luisa Terry, was commemorated in at least one publication in the high comb, mantilla and long silver earrings of the Andalusian señorita. In another portrait, this time of Carina Uncita, the sitter might have been dressed by Goya.[25] But, despite the popularity of folkloric references in the *costumbrista* cinema of the period, other looks were more common. Falangist magazines, with their illustrations of hats, tailored suits, and impractical court shoes made it quite clear that the favoured aspirational model was the bourgeois lady. This was part of the reassertion of social order: during the war hats had disappeared from Republican Spain, along with other forms of bourgeois dress (Lannon 1991: 216–17). Hats returned alongside overt class distinction after 1939, but they were never to regain their pre-war ubiquity.

Despite the rhetoric of autarky, out-of-uniform Falangist women never seem to have challenged the imperatives of fashion. Nor did the Catholic

Church appear able to counter fashions few outside the priesthood perceived as shocking. Shorter skirts, for instance, had been widely worn in urban bourgeois Spain throughout the 1920s, despite the fulminations of various clerics. Injunctions against frivolity – whether produced by Church or Party – appear to have had even less impact than those against scandal. Throughout the 1930s and 1940s, affluent women plucked their eyebrows, wore sheer stockings (when available) and used cosmetics (de la Mora 1977: 59, 61; also Roberts 1993 and 1994; Lannon 1999). Falangist girls were told that the use of perms was acceptable but not hair dye; lipstick of an appropriate shade could enhance the appearance but nail varnish did not.[26] The economic privation of post-war Spain would have restricted the purchase of beauty products, even among the middle classes. But, at least as aspirational goods, they were well established. Mass consumption had brought with it American models of fashion, beauty, and marketing. No area of life was impervious to these, as Spain's supposedly distinctive Falangist and Catholic women's press showed. Advertisements for beauty products crowded its pages, indicating just how central makeup now was to female identity (Peiss 1996).

In the new fashions for both clothes and cosmetics, Hollywood reigned supreme. Cinemas were well established as Europe's most popular form of entertainment, with most filmgoers preferring American blockbusters (de Grazia 1989).[27] Cinema columns were a staple of newspapers and magazines, while images of the stars – quickly copied by advertisers and retailers – brought *haute couture*, obvious make-up and studio gestures to an international, multi-class audience (Smith 1989: 444–7; Steele 1998: 258–9; Eckert 1990). Fashion illustrators introduced exotic garments such as negligées and lounge pyjamas to magazine readers, while makeup artists announced their methods to be 'based on cinema technique'. Articles such as these, of course, emphasized the fantasy, both of Hollywood and of advertising. Fashion models were styled to look like Lauren Bacall, cover girls like Bette Davis. Face creams were sold by platinum blondes reclining on curvaceous sofas in the best traditions of Jean Harlow or even Mae West.[28] The studio props and cosmetic aids used to create these images (flowers, false eye lashes, peroxide) rendered them essentially artificial. Permanent waves and heavily plucked eyebrows were imitated by women the world over, eventually becoming incorporated into the ordinary image of the well-dressed woman, an expected accessory, like a handbag and matching shoes. Consumption had become aspirational. Before the First World War, artifice had been used to aid 'natural' beauty with obvious paint or dye reserved for the unrespectable. But by 1940, even in Catholic Spain, artifice reigned supreme.

Wearing lipstick with Falangist uniform, even in church, was not proscribed or, one suspects, unusual. But that did not mean that the lure of Hollywood went unchallenged. Church and Party hierarchies were convinced of the need to resist decadence. Under the Republic, fascist activists disrupted cinemas in Madrid by throwing ink at images of Stalin; in 1946 they threw ink at Rita Hayworth's *Gilda*, whose Jean Louis sheath-dress featured prominently in the publicity posters. Women's dress bore great symbolic weight in Francoist Spain. Episcopal authority, often backed up by public authority, attempted to keep Spanish women demure and covered. Like the ink-throwing Falangists, the bishops were essentially attempting to hold out against the forces of mass consumption, Americanization, and commercial leisure. Both were doomed to failure: commerce and the lure of Hollywood-style consumption undercut the Nationalist 'Crusade' more effectively and invidiously than communism ever did.

Neither Church nor Party could dictate what women wore to the extent they wanted to, in part because of competition between them. Such tension surfaced occasionally, notably over the issue of physical education for girls. From the 1920s, sports had become a major influence on fashion design. Freedom of movement and simplicity of design contributed to the image of the modern woman (Steele 1998: 251–3; Roberts 1994: 77–81; Smith 1989: 325–30). Spain's Lilí Alvarez – a three-times finalist – scandalized Wimbledon in 1931 by appearing on court in culottes. A devout Catholic, Alvarez exhibited no moral qualms over divided skirts, higher hemlines or bobbed hair (Alcalde 1996: between 64 and 65). Her later collaboration with the Sección Femenina suggested that Falangist women paid little heed to outmoded clerical strictures on modesty and decorum, which some considered incompatible with physical exercise for girls. One former member recollected how

> There were bishops who did not look at us with a kind eye; they would even say to us that we were perverting the youth . . . a priest, who had confessed me, said that if I did not leave the Sección Femenina, that my soul was in danger. Certainly I didn't ever return to confess with that man. (Enders 1999: 384)

It would appear that, in this particular skirmish between Party and Church, the Party won. But the woman is essentially making choices for herself, shopping around to find a course of action which best suits both her wishes and the dictates of her conscience. Here, neither Party nor Church could ultimately hold sway.

The Cult of the Body

Women who grew from Francoism to feminism remember a rivalry between the Sección Femenina games' teachers and the nuns who taught all other subjects, as well as the greater attraction of the former (Alcalde 1996: 81). Physical education (PE) was introduced into all Spanish schools after 1939, at the behest of the Falange. Co-education was banned and, in PE as in every other aspect of the curriculum, girls and boys were taught separately and differently (Also de Grazia 1992: 158–9). Exercise for girls encouraged balance, poise, and grace: rhythmic gymnastics and 'Greek' dancing were popular, while folk-dances replaced the boys' *gimnasia fuerte*. Sport for both sexes was to make them 'healthy, agile and happy'. No longer was the object to create 'a stadium youth, . . . strong and clean-shaven', though pre-military training remained key to boys' physical education (Jato 1953: 101).

Physical education and the kind of massed sporting displays favoured in fascist states demonstrated the vigour of youth and paradoxically drew on the language of virility. Training the bodies of a generation would ensure the future of the fatherland by providing both soldiers to attest to its glory and mothers to ensure its continuity. The strength of current generations was thus associated with those to come. The primacy of this patriotic task broke numerous cultural taboos. Girls who, before the Civil War had even been prevented from riding bicycles in some parts of Spain, were now encouraged to take part in physical activity, not least in order to strengthen the 'race' (P. Primo de Rivera 1983: 279–81; Suárez Fernández 1993: 155–7). The Sección Femenina organized competitions in skiing and swimming as well as in team games, such as basketball and hockey. In the skiers, fascist Spain finally produced women in trousers; though few in number, pictures and reports of their achievements were widely reproduced in newspapers and magazines.[29]

Games' clothes were now finally seen on girls throughout Spain and, while great care was taken not to offend accepted social norms, resistance was not uncommon. Gymslips and games skirts had to end five centimetres below the knee; bathing costumes were always skirted; overcoats had to be worn over sports' clothes in the street. Knee-length gym knickers were compulsory for every kind of exercise, games or dance. Even though these were sufficiently voluminous to be taken for 'flared skirts', they were still considered 'provocative; and the mothers of the girls wouldn't let them put on bloomers'.[30]

Falangists, clergy, and worried parents all agreed that sport should not lead to scandal; their differences came over where to draw the line.

For the fascist party, body and spirit had to develop together: serving Spain demanded strength and discipline.[31] But strengthening the will, encouraging a competitive spirit, and developing the physique of the mothers of tomorrow always coexisted with less political aims. Summer fashion spreads featured divided skirts that permitted the wearer to ride a bicycle while maintaining 'a perfectly feminine appearance' and explained how coloured jumpers would brighten up tennis whites. Above-the-knee tennis dresses that allowed the wearer 'to move easily, run, jump etc.' encouraged women to exercise, not only for health but also to help keep a trim figure. As popularized by beauty magazines, ten minutes of exercises before showering would ensure 'flexibility and slenderness'.[32]

It is hard to credit this kind of advice with the same seriousness of purpose espoused by those who penned fulminating editorials against 'frivolity'.[33] Nor does it easily square with the subordination to Catholic social norms so often assumed by historians of the Sección Femenina (Gallego Méndez 1983: 74). Urging young women into underwear that scandalized their mothers fed fascism's demand for active citizens and disciplined cadres but it did nothing to reinforce the family hierarchies on which Spanish society was legally based. Such tensions ultimately undermined the ideological underpinnings of the Francoist state just as Americanized consumerism undercut the rhetorical strategies of national-Catholicism. Despite the grandiloquent claims of Franco's Crusade, post-war Spain was never 'the spiritual reserve of the West' unaffected by cultural or economic cross-border currents.

The post-war Falange was an institutional prop for an authoritarian regime which shrugged off associations with fascism once Allied victory in the Second World War seemed assured. Rivalries between *camisas viejas* and *camisas nuevas* were soon allayed, although some 'old shirts' did move into opposition. However, most Falangists, including Pilar Primo de Rivera, were happy to support the regime. They provided its style, the elaborate victory demonstrations, the endless displays of patriotic and sporting achievement. The Falange's main concern was thus with clothing the body politic. Donning blue shirts and embroidered armbands fashioned a collectivity, demonstrating the strength of a generation, not the personality of an individual. This strength depended on health and with a new emphasis on fitness went a new sense of the physical. Bodies were now on display as never before in Spain. They were exercised and observed, not only because of a medicalized belief in health, but also as a demonstration of national strength.

But the Falange never controlled the language of clothes. In clothing the body politic they also clothed the body physical. In a culture where nudity was taboo and carnality widely equated with sinfulness, this assertion of the physical had profound effects. The Falange's original anti-bourgeios rhetoric – while never reflected in its membership – sat ill with the consumerism and conventional social respectability of the post-civil war period in Spain. The party's preferred solution of economic autarky was undermined from the start by American-style consumerism. Protected by the black market from the hunger and poverty experienced by the working classes in the immediate aftermath of the war, some Spanish women began to think of themselves as modern consumers, copying fashions that began far away. Both the artifice of Hollywood and the physicality of fascism brought with them a new sense of what the body was and how it should be dressed. Though legally subordinated to men in every walk of life, the way in which Falangist women were coming to use the language of clothes suggested an increasingly informed individual choice that subverted political, familial, and religious strictures on dress and, in so doing, subverted a great deal more.

Acknowledgement

I would like to thank Karen Harvey, Paul Heywood, Wendy Parkins and Mike Richards for their comment on earlier drafts of this chapter.

Notes

1. This reflects a more general lack of attention; Graham and Labanyi (1995) has nothing on dress or fashion while Rodgers (1999) has a single entry.
2. Under the Second Republic (1931–6), Spain experienced pronounced and rapid political polarization. The largest force on the right was the parliamentary Catholic party (CEDA) whose youth wing, the JAP, easily eclipsed the Falange in numerical terms. The CEDA's legalist tactic for winning control of the Republican state was seen to have failed after the party lost the February 1936 elections. Thereafter, distinctions between the violent and legalist right became blurred as preparations for the military coup, which would plunge the country into Civil War (1936–9), began immediately.
3. Testimony in Fraser (1979: 339).

4. The full *mono*, which was never worn by the Falange (except as prisoners in Republican gaols) became the 'uniform' of the Republican militias in the first days of the Civil War.

5. 'El uniforme', Sección Femenina, *El libro de las Margaritas* (1940) reproduced Otero (1999: 78).

6. Sección Femenina Tradicionalista y de las JONS, *Formación Política: Lecciones para las Flechas* (Madrid: n.d. but sixth reprinting), 34, quoting José Antonio. Blue, albeit in a different shade, is also the colour associated with the Virgin Mary. I have found no direct allusions to this symbolic connection but it is probably not coincidence that the fascist movements in Spain, Ireland and Portugal all chose blue shirts.

7. M. García i García, Catalogue of the Exhibition *La guerra civil española* (Madrid: Ministerio de Cultura, 1981) quoted Ellwood (1987), 35. Catholicism provided another idiom for public display, though there was substantial overlap between the two.

8. Sección Femenina, *Formación Política*, 36–8. The lyrics were written by 'the Falange's poets', young men including Dionisio Ridruejo and Agustín de Foxá.

9. Marjorie Munden, a founder member of the SF and a British subject, bought arms abroad.

10. The SF had c. 580,000 members by 1939, Payne (1999: 301).

11. '"Y" roja colectiva a la Sección Femenina de Mallorca', Sección Femenina de Falange Española Tradicionalista y de las JONS, *Anuario de 1940* (np, nd: 232).

12. A handful of men, presumably tailors, also worked there.

13. 'Lavaderos de frente' and ''Mutilada de Guerra', Sección Femenina, *Anuario de 1940,* 104: 66; see also Gallego Méndez (1983: 56); P. Primo de Rivera (1983: 151).

14. '18 de julio', *Medina* (Semanario de la Sección Femenina*)* 19 July 1942.

15. Borras (1965: 25); speech made at the Consejo Nacional de la Sección Femenina, Zamora, January 1939, quoted Pastor (1984: 23).

16. *Medina* 1 (March, 1941); for the war dead see Suárez Fernández (1993: 101–4); P. Primo de Rivera (1983: 138–9).

17. Sección Femenina, *Formación Política*, 34.

18. Sección Femenina de FET y de las JONS, *Formación Familiar y Social* (Madrid, 1943: 9).

19. Juan Bosch Marín, 'Por qué mueren los niños de España', *Medina,* 3 April 1941; see also Nash (1991).

20. The continuing importance of such ideas may undermine Mary Nash's claim that 'conventual life no longer constituted a valid model of femininity', Nash (1999: 27).
21. Florence Farmborough, 'A Shining Light', in Fyrth and Alexander, (1991: 317). She appears to refer to 'blouses' simply because they were worn by women.
22. 'Juquemos a ser amas de casa', *Bazar* (Revista de la SF de FET y de las JONS para las Juventudes) 1 (January 1947), 4 (April–May 1947). The issue covered two months due to paper shortages.
23. Sección Femenina, *Formación Política*, 31–3; quote at Suárez Fernández (1993: 87). See also Payne (1999: 63).
24. Sección Femenina, *Formación familial y social*, 252, 243–9.
25. *Anuario de 1940*, 22–3; Borras (1965), 34. Carina Unciti's sister, Mª Paz, founded *Auxilio Azul* and was executed during the war.
26. Sección Femenina, *Formación familial y social*, 250–1.
27. Filmgoing was highly popular by the 1930s (Spain had 3,337 cinemas by 1935) and, while the number of American films released in Spain fell from 77 in 1940 to 28 in 1942, it recovered to 120 in 1944 and 138 in 1945 (Besas 1985: 9, 18, 25).
28. 'Para estar en casa' and 'Peinado y maquillaje', *Mujer* June 1937; 'Sombreros', *Medina* 17 April 1941; *Mujer* September 1937; advertisement for 'Visnú', *Medina* 24 April 1941.
29. Though not those of Lilí Alvarez, who was stripped of her 1941gold medal for accusing the jury of *machismo*. In 1946, only 27 girls took part in the ski competitions and 98 in swimming galas but there were 82 basketball teams and 188 gym teams, *Bazar*, 1 (Jan. 1947).
30. Interview with Enders cited in (1999: 384); Delegación Nacional de la Sección Femenina: Circular no. 206 (June 1943), 'Normas para movilizaciones', reproduced Otero (1999: 144); Suárez Fernández (1993: 124–5). Infringement of the dress code resulted in immediate disqualification.
31. 'Campamentos femeninos', *Consigna* (Revista Pedagógica de la Sección Femenina de FET y de las JONS), 5 (April 1941).
32. 'Vacaciones', *Medina*, 10 July 1941, 'La falda pantalon', *Medina* 19 July 1942; *Formación familiar y social*, 221–4 at 223.
33. 'La frivolidad y la mujer falangista', *Medina* 12 June 1941.

–9–

Blankets: The Visible Politics of Indigenous Clothing

Margaret Maynard

The 'Corroboree 2000' marches and intensifying debates on reconciliation in Australia mark a useful staring point for a discussion of the issue of indigenous citizenship and the politics of clothing. Although no national body today exists with full authority to speak for all indigenous Australians, the Council for Reconciliation seeks to redress the political, economic, social or cultural imbalances that have existed between the races in Australia for two centuries. The visibility that is increasingly accorded to indigenous issues, partly as a result of the work of the Council and other agencies, has brought the politics of Aboriginality to the centre of the national agenda, although to date indigenous people remain positioned outside the boundaries of full Australian citizenship (Day 1998: 187). Dress and reconciliation might at first seem to have little in common, but it is partly the purpose of this essay to show that the study of indigenous attire and body covering generally can tell us much about the workings of the political and thus about relations between Australia's black cultures, citizenship and the structures of white power.

Wayne Hudson has recently argued against accepting a model of citizenship in Australia that restricts civic identities to a single concept (Hudson 1998). In line with many theorists seeking to move beyond strictly bounded notions of culture and politics, he proposes a differential model of 'sphere' and 'domain' distinctions that can exist quite widely beyond nationality. In this model the exercising of civic capacities can occur outside a single national citizenship, and can differ widely according to specific sites. Bearing in mind such a differential and site-specific notion, it is worth exploring changes in the nature of clothing visibilities in relation to various cultural groups, in particular indigenous peoples. Radical federal policies adopted by the Whitlam government between 1972–5, reversing earlier doctrines of protection and assimilation (the latter aiming in part to encourage indigenous people to adopt white patterns of consumption including clothing), attempted to rehabilitate Aborigines, but as a marginal people with an independent culture. Thus, over the last two decades or so, Australia has transformed its colonial subjects situated inside the state yet outside the nation into a legitimate yet minority constituency of citizens who lack complete acceptance. Indigenous people are now fully included within the nation and with the right to vote, but are in a sense still disenfranchised: many are economically bereft, lacking the full benefits and rights of other Australians citizens and remain, to a greater or lesser degree, dependent on the prevailing political system (Beckett 1988: 17).

According to customary social procedures in Western society, a fundamental part of the so-called civilizing process is the adoption of acceptable clothing codes and related etiquette and behaviours. Whilst dress is clearly a matter of practical body covering, it is at the same time a public cultural practice that demonstrates social and aesthetic tastes, group membership, acceptable moral standards, status demarcation and appropriate levels of consumption. A significant aspect of past European interventionist policies in relation to the 'indigenous problem' was the dispensing of clothing. This was undertaken in various ways and for a variety of reasons from the time of early settlement, a practice that ultimately obliterated most forms of traditional attire.

By considering Australia's extremely small indigenous minority, both in the light of Hudson's differential model and the wider frame of so-called civilized society, this essay argues that the study of dress, as the private made public, enlarges our understandings of citizenship and racial politics in Australia. It shows that clothing can provide important new ways to read the nature and workings of gendered social relationships between the two cultures. Furthermore it demonstrates that indigenous clothing as a fluctuating sign has functioned in this country in ways that have visibly marked out the struggle for an indigenous identity both in colonial and more recent culture.

Dress Systems

Clothing is a complex and generally gender-specific bodily covering, which may be read in many ways. Its multiple and various meanings differ widely between the wearer's intentions and other people's perceptions about what is worn. It is thus an aspect of material culture that has serious public implications, for it is one of the ways whereby a culture projects ideas, organizes itself or is brought under the control of another society socially, economically and politically. Importantly it is also one of the ways in which both cultural identity and individual subjectivity is denoted. In the shifts that have taken place for indigenous people from being colonial subjects to part citizens it is useful to analyse how these changes have been visibly expressed through bodily decoration and dress. It is also pertinent to examine the changing tactics or negotiated claims made by indigenous people through dress as they seek to achieve some accommodation to the prevailing status of their citizenship.

Dress and fashion theory has traditionally centred on the role of fashion as the purview of the elite within civilized nations; it is considered part of the modern civilizing process itself. Craik has argued that dress and adornment function as part of a body-clothing complex which is constituted by and operates in ways that are consistent with a particular social milieu or habitus (Craik 1994: 10). The absence of clothing has been regarded dialectically as a lack of, or sign of, that which exists outside of the civilized, that is it inhabits the realm of non-fashion or the 'primitive'. Recently definitions of fashion have increasingly been placed under scrutiny, and the study of fashion and indeed clothing shifted from something that is condemned as superficial to a study central to our understandings of cultures and ethnicity. Traditional clothing systems are no longer considered to be static but can undergo alterations, and form hybrid types of attire that themselves shift and change (Craik 1996: 156). Exposure to Western commodities has not meant unequivocal acceptance of modern garb, but rather an uneven process of commoditization (Comaroff 1996: 37). Because of the active interconnectedness of culture and economics, we need to stop thinking of traditional versus non-traditional clothing, and more about mediated social interaction and exchange systems.

In order to understand something of these interconnected processes, I detail two particular examples of clothing practices of indigenous Australians that occurred a little under one hundred years apart, in vastly different social climates. I deal in particular with practices in New South Wales (NSW) and Queensland. I begin with the symbolic annual blanket ration (a fixed or allotted portion) issued by colonial authorities to blacks. For many reasons Europeans feared black nakedness as an uncomfortably barbaric and primitive state, although this form of exposure had entirely different meanings for indigenous people. Their state of undress was believed to require remedial action by colonial officials and mission officials. This took the form of dispensing blanket coverings (and loose slop clothing – dress of a basic generic kind), at first to conciliate with Aborigines, and later with more visibly charitable and paternalistic intent. Whilst colonial photographers engaged in scientific projects to categorize indigenous peoples encouraged them to be represented naked, to stress their 'primitive' place in social evolution (Maxwell 1999: 42), the dispensing of blankets was undertaken with different intent. Effectively it was a means of neutralizing the sight of unclothed 'natives', and rendering indigenous men, women and children non-gendered, even non-existent by the covering of their bodies. One could go so far as to suggest that gifted blankets were a gesture of disempowerment; a material equivalent to policies of racial exclusion or protection. This attempt to generally render bodies absent must be seen in relation to quite separate and sharply gender differentiated European clothing practices in Australia, derived in large part from Victorian Britain. The punctilious use of this latter clothing was intended as a key marker of decorum and of the civilized way of life in the distant colony.

Blanket coverings, often used as a form of attire by indigenous people, will be compared to more recent and visibly dramatic appearances of indigenous activists since the 1970s, especially those associated with the Brisbane Commonwealth Games and anti-bicentennial protests of 1982 and 1988. From this time political statements made by indigenous people using T-shirts, headbands and hats, even representations of traditional unclothed appearances, have been a deliberate attempt to communicate political self-empowerment and identity. Self-styled statements, made through dress and adornment, bring a political visibility to the cause, securing a distinctive clothed identity and thus signalling claims to a civic position on indigenous terms. Aboriginal people are re-evaluating their clothing dependency of the past, and performatively using their attire and bodies as a way of asserting their own cultural visibility.

Obviously, I in no way suggest these two vastly different examples cover the entire range of indigenous clothing practices, or that these events explain the complex clothing relationships that have existed historically between white and black. Rather I use them as a way of dramatizing a set of issues in relation to dress, power and the political visibility of indigenous peoples within two specific cultural frames. This has been a radical shift in the nature of dressing, but ironically the latter clothing practices remain largely specular, rendered visible essentially via their media coverage. Paradoxically, this very assertive visibility demonstrates a political position that remains outside the parameters of everyday European citizenship, except to the extent that non-indigenous political sympathizers may on occasion assume some aspects of this attire. In as much as the ragged European style clothes worn today in the Northern Territory, Queensland, Western Australia and in all deprived areas of indigenous habitation (little different from those in the nineteenth century) are political, the very visibility of overtly political dress further contributes to the nature of being 'outside', as signs of those who are still negotiating acceptance as full citizens.

Blanketing

Official issue to blacks of British-made rough shoddy blankets (an inferior made-up textile) was originally a colonial practice that until recently was believed to have commenced in NSW at Governor Macquarie's first annual Parramatta Feast in December 1816. The giving of blankets was a complex relationship that Europeans entered into with Aborigines in exchange for certain acceptable behaviours and for whom blankets apparently replaced indigenous gift exchanges of traditionally crafted possum rugs and cloaks and, in Queensland, the making of bark blankets. Recent research shows that the annual giving of blankets commenced independently under the Governor of NSW Lieutenant-General Darling in 1826, building on the gift giving precedent of Parramatta. The express purpose was to reduce violence, gain control of and secure the frontier (Smithson 1992: 75). At this point dispensing of blankets, seemingly highly desired by Aborigines, became the major tool of social cohesion and reconciliation for Darling, and was not in any sense a charitable act. The activity was taken up by other States and in 1839 South Australian Governor Gawler began to dispense clothes and food to the Kaurna people of the Spencer region on the coastal plain around Adelaide, also as a technique of frontier governance (Rowse 1998: 17). Issues continued to be maintained, under a variety of different circumstances and institutional bodies, well into the twentieth century. In NSW blanket issue was transferred to the Aborigines Welfare Board (established in 1940) and finally to Child Welfare and Social Welfare in 1962, when it is last mentioned in the records.

In several important texts on the complex issues surrounding rationing and attendant social relationships, Tim Rowse has analysed the problematic and fluctuating nature of Aboriginal/ European relations in the politics of the rationing process, although he has not dealt specifically with clothing. To ration is to predetermine that which is supposedly needed but it is also attended by certain expectations on both sides. The work of Rowse and indeed Nicholas Thomas shows that in cross-cultural relationships, gift giving cannot be regarded as an equal transaction, and parties involved do not necessarily have common understandings of the meaning of the goods, or the behaviour that may attend the action (Thomas 1991). The relationship itself may be signified by the goods as they are given, but there is not necessarily a shared cultural understanding of what the gift might mean (Rowse 1998: 207). To ration goods, argues Rowse, is different from bartering. Bartering, he suggests, is a more transparent, agreed engagement between parties, compared with rationing, which is more complex, less well defined, its attached expectations more diffuse and perhaps open to abuse. He terms rationing a more opaque process, in which acceptance of goods also meant acquiescence to the new, imposed social order (1998: 20). This clearly underpins the nature of blanket rationing to Australia's indigenous peoples.

A blanket is a large, warm multi-purpose textile covering, of variable quality used normally in Western culture as an article of bedding. But the European term 'blanket' or 'to blanket' is worth some analysis. It is a generic one and implies a blank-ness or a blandness that blanks out, shrouds or obliterates the person involved, their age and gender, and in some sense hides or covers them up. Blanketing individuals with government issue, men, women and children, is in a sense to render all these persons undifferentiated. To dispense official rations (be they slops or blankets) that cover up or erase is a symbolic act of great political significance, especially in light of the widespread view held by the end of the 1840s that Aboriginal people were a dying race.

Although they had many other uses beyond clothing, blankets mark the extreme opposite to European civilian dress of the nineteenth century. The latter attire, brought out to Australia or imported from Britain, but sometimes also made locally, stressed the separation of the social spheres of the activities of men and women. Women's dress was bright or strongly coloured, ornamented in various ways and with voluminous skirts, whereas that of urban men consisted normally of dark cloth suits and hats. Bush clothing and informal dress for both men and women had other characteristics of course. But it was the sharp contrast between the dress of the colonizer and that of the colonized that helped to strengthen racial differences and hence to harden social attitudes.

Thus the function of blanket issue was far more than a question of charity and the clothing of indigenous nakedness. There were important additional elements of social control and moral probity embedded in the practice. This is evident in the nature of blanket dispensement as it changed with historical circumstances. The eating and drinking that initially accompanied the issue of European goods at the annual Parramatta Feast were abolished in 1835 by Governor Bourke who replaced them with an annual issue from police stations (Maynard 1994: 65). Removing blanket issue to places of petty sessions ensured dispensement remained in the hands of government officials such as magistrates and the police, and it did not fall to pastoralists under whom the government felt the practice might be abused. So depots from where issues were made became gathering places, but importantly official centres from where government instructions could easily be communicated. Recording the distribution of blankets at Mount Brown in 1854, the South Australian Sub-Protector of Aborigines noted, 'It brought many natives within my reach that continually avoided me, and over whom, by means of a blanket, I was able to gain a little influence, and to caution and advise them as they required' (Foster 1989: 74).

Aborigines used blankets for warmth, for covering their bodies and for carrying offspring, as well as for sleeping but they were also articles easy to adapt to other uses.[1] Aborigines valued them as currency of exchange, as did whites who certainly acquired them illegally if they could. Significantly, blankets, like other rations, were a means whereby whites could reward, encourage, pacify, compensate, keep track of, estimate numbers and influence, manage contact with, control and monitor the behaviour, travel and general population movements of blacks. The proposal by Walter Roth, Northern Protector of Queensland Aborigines and later Chief Protector (1897–1906)[2] to close the issue centre at Cooktown in 1903 was expressly intended to deny blacks any reason to congregate at the outskirts of the town for the weeks beforehand (Annual Report 1902 QPP 1903 2: 4).

Issues took place annually on the Queen's Birthday (1 May) usually in the presence of the Queen's representative, and thus were gifts made on behalf of an absent ruler, supposedly symbolizing her concern for her distant subjects. In 1879 at the blanket issue to Aborigines at Townsville, when the Townsville Reserve was on the point of closure, the recipients were requested to give 'Three regular "British" Cheers' for the Queen's substitute, the Visiting Governor (Evans 1971: 8). In Queensland the annual blanket issue was regularly reported to the Queensland Parliament and often made the pages of daily newspapers. In 1899 Walter Roth carefully noted in his report to Parliament the customary annual blanket issue to indigenous people had taken place; 900 at Cairns, 250 at Atherton and 1250 at Cooktown (Annual Report1899 QVP 1900 5: 583). In 1902 Roth again noted, with the accuracy of a census gatherer, that blankets were that year dispensed at sixty-two centres, to 2,777 men 2,311 women, 765 children under sixteen and to two unspecified persons (Annual Report 1902 QPP 2 1903: 4).

After the middle of the century, the annual habit of blanket giving was accompanied by the making of an official representation of the event. So the public importance of blanket issue was customarily signalled by the taking of an official photograph to record the important procedure. The ceremonial handing over of these articles of erasure was a well-documented ritual and intended to reinforce the nature and extent of colonial powers. An official photograph taken at Cedar Creek, Herberton illustrating the Protector's Annual Report to the Queensland Parliament for 1911 unequivocally demonstrates the inequitous power relations implicit in blanket gifting. The image shows a symbolic moment when Richard Howard, Chief Protector of Aboriginals, gives a blanket to an Aboriginal man, so-called 'King George VI' of Ravensbourne. The latter wears a demeaning King Plate, a token of brass inscribed with a grandiose European title. Perhaps the intention was to instil in indigenous people the concept of hierarchy absent in their cultures, but this overt 'naming' was inevitably a way of mocking the wearer's lowly social status. The blanket is clearly stamped with a large Q and the broad arrow of Government issue, so that all who used it would constantly be reminded of the presence of white colonial rule (Annual Report 1911 QPP 3 1912: 1002).

The early issues of blankets took the form of an exchange, but the nature of gifting changed in the 1840s. By then, following alterations in attitude toward charity in Britain, blanket issue came to be seen as a

Figure 9.1. 'King George VI' of Ravensbourne, Cedar Creek, receives his government blanket from the Protector, 1912.

significant aspect of official philanthropy, intended to provide bodily covering, modesty and warmth and general 'relief' to needy Aboriginal people, men, women and children of all ages. So, after temporarily ceasing in 1844 due to economic pressures, issues were reinstated as a charitable gesture in 1848 by Sir Charles Fitzroy in the settled areas of NSW and Moreton Bay. It was now believed that the Aboriginal people were dying out and that the need for blanket issue was unlikely to survive all that long as a practice. There is some irony to the fact that the practice did not diminish, but grew increasingly extensive, and in 1880, for instance 8,400 blankets were issued at 86 NSW centres (Smithson: 106). By now blankets were regarded as health preserving, and it was felt weak and infirm Aborigines required them. Thus any attempt to alter the rations became even more morally problematic, for the failure to dispense blankets was believed to cause deterioration in the health of indigenous people.

The offer, or subsequent withdrawal, of blankets was clearly more than a matter of clothing. The political and social implications were far reaching. In 1902, in a cost cutting measure, Roth proposed to reduce the blankets issue by 25 per cent the following year, except on Mission Stations, and to refuse blankets to healthy Aborigines. This proposal did not eventuate. When offered other consumable goods in their place, blacks resisted and refused to accept them. Again in 1905, attempts to reduce the issue were unsuccessful. Roth tried to give out print dresses and fishing lines instead of blankets, but collective pressure from blacks meant blankets had to be reinstated. So blanket issue remained as an accepted practice in Queensland; in the 1920s blankets were still being distributed by the then Sub-Department of Aboriginals. Yet substitutes were gradually agreed upon and in 1929, for instance, where found to be more suitable, dresses, trousers, shirts, prints and tobacco were dispensed instead. In an important sense blanket issue had come therefore to be regarded as a right and could be effectively used as a form of bargaining chip with the government.

Rationing and Monitoring

Clothing was a significant material element of European control of indigenous peoples, and thus a way in which paternalistic relations could be maintained. For the most part Europeans allowed indigenous fringe dwellers access to town, mission or station areas only if they wore clothing of some kind. Insisting on a supposedly civilized appearance was an important way of influencing movement of blacks, for nakedness was not tolerated in urban areas, most particularly if women were present.

By the end of the nineteenth century these attitudes to nakedness were complicated by a counter rhetoric that suggested the indigenous weakness for the 'white man's goods', including clothes, would hasten their social collapse. According to Rowse, by suggesting the receiver was degraded, the power of the giver was enhanced (1990: 144). He uses an example from Robert Croll's book *Wide Horizons. Wanderings in Central Australia* published in 1937 to illustrate his point.

In his text, Croll discusses his experiences with the Luritja people, the neighbours of the Arunta near Hermannsburg Mission. His frontispiece is a photograph of a so-termed 'primitive' Aboriginal man, fully naked, holding shield and spear, standing on a rock and with a heroic, distant look on his face. It is captioned 'Uncivilized', and according to Croll's somewhat romantic view of the 'primitive', said to possess a natural and attractive dignity. Later in the text itself, Croll uses a contrasting set of two images entitled 'Civilized'. These show what he believed to be unfortunate Aborigines entirely spoilt by contact with whites, wearing ragged European slops and rags. 'To obey the missionary convention in approaching the station, they must put on clothes. That act transformed them from kings to beggars; the borrowed rags were an ass's head upon the natural man' (Croll 1937: 130). The very activity that was required of indigenous people in order to participate in white civilized existence had now become the very thing that damned them in the eyes of commentators like Croll. The clothes that gave the white man status and access to the benefits of civilized life were believed to be the very things that demoralized blacks, and forced them to forget their own traditions.

Clothes worn by Aborigines engendered mixed feelings among whites. Worn appropriately they were a sign of approximation to the parent culture, but also a sign of weakness for the materials of civilization. Clothes had further uses for Europeans. They were something that could be used as a form of payment instead of currency, although any transaction brought with it certain obligations and meant a further fostering of dependency. Alfie Deakin, an Aboriginal stockman who worked in the East Kimberley region, told Bruce Shaw how when he was a young boy (probably about 1945), 'as soon as I got some of a moustache I started working. In those days we used to work just for shirt and trousers, blanket and calico – no money at all – hat and boots and two sticks of tobacco' (Shaw 1992: 129). Here we see how payment in food and clothing, instead of cash, locks the receiver into a system of dependency that suggests indigenous labour is less valuable than that of white workers.

Thus clothing, and attire generally, bound indigenous people to Europeans in a web of relationships. This was especially the case in reserves and missions which were, in the latter case, training grounds for citizenship. Movement in and out was controlled and the way clothes were kept and worn carefully monitored. Yarrabah Mission set up in 1892 originally for the Yidinjdji people was one such place of control, a place that grew increasingly harsh with the years. Proclaimed a reformatory in 1901, inmates could only leave if they received one of the rare exemption tickets, ran away, were removed, or married someone outside the establishment. Mission men worked for board and meagre rations, often having to find other kinds of food off the land. In 1901 a minimum wage for Mission adults was set by amendment, but all wages were held in trust by either the Protector, or his representative the Superintendent, and inmates given pocket money only (Thomson 1989: 66).

The ways in which clothing was monitored at the Yarrabah Mission shows the degree of humiliation to which Aboriginal people were subjected. Writing up his Annual Report on Aborigines for the Queensland Parliament in 1902, the Protector noted with pride how precisely regulations there were being observed. The Mission had a special clothes room where on Sunday mornings clothes were hung on a rail to be fetched by single men and boys. After their 'matutinal' bath they left their dirty clothes at the door. On the Monday clean weekday clothes were hung on the same rail and the Sunday ones left at the door for washing. The supply of women's and children's clothes was the responsibility of the ladies of the Mission but if a married man needed a coat or trousers he must produce the whole wardrobe to satisfy the storekeeper that he needed the clothes. From time to time parades were held and each man had to fall into line with his bundle of clothes, which were examined and requirements noted. Unfit garments were burnt (Annual Report 1902 QPP 2 1903: 469).

For Europeans clothing was imbued with moral and material values and was a symbol of white civilization they believed should be respected. Indigenous people did not necessarily share their views of its significance. When blacks passed garments from a man to his wife and then on to a friend it was possible for Europeans to interpret this as a light regard for property. As Rowse shows some goods had greater value for indigenous people than others (1998: 23) and it is impossible to understand the precise attitude that indigenous people attached to white clothing. What we can say is that whites were able to use dress as a powerful tool of social control, but at times blacks were able to disrupt some convictions about dressing using European clothes in ways that were regarded as inappropriate, and even to show resistance to certain impositions.

Europeans believed that the material products of their culture, including dress, were a crucial aspect of the ways in which relationships with

Aborigines could be mediated. Rationing of clothing was integral to the policies of assimilation that developed from the late 1930s – a process that induced indigenous peoples to take up citizenship. As part of assimilation blanket issue was gradually superceded by cash payments, as recipients were eventually deemed entitled to have them. The entire practice of rationing was finally replaced in the 1960s and 1970s when full social security benefits were granted, a different form of 'security blanket' (Rowse 1998: 3).

Protest Clothing

More recent examples of indigenous dress occupy an entirely different social, political and cultural frame of reference from the past. In colonial times blankets and slops imposed on Aborigines enshrouded bodies, but in the last thirty years indigenous people have reclaimed these former practices and are now using attire as a strategic method of telling the story of their own identity. Despite these assertive gestures, one could argue that dress reclamation whilst 'domain' specific in Hudson's terms, has remained at the level of performance or signage only, with little substantive change in indigenous lives and conditions.

The history of the Aboriginal protest movement goes back to the 1960s, but the sense that indigenous people were taking control of their clothed identities within the public arena emerges in association with the Aboriginal Tent Embassy set up on the lawns of Parliament House on Australia Day 1972. Here, flying the Aboriginal flag newly designed by Harold Thomas, was a symbolic and inspirational moment in the quest for land restitution, and the result of ten years of debate over the political goals of indigenous people. Associated with this moment of protest were public expressions and assertions of indigenous identity figured through clothing. Starting initially with red head bands, protest clothes now include printed T-shirts, striped beanies and dramatic, broad-brimmed hats often black and similar to stockmen's hats worn by women as well as by men.

T-shirts with their textual and other logos are proud statements of indigenous identity and are a key part of indigenous political strategies to counter their past clothing history. These garments are a particularly effective ephemeral cultural news sheet, cheap and easy to produce, and able to display the topical and the contingent through temporary signs and commentary. Gender unspecific, ephemeral and unpretentious, they are nevertheless highly meaningful in their capacity to annunciate political views and opinions. Richard Martin has shown that T-shirts are the modern equivalent of a calendar because they can act like markers to signify the

Figure 9.2. Vincent Brady leading a protest march to bring attention to Aboriginal opposition to the bicentenary celebrations, Brisbane, 1987.

passing of historical events and changing political viewpoints. Their capacity to display temporary logos and text make them ideally suited to conveying a sense of group solidarity and political resistance and to play a role in communicating rapidly changing ideas and meanings. But as Martin shows, there is more to shirts than simply a time line or message bank. Whilst these clothes are 'newsworthy', they are not just documents or journalistic texts, for 'the articulate T-shirt can also take its place as a principal player in the modern drama' (Martin 1992: 27–9). In other words these articles have the capacity to change the ways in which people think and act in the world.

T shirts have been used by indigenous people at numerous important cultural and political events. In fact it is in the public cultural arena, where subjectivities are performative and unfixed, that shirts, so amenable to change and alteration, can play their most important role. Some of the most significant are those inscribed shirts marking political protest in the 1980s such as Lands Council shirts, shirts worn at events like the handover of title to Uluru in 1985, or shirts printed to protest Aboriginal deaths in Custody in 1986–7 (Dewdney 1994: 128–33). Some of the earliest examples of political T-shirts were North Queensland Lands Council shirts distributed in 1980 by FAIRA (Foundation for Aboriginal and Islander Research Action) and those worn at marches organized by the Black Protest Committee during the 1982 Commonwealth Games in Brisbane. Under their auspices in September an incident-free march of 2000 people took place from Brisbane's Roma Street Forum to Musgrave Park and the following day a march to QEII Stadium. Land Rights T-shirts were worn on both occasions (Watson 1988: 40).

It is useful to compare the 1982 clothing to dress worn at the January 1988 bicentennial protest march in Sydney some six years later, when the world spotlight was again on Aboriginal protest claims. The Australian bicentenary of first settlement celebrated in 1988 was, according to cultural historian Graeme Turner, an uncomfortable and artificially constructed event, but as he strongly argues, its failure to construct a seamless image of national unity was the very basis of its success. It was, he feels, a complex occasion during which Australians were asked to sort through various competing versions and claims on their identity (Turner 1994: 72). Aboriginal people were unable to support the bicentenary festivities because of what they felt to be the failure of the federal government to accord them basic political and civil rights, rights to land, rights of determination, rights of prior ownership and also compensation (Watson 1988: 28). So part of the complexity of the bicentenary, and associated events, was that it was a festive occasion for Anglo-Australians, but an indigenous mourning about white invasion, as well as a strengthening of indigenous political will.

Australia Day 1988, renamed by indigenous people as Invasion Day, was marked by a large and peaceful 10,000 strong anti-bicentenary march in Sydney. This was labelled the 'Justice, Freedom and Hope' march, and took place from Redfern Oval to Belmore Park. It was a conciliatory march, although far smaller than the more recent Corroborree 2000 march over Sydney Harbour Bridge, the latter event calling on the government to reconcile with Aboriginal people. The 'Justice, Freedom and Hope' march was, at the time, regarded as the biggest and perhaps most unified gathering of indigenous people in their history, and according to Turner was given wide exposure through the media. It became a political event of some moment, turning out to be more a celebration of a coming together of Aboriginal people on their own terms, rather than simply a mourning about the past. The clothing worn was an important aspect of the march, the spirit of the occasion captured in 'The Justice, Freedom and Hope' photographic mural with original photographs by Huw Davies. (Dewdney 1994: 151–8). Memorable photographs by Brenda Croft include a line of men and women in T-shirts carrying a banner inscribed 'Our Land Our Life' and a vivid image of Michael Watson with his face painted, wearing a head band inscribed 'We have survived'. His T-shirt was emblazoned with the Aboriginal flag and inscribed 'Cook Who Coo-oo' (Dewdney 1994: 118-22). Children on the march wore T-shirts inscribed with the words 'I am a little black, yellow and red Aussie', older indigenous people wore headbands inscribed with the words 'our land', and tribal elders from the Northern Territory carrying spears and chanting and clapping sticks walked wearing only loin cloths, their bodies marked in traditional manner with feathers and ochre.

Playing to the media was and is a major ingredient of these protests, although the mainstream media are, of course, not neutral, constantly managing and manipulating notions of citizenship and identity. But indigenous protest clothing, heightened by its visibility in the media, is a sign that the former colonial practice of photographing blanket issue has been resituated and reversed. The work of indigenous photographers like Brenda Croft, Mervyn Bishop, Michael Aird and Ricky Maynard, who have taken some control of the process of representation of indigenous people, also marks a significant reversal of colonial practices. According to Meadows and van Vuuren any formation of indigenous citizenship needs to be linked to their identity as it is created through dialogue with white culture (Meadows and van Vuuren 1998: 98). But so little dialogue has occurred in the past that even admitting the existence of indigenous identity has remained at the edge of citizenship debates especially in recent years. Clearly dress is merely one aspect of a large and contested field relating to questions of citizenship for indigenous peoples whose lives have been so marginalized in our culture. The wearing of politicized clothes that mark out a special place and visibility for their cause is simply one step on a larger journey toward the presence of indigenous peoples as full and equal citizens of Australia.

Acknowledgements

I would like to acknowledge the work that was undertaken by Faith Walker, who has studied Queensland blanket issue in some depth.

Notes

1. Blankets used for canoe sails were reported by Coen Police in Annual Report of the Northern Protector of Aboriginals for 1903, QPP 1904: 853.
2. Roth was empowered under the 1897 Queensland Aboriginal Protection and Restriction of Opium Act that remained the main Act administering Aboriginal affairs until 1939.

10

Children's Day: The Fashionable Performance of Modern Citizenship in China

Stephanie Hemelryk Donald

Introduction

This essay is concerned with the performance of citizenship in China, an authoritarian collective society in transition to a market economy with socialist characteristics. I argue that the performance of citizenship here refers to the ways in which fashion is used by urban children as an articulation of their relation to the state, its norms and histories, but also to their wider social sphere. Given the high level of adult gatekeeping in children's access to fashion, to public spaces and to material goods in general, I acknowledge that the examples used below refer as much to adult ideas about children's proto-citizenship modes as they speak to the children's own articulated experience. Citizenship is here understood as an ideal state-society relationship model that is differently conceived according to location, class, gender, group identity and education. The model does not prioritize Western and liberal-democratic particularities in definitions of citizenship in political legislation. As David Brown has argued:

> 'Citizenship' functions as a normative ideal to provide the individual with formulas of identity, virtue and morality that convey visions of the nation in which the individual is ethically embedded as a just society. These resolve the individual's sense of insecurity and uncertainty. Citizenship also establishes a basis for social control by invoking ideas of duty, obligation and conformity. (Brown 2001)[1]

Children's fashion is likely to be a mixture of adult fantasy, role playing, cultural appropriateness and functionality (Higonnet 1997). It is not necessarily tied to individual choices, nor to street wear. Children 'do fashion' at school, in play zones, and as part of their play. Whilst parents might purchase special smart or ceremonial garments for them, they must also accede to school uniform regulations, to the needs of rough play, and to the pressures of their friends. In this chapter, I want to explore how these various fashion spaces are produced in China, and to examine the complexities which they illustrate in relation to China's emergent status as a socialist-capitalist economy.

In places where state education is available, and especially where the reproduction of a national ethos is prioritized, much of a child's clothing will be school uniform. In Australia, state school uniforms are fairly relaxed, usually restricted to a particular colour of skirt or trouser (light blue, green and gold, red and so forth), a large sun hat with a school crest, and a school back pack. In the US, France and the UK, many state schools have no uniform at all. It is often the private school sector that insists on complicated uniform codes, as a way of distinguishing their students, and insisting on an exclusive presence for their values and standards.[2] In the Asian region state school uniforms tend to be standard across the country, and many of the designs between countries are surprisingly similar. In Japan, Taiwan, the People's Republic of China (PRC) and Hong Kong there are various versions of blue-and-white uniforms, with gradations in style to indicate a child's school age and status. It appears that, despite strong ideological differences between national agendas, dark blue is a preferred colour and always matched with a white shirt. There are of course notable details, which mark the particularity of the national as invested in the maturing child. Male top graders in Japan wear a dark, almost black, military style jacket in opposition to the kindergarten's bright yellow capes. Brian McVeigh has argued that in Japan 'it seems as if everyone is in uniform' (McVeigh 1997: 191). He goes on to argue that the maintenance of the deep ideology of the Japanese nation state depends in great measure on the adherence of its citizens to normative codes of conduct, exemplified in dress codes (McVeigh 1997: 195). Although there are no state-level rules about uniforms in school, the permeation of the needs and expectations of the state to almost all levels of society ensures that they exist. Conversely, one could argue that social norms have permeated state organization to the point where the modern nation-state in Japan has exceeded global patterns of bureaucratization to rely on ritualized cultural artefacts for its cohesion.

In China, there are uniforms too, although the differentiations across school ages and levels are subordinated to marks of personal revolutionary achievement. First, all children in the PRC expect to be granted leave to wear a Young Pioneer (*shaoxianduiyuan*) red scarf as part of their uniform (and some also wear it out of school). The Young Pioneer scarf 'symbolizes a corner of the national flag, stained red by the blood of revolutionary martyrs' (Donald 1999: 85). It has to be earned by appropriate skills, attitudes and behaviour. As Mary Farquhar has noted, the Young Pioneers movement has supported other educational activities as a thematic and a motivating concept (Farquhar 1999: 251).

Children who are particularly competent in social and political skills may also earn red stripes on their school shirts, which denote varying levels of class leadership. Teenagers may apply to join the Communist Youth League (which brings them a small gold badge). These marks of success are often gained in a fairly predictable age pattern, but are nonetheless predicated upon political-social behaviour rather than simply on belonging to the group in a national context. The children's book *How Luo Wenying became a Young Pioneer*, tells how a young boy overcomes his laziness through hard work and the help of a study group formed by his school friends. In this progress of collective endeavour, he manages to gain his membership and the coveted red scarf (Farquhar 1999: 260). This follows long-standing habits in China of combining nationalism, political identification and dress, particularly male dress (Finnane 1996: 99–101). As Annie Chan has also argued, in Hong Kong the choice between Western and Chinese dress styles was a significant marker of both Chinese consumption and of post-colonial identity, whereby Chinese dress still signifies an anti-modern servility (Chan 2000: 304–5). Children in both Hong Kong and China might still be wrapped in Chinese style open-bottom baby wear but they shift to Western-based clothes as soon as they move into the public sphere of education.

Outside school wear depends not just on style but also on children's experience as consumers, and international brand names spread rapidly across national borders. The ubiquitous *Hello Kitty* design is found on children's outfits and accessories in Japan (where the design is patented),[3] Malaysia, Hong Kong, Taiwan, PRC, South Korea, and doubtless elsewhere in the region. I have also seen several non-patented versions, where an exclamation mark replaces the second 'l' : *Hel!o Kitty*! Disney motifs, cute approximations of branded names (*Jiahui, Lanmao*) and appliqué animals are all staple design features in children's clothing. Girls' clothes, particularly in the PRC, tend towards extreme frilliness (especially in socks!), and boy's gear has a tendency to the military cargo look, which is also familiar to Australian and American shoppers. These observations are only pertinent, however, if they are considered in relation to the environment in which they are worn. The arrival of Disney socks might (simply) herald the success of a globalizing consumer economy. In Hong Kong SAR, after all, the biggest tourist venture for 2001 is the building of Asia's Disney World. Yet, when the children who wear those Disney socks, or visit Disney World on a school trip, are also wearing their school uniform and a Young Pioneer scarf, what history of succession and compromise do they tell us?

Revolutionary Chic

> At a time when everyone in the nation was being urged to focus on the noble goals of self-reliance, thrift, and hard work for the sake of strengthening the country, how could I feel proud of a mother who wore fashionable dresses and high heels? (Chen 1999: 112)

Writing on fashion in the context of revolutionary China requires the political and subjective nuance of ambiguity. In the above quotation, Chen Xiaomei reflects on her mixture of feelings towards her mother, a successful and glamorous revolutionary actress. Chen remembers adoring her mother's chic, beauty and poise, but, as a teenager and young adult during the Cultural Revolution (1966–76), she also recalls feeling embarrassed by those same attributes. At moments of youthful ideological austerity, what was fashionable was not necessarily glamorous. Dressing down was a signifier of moral, rebel revolutionary fibre and that was a valuable social asset. Western writers on fashion have also described ideological dressing down, perhaps wearing jeans as a statement of working-class pride, or wannabe working-class chic (Barnard 1996: 127–9). Anti-fashion and sub-cultural grunge is also usually the preserve of the young in these accounts. Chen's comments, however, remind us of the absolute contrasts, across and within generations, which emerge in cultures with high levels of political coding. In China after Liberation, fashion was a difficult game to play. At what point does dress sense become bourgeois? When does femininity become a problem? Or rather, can it be articulated in ways which incorporate the political? These questions of femininity and state socialism are not the core theme of this chapter but they do need to be considered as an historical foil to modern Chinese consumption.

In the 1997 exhibition of Chinese dress at the Powerhouse Gallery in Sydney, Australia, there was a 1950s floral frock on display, based on a Soviet design (*bulaji*). It came from the Communist bloc, it avoided the connotations of Western pre-Liberation decadence and Chinese traditionalism, and it was pretty, popular and wearable (Roberts 1997: 24).

The curators of the exhibition, Claire Roberts and Sang Ye, also incorporated workers' overalls and subdued two-piece Mao suits in the display. Versions of the latter (which were often blue or blue and grey) are still worn by older members of the population in contemporary China. The familiar army-look suits worn in the late 1960s are less restrained. Instead of shapeless reticence, they suggest baggy, barely restrained fury and energy. With hindsight, and with the easy nostalgia of non-involvement, the PLA-khaki square-cut jacket and baggy trousers, complete with natty red badges and armbands, of the Cultural Revolution period seem to be the epitome of grunge chic. It is not hard to appreciate why young rebel revolutionaries preferred to express their morality in the asexual uniform of the soldier hero rather than in the floral pastels worn by their mothers in the 1950s.[4] The so-called 'Mao' suit was actually based on an outfit (*Zhongshan zhuan*) developed by Dr Sun Yatsen (the leader of the Republican revolution in 1912). It was an adaptation of military uniform, Western men's suits, and overseas Chinese styles (Roberts 1997: 12). As Sun had spent considerable time as a student in Japan, the echoes of a Japanese boy's high-school uniform are not spurious. Given the crossover between the regular Sun Yat-sen suit, the PLA (People's Liberation Army) uniform and the outfit worn by Little Red Guards, this is a nice irony. Rebel revolutionaries and the reviled Japanese (still represented as war criminals in the 1960s and 1970s) are contrapuntally sharing the iconic anchors of the century in their dress codes. The suit is now in abeyance in China amongst the young, however. Bohemian artists might dip into retro revolutionary chic, but schoolchildren do not (Hou 1996: 46).[5] The suit as a general costume has become another mundane cipher in consumer semiotics. Not in the exhibition, but visible all over Beijing, is the 'suit' worn by waiters and waitresses. Many restaurants clothe their staff in severely cut two pieces in a uniform colour. Of course, the better the restaurant, the nicer the cut and the colour, for the association between uniform and good quality food is an easy code for the consumer to grasp. Nonetheless it is a strangely dull turn for the two-piece to take in post-socialism, and, given its history, possibly not its last move.

I wish to consider the juxtapositions on show in the Children's Day event, described below, in the context of consumerism in contemporary China. In particular, I will make reference to the idea of modern citizenship and the ways in which fashion contributes to its formation. In this regard I suggest that the notion of culture as praxis (Bauman 2000) is helpful in thinking through the constructive anomaly of street-smart fashion consciousness (designer leggings), historical reverence (the legacy of the Mao suit) and nationalism. Culture as doing is the basic concept in Bauman's thesis of dynamic self-assertion in social life. Doing culture, and particularly doing fashion,[6] allows for quick changes in a turbulent situation.

Children's Day

Children's Day (*liu yi* or *ertong jie*) celebrates the importance of youth to the future of China. A young university professor in his twenties (Sheng) from Shandong province recalled for me in a recent interview (2001):

> As to Children's Day, I believe it is an international day and that there must be some international meaning attached to it, as well as related regulations for the welfare of children. The Chinese Government pays a great deal of attention to this Day and has done a lot to ensure children's rights and benefits. Children's Day is one of the most important festivals for the Chinese children. I remember when I was very young, we used to prepare various programs for the occasion long before the Day every year until I went to high school (junior).We would start very early that day, sometimes it was still very dark. We would walk two and a half kilometers to the central primary school in our community. We would bring our own lunch with us and it used to last till 2 or 3 o'clock in the afternoon. Children are encouraged to do good deeds for others and for the society like Lei Feng did, especially in the earlier days – but there is no necessary connection between Children's Day and Lei Feng.

Although based in pride and affection for the nation's (and one's own) children, the day also mobilizes that sentiment into a declaration of national regeneration. Children are given a day off school, but many are also required to perform in carnivals and parades. The biggest of these parades, in Tiananmen and other civic central squares and parks across China, are given heavy media coverage. Children's Day is then a day for the exhibition of youthful accomplishment in a strongly nationalistic context.

The day is not divorced from other festivals and practices of Children's Day around the globe, however. International Children's Day(s) were inaugurated after the 1925 Geneva Conference for the Protection of Children, which sought to improve the lives of children worldwide. In Taiwan, Republic of China, the festival is celebrated on 4 April and is 'marked by the Children's Day Celebration honoring model students from around Taiwan'.[7] In the US, Children's Day (around 12 October) tends to be a multicultural festival with a strong emphasis on Asian American and African American cultures. It involves dressing up, face painting and the chance to 'experience different cultures, learn a little tolerance, and connect with [other] kids'.[8] In Japan, Children's Day is a gender friendly adaptation of the older 'Boys' Festival' and is celebrated on 5 May. It forms part of a week of national celebrations, 'Golden Week', along with Greenery Day and Constitution Day.[9] There has also been a media focussed 'International Children's Day of Broadcasting' (1992 until the most recent, 10 December 2000), organized by UNESCO, which responds directly to the 1925 conference, by giving children a voice in the articulation of world events.[10]

In different ways the Children's Days celebrations are all as much about how a nation likes to think about itself as they are about the rights of children. The various celebrations all focus on cultural citizenship, but they do so through the expressive tropes appropriate to the values of the nation concerned: model behaviour, multiculturalism, a gender-free embrace of traditionalism in a civic context, and so on. In the People's Republic of China, Children's Day is interesting because it has not yet fully assimilated political culture into modern cultural performances of national identity as a formation of consumerism. There are fissures evident in the structure of the children's house. This year (2000) much of the media coverage of *Liu Yi* dealt not so much with national glory as with family issues (the pressure of work on parents, single-parent families) and details of consumption choices. Nevertheless, the photographs used were taken from the spectacular moments of performance in large national spaces. The newspapers preferred typical images of children moving in perfectly choreographed harmony, dressed in red.

A daily paper in Beijing gave a full-colour image over to the choreography of youth in Tiananmen. The text was concerned, however, with the fact that children had kept away from playgrounds in favour of the zoo, the swim pool and seaside play areas. The article noted that children were consuming space in different ways, picking commodified and expensive treats against the state provided children's palaces. Meanwhile, stores throughout the major cities geared up to do a rousing business in toys, games and clothes. In the paper's report this point was tied to comments from parents that Children's Day was their only chance to spend quality time (and quality cash) with their families. The relationship between the various uses and meanings of Children's Day is therefore difficult to pin down. Is it any longer a national celebration of China's new generation, or is it akin to Christmas: a chance to marvel at your child's performance and then spend money on her?

On 1 June 2000 I attended a Children's Day celebration at Qinghua Linked Primary School in Beijing. This is a school based in a large university compound. It has a high proportion of pupils whose parents work in the university or in the associated service sectors. In other places it might be described as a high achieving middle-class school with strong affiliations with the status quo. That information is necessary for readers to understand that this chapter is talking about the fashionable behaviour of a particular sector of Chinese urban society. Many rural children might not have access to the money or to the shops where new fashions are sold (although many rural township enterprises will be making the clothes that Westerners buy from their own high street outlets). Poorer children in major cities, especially those dispossessed by internal migration, will not be attending school at all. The middle class élite is, however, a sector with a high level of influence in consumer purchasing patterns and media output. The ways in which its children play with culture is significant to an understanding of the logic of consumption in the state more generally. The association of consumption, fashion and a national festival, which I observed at the school's celebration, indicates a paradoxically collective and nationally sensitive relation to global influences.

The show started at 8.30am and finished around 11am. It was a hot day but the school-yard was full of proud parents and exhilarated children. Children aged six to ten years performed songs and dances and engaged in displays of sporting skills and martial arts. Sports included traditional games (hoops and balls) and new fads (roller blading). There were two items on the program which I found especially interesting. Both were fashion shows of a kind.

The first item was a parade of girls wearing brightly coloured folk costumes of China's minority peoples. There are fifty-five designated minority peoples (*shaoshu minzu*) in the People's Republic of China, making up 9 per cent of the total population. Of those, 17 peoples have a population of more than one million. The largest concentrations are in the far west and in the south of the territory (Benewick and Donald 1999: 20–1). The children's endearing ethnic show was part of a long and wide continuum of condescension towards non-Han cultures in the mainstream media. Although these peoples have vastly differing backgrounds, religious affiliations and local histories, the Chinese popular media (and the state) tend to describe them only in terms of block colourful ethnicity. Each New Year a 'special' TV show will include dancers and singers from minorities, dressed up to the traditional nines and entertaining the average Chinese spectator with a version of highly commodified difference. Roxanna Lilley has described how the same habit appeared in television spectaculars celebrating the Hong Kong handover in 1997:

> A woman clad in a diaphanous evening dress, resplendent with glittering beehive hairdo, croons a romantic song. She is immediately replaced by a

chorus of male dancers, acrobatically traversing a set that evokes a sanitized construction site ... Enter a group of children dressed in the costumes of minority nationalities, familiar to us all through the efforts of glossy tourism brochures. The children exit and we are treated to a space-age fashion parade evoking a science fiction image of detribalised Chinese grunge. (Lilley 2000: 169–70)

More often, when minority cultures are not deemed necessary to establish China's diversity, regular shows vie with one another to produce fashionably global Han presenters and entertainers. The extremely popular magazine programme, *Joyful Gathering* (*Huanju yi tang*), ran a show on 'beautiful women' (CCTV 4, 2 July 2000). All the women were mainstream 'Han' and none wore anything remotely resembling a national costume. The show's maxims were that feminine beauty centred around up-market designer labels (and up-market figures), drinking pure water instead of coke, keeping young after producing beautiful triplets – now twelve years old – and being able to paint, quote poetry in argument, and do the can-can (the finale). A racial extension of this discourse of the modern cool as a reinvention of the mainstream feminine is an obsession with whiteness (white has long been considered the colour of aristocratic beauty) (Schein 1994). In many cases minority peoples are not white skinned (who is?) and are written out of this discourse, which, although not as invidious as European versions of whiteness, are still steeped in internal orientalism. In 2000 CCTV (Chinese Central Television) and BTV (Beijing Television) ran advertisements for almond milk, which claimed that it whitened skin. My own children were stopped in the street on several occasions in June 2000 and the younger (very pale-skinned daughter) was asked if she liked almond milk. Bev Hooper (2000) has noted that this sales angle is pursued by Japanese companies too:

With its prestigious 'Beautiful White Series', Shiseido had a head start over Western brands in the booming market for skin-whitening products which it had already produced for the Japanese market and which have appealed to a similar Chinese/Oriental beauty discourse of the desirability of 'fair skin.' (Hooper 2000: 459 / Johannsson 1998–9)

The children's minority ethnicities item was caught in a cycle of authenticity and fashionable demotion, which is familiar territory for indigenous and minority ethnicities. Although racism is supposedly outlawed in Chinese society, consumer choices that relate fashion to urban mainstream preferences do work against minority culture choices and necessities. That is not to say that consumption is heading invariably towards Western models. New habits of consumption and advertisement are de-linking beauty from the Western fetish. As Hooper argues, the desire to buy local goods as opposed to imported brand names is increasing as consumer confidence grows.

The second item that caught my attention was a fashion parade, with children wearing various 'styles' and sauntering across the school podium as though it were a catwalk. Delighted applause greeted each new mannequin. Children shimmied one by one (or in colour co-ordinated pairs) across the stage. Each outfit was evidently an expression of the child's personality, and hoots from friends in the audience demonstrated the wit and self-irony on display. One rather little boy sported a tweedy jacket, faun trousers and a homburg-esque hat. He was 'doing' the English gentleman. Others strutted around in baseball hats and jeans. Some girls wore gear that the Spice Girls might have liked, while others dressed demurely in frills and flounces. Whatever their choice, the demure and the raunchy were clearly playing a role in a continuing exploration of what it might mean to do fashion. Yet, as Michael Dutton has argued, doing fashion in the PRC is not in fact best understood as a statement of individuality. It is a statement of wisdom, knowing what means what to whom, and thus aligning oneself with a superior collective. That is, of course, also an explanation of fashionable and snobbish behaviour elsewhere. The differences are, perhaps, that limited numbers are not a fashionable requirement in the Chinese case, and that the collective is just that, and not a collection of loosely affiliated individuals in the same mall.

> For these Chinese, fashion is not constructed to mark out one's individuality, but to mark out one's success . . . One has chosen wisely for one has made 'the popular choice'. Not for these Chinese the transparent delusion of individuality that Western fashion victims entertain. The Chinese, in this one, crucial, respect have never really changed out of their Mao suits. (Dutton 1998: 274)

Fashion collectives might prove self-limiting as fashionable decisions increasingly rely on money as well as political nouse. However, Dutton's argument contends that the seeming juxtaposition between collective self and fashionable self is a false one, because it relies on the delusory arrogance of individualism in Western consumer performance. What, though, of the convergence of consumer capitalism and historical memory? How does the value system of a revolutionary society cope with the stratified materialism of capital?

Directly after this item the audience were settled down again: a group of third graders dressed in pale blue school uniform sang in praise of the model soldier Lei Feng. Lei Feng was glorified after an early death in the service of his country. He is remembered for his numerous good deeds and utter selflessness in favour of the collective. Children have been emulating his model behaviour since the early 1960s. It was a surprise, though, to see his image on 1 June 2000, and to listen to the earnest song in his praise. To my literal Western eyes, it looked like a contradiction. How could the children relate the materialism of the fashion show to a paean to an old-style hero? The simple answer is that they don't. The collective impulse, which Dutton notes is embedded in Chinese social practice and self-expectation, allows a continuum between performances. Doing culture now involves doing revolutionary reverence as much as it encourages doing dressing up in the latest department-store styles.

The show and its items worked as a descriptive and performative metaphor of the theatrical progression of contrasts in Chinese socialist capitalism. Each item on the programme demands a quick change as the students' costume signal shifts from trendy roller-bladers to serious choristers of the nation. The children who sport new fashions are participating in the consumption of Western styles, Chinese domination in the mass garment industries, and, crucially, in the production of the individual as a dressed fetish. The same children, or their classmates, are doing something rather different in terms of cultural politics when they change into pale blue straight dresses and shorts, white shirts and red Young Pioneer scarves. They are doing succession and revolutionary continuity (Donald 1999: 85, Chan 1985: 28–9).

I am still uncertain as to the nature of that succession. Despite songs to Lei Feng, many children have not experienced economic socialism or the welfare state (Cook 1999). And, of course, teachers decide what songs are sung on open days at school. Also, not all children are at school for much of the time anyway. Children outside the safety net of a steady income are prey to the travails of parental migration, to huge unemployment concerns, and to a fast-thinning faith in communist ideology. As Sally Sargeson has suggested, the rural poor are working much too hard in the new economy to have much time to put aside for identity politics (Sargeson 1999). I defined citizenship as a concept defining an ideal relationship between the state and the individual, or group member. It remains to be seen how that relationship develops in the wake of capitalization and economic upheaval. How will the Chinese nation state fare in the face of regional interests, localized poverty and unrest? The slip between fashion and faith was a startling fugue in the Children's

Day show, 2000. The performance of citizenship, as a statement of proto-citizenship amongst middle-class urban children, was relaxed and stylish. In future years and in the wider reaches of the territory it may be less easy to carry off.

Notes

1. Unpublished proposal written by David Brown, Sally Sargeson and the author.
2. In China most state schools are not free of charge. At least 80 per cent have to find ways of supporting themselves. In 1997 12.9 per cent of income went towards education costs. There is also a fast developing private sector, which competes with locally supported schools.
3. Websites: http://www.sanrio.com/ and http://www.sanrio.co.jp/world/ world.html (the official market place portals but there are also many fansites and especially Taiwan-based sites).
4. Today, twenty-something Beijingers associate floral prints with visiting female foreigners with little taste.
5. However, for an impression of the continuity of severity in dress styles, see Zhang Xiaogang's 'The Big Family', 'Bloodline' and 'Comrades' series (*Reckoning with the Past: Contemporary Chinese Painting*, curated at The Fruitmarket Gallery, Edinburgh, 1996).
6. Thanks to Hsin-yen Belynda Sim for bringing this to my attention.
7. Children's Day, Govern,ment information Office, ROC, http://www.gio.gov.tw/info/festival_c/child_c/child.htm.
8. Greg Reinholt, director of The Fox Point Boys' and Girls' Club, 'At Children's Day, The Playing is the Thing' http://netspace.org/herald/issues/120595/childday.f.html.
9. Children's Day (Boys' Festival) http://www1.corainet.or.jp/kinsan/tango.htm See also Janet Riehecky, *Japanese Boy's Festival*, Children's Press, Chicago, 1994.
10. http://www.unicef.org/icdb/.

11

Afterthought: Redressing the Balance in Historiography
Roger Griffin

I ask readers to excuse yet another sartorial pun, especially since the point of this brief postscript is to stress just how erroneous it would be to dismiss a scholarly concern with the socio-historical implications of clothing as a passing fad. Instead, the significance attached to clothing in *Fashioning the Body Politic* is symptomatic of a slow but profound transformation that is taking place in the way history is being understood by the humanities. The essays in this collection speak eloquently for themselves, so it is this transformation that I propose to concentrate on, because it imparts a resonance to them far beyond their immediate subject.

When in the late nineteenth century historiography finally established itself in the Europeanized world as an examinable discipline and an academic career, its purportedly universal concern with 'what actually happened' was limited in practice by a prevailing paradigm that not only contained built-in blind spots such as Eurocentrism, male chauvinism, and an ecologically catastrophic myth of progress, but that privileged the written word as the basis of documentation. Bound up with this Enlightenment prejudice was its conception of motivation in an essentially rationalist key, even if the 'reason' in question was shaped by the imperatives of state, national or class interests, personal ambition, or sheer survival. The human need to overcome *anomie* posited by Durkheim in some form of communal ideology or the instinctive urge to project magical significance onto an essentially meaningless world identified by Weber was the province of 'sociology'.

As for Friedrich Nietzsche's vision of an alternative history of the West driven by conflicting metaphysical and moral reactions to an essentially godless universe, or Georges Sorel's emphasis on the central role of mobilizing myths, whatever their intrinsic absurdity from a rationalist perspective, in generating historical transformation on an epic scale, these were generally ignored by professional historians as the lucubrations of intellectual misfits. Such outsiders did not even seek asylum in an established discipline because their concern was not 'the facts' about the past. Rather they sought in their own way to bring about Europe's salvation from what they saw as the encroaching decline of the life force, of which the hegemony of positivism within academia was but one symptom. Their irrationalist assumptions about the structural forces shaping history remained as remote from the concerns of 'real historians' as the lives of the poor, workers, women, children, the mentally or physically disabled, the unique cultures of non-European humanity, or the fragile miracle of the planet that 'Man' had so imperiously made 'his' home.

In this context the history of the French Revolution can be seen as paradigmatic. Until the 1960s the dispute between the 'orthodox' (sophisticated Marxist) and 'revisionist' (liberal) schools still centred on the role played by cohesive class resentment of the *ancien régime*, the interaction of economic, social and political crises, and Enlightenment ideas of human rights. It was not till the 1970s that the French scholar Mona Ozouf demonstrated the existence of a genuine 'third way' to account for some of the seismic changes that affected France in the last decade of the eighteenth century, namely by highlighting the significance of the rituals and festivals that were either instituted from above by the Republic, or that welled up spontaneously from below as the externalization of authentic populist energies. In both cases they were enacting the collective experience of the Revolution as a historical watershed between two eras of humanity. *La fête révolutionnaire* (1976)[1] was more than an attempt to reconstruct the Zeitgeist or to penetrate the 'mentality' of the period. It was the application to a pivotal event in Western history of the insight that even in the 'modern world', a major factor in socio-political transformations is the unleashing of collective mythic energies whose most eloquent expression is to be found not in speeches and manifestos but in symbols and ritual behaviour. Thus the famed 'rationalism' of the revolutionaries paradoxically turned out to have a deeply irrational tap root. The French Revolution, putative child of the Enlightenment, displayed in the cult of the allegorical figure Marianne, the reform of the calendar, or the myth of the 'new man', a much more venerable ancestry. It marked as much the appearance of a new political religion as it did the formation of a new type of state.

That Ozouf's book epitomized a wider, largely subliminal, paradigm shift in the West's historical imagination is suggested by the fact that a year earlier the American scholar George Mosse had published *The Nationalization of the Masses* (1975), which located a vital factor in the origins of the Third Reich in the emergence of a cult of the nation. He showed that the sacralization of the German nation, the apotheosis of the Volk, had started long before unification became a reality, and manifested itself not just in highly quotable anthems and poetry, but in liturgical ceremonies and architectural symbols designed to associate the nation with a sense of sacred time and space. Mosse's assumptions about the historical process had been influenced by Benedetto Croce and Johan Huizinga, both of whom in different ways made the dominant worldview central to explaining 'external' social and political realities. Whereas conventional attempts to account for Nazism focused on Germany's imperialist tradition, the aberrations and traumas of its 'special path' to nationhood, the dysfunction of its capitalism, or the pathologies of Adolf Hitler and his henchmen, Mosse's approach was informed by the assumption that 'the historian's function must be to understand the myths that people live by' (1978: 29). This approach moves 'cultural history' from the wings to the centre stage of historical analysis, as long as 'culture' is understood as a 'totality' that can be accessed by paying particular attention to 'the perceptions of men and women, and how these are shaped and enlisted in politics at a particular place and time' (1999: xi).

In the case of fascism this meant considering it primarily 'as a cultural movement', in other words, seeing it 'as it saw itself and as followers saw it' (Mosse 1999: x). Applying the principle of methodological empathy even to something as morally abhorrent as the Third Reich leads away from the causal explanations of traditional historiography to an appreciation of why 'considerations of beauty usually not thought of as an element of politics played such an important role in defining the political liturgy as well as the human stereotypes used as symbols of the movement', and why 'the visual expression of fascism in architecture, art and city planning played a leading role as expression's of the movement's political thought' (Mosse 1999: x–xi). It was this 'anthropological' approach to history that enabled Mosse to identify the key to Nazism's 'seizure of power' in the way the political and cultural crisis of Weimar Germany after 1929 enabled the longings of millions of Germans for a new age to be projected onto Hitler (1978: 34). In fact the NSDAP deliberately set out to infuse politics with a collective mood of euphoria, celebration, and festivity. Electoral programmes and internecine machinations were eclipsed in importance by a constant flow of performative acts, liturgical events, and concrete symbols.

In the last twenty-five years the 'culturalist' approach to history has become increasingly established as part of the common sense of the discipline. In the US Lynn Hunt has demonstrated its fertility for studying the French Revolution to an Anglophone readership (for example Hunt

1984), while the last ten years have seen a spate of works exploring the cultural and aesthetic dimension not just of fascism,[2] but of communist regimes as well.[3] Perhaps the culmination of this trend is a recent definition of 'totalitarianism' that marks a decisive break with the ideal type emphasizing the state monopoly of ideological, political, and military power for its own sake which dominated political science for most of the post-war era. For Emilio Gentile the totalitarian regime's 'monopoly of power' and 'conquest of society' aims at 'the integral politicization of existence . . . interpreted according to the categories, the myths and the values of a *palingenetic ideology*, institutionalized in the form of a *political religion*, that aims to shape the individual and the masses through an *anthropological revolution* in order to regenerate the human being and create a *new man'* (2000: 19).

The realization that the revolution that all modern ideologues seek to bring about is at bottom a 'cultural' and 'anthropological' rather than economic or political one has a profound bearing as well on post-revolutionary societies in their non-revolutionary or 'steady state' phase (what Saint-Simon called their 'organic' as opposed to 'critical' state). The 'normalization' of an exceptional state, the routinization of charisma, the hardening of the molten magma that flows from a historical vulcano into the solid tufa of institutional structures, proceeds not primarily ideologically in the sense of formally articulated doctrine, but semiotically. It is gradually being realized by historians, so long concerned with diplomacy, militarism, political elites, and economic systems, that the claim in a recent advertisement on British TV (for a type of credit card!) that 'only 7% of communication is verbal', applies to the entire history of humanity. In what can be seen as a Copernican revolution in reverse, a younger generation of academics is increasingly concerned with aspects of human reality that become invisible when the sun of deductive reasoning burns too bright, but that come out like stars when the right lobe of the human brain comes into its own. The ephemeral tactile world of festivities[4] and even smells,[5] the lunar realm of dreams, longings, intuitions, and myths, including the metaphysical anxieties and nightmares associated with the 'dark side of the moon', is being increasingly recognized to play a decisive role in determining what happens in the social and political realm. There is every prospect that in the twenty-first century it will become the norm for historians to apply the principle of methodological empathy that makes the analysis of the cosmology and mindsets of the actors (too long referred to by mainstream historians pejoratively as 'psychohistory') an integral part of causal explanation.

As the one-sidedness of conventional history disappears, a new phase of this velvet revolution promises to be a deeper awareness that the emotions and aspirations of the most modern citizens are structured atavistically by mythic narratives, articulated by ritualistic forms of behaviour, experienced in terms of qualitatively different types of time,[6] and expressed symbolically, visually, semiotically. The impact of 'continental' post-structuralism and post-modernism on the Anglophone human sciences in the 1990s gave a powerful momentum and spin to this development. As the Cambridge historian, Richard Evans, one of the most acute observers of the challenge mounted to traditional historiography by what has become known as the 'linguistic turn' (Vernon 1994: 81–97), wrote:

> At its best, the work that is now appearing under the influence of postmodernist theory provides a new dimension of understanding that moves well beyond the limitations of social history. Studies of popular mentalities, of memory, commemoration and celebrations, of the cultural dimensions of power and authority, of gender and the micropolitics of everyday life, and of many other subject, have added significantly to historical knowledge. The achievement of cultural history in the postmodern mode is not merely additive; it has helped reorient our understanding of many areas of politics and social history, from the French Revolution to the First World War and beyond. (Evans 1997: 184)

However, Evans is equally eloquent in expounding the dangers that, taken to extremes applying the postmodernist preoccupation with 'discourse' instead of causes to historiography can lead to a past-denying subjectivism, a nihilistic relativism, a self-gratifying narcissism, and boundless trivialization, thereby subverting the essence of the discipline (not that the post-modern mindset can abide 'essences'). Personally I would be relieved if the 'culturalist' trend in historiography were to be informed less by the heirs of structuralism, and more by 'real' historians such as Lynn Hunt and George Mosse, and by sophisticated cultural anthropologists such as Victor Turner and Clifford Geertz. Should additional theoretical underpinning be required I would recommend for consideration two concepts already well established in the social sciences which I believe could acquire new importance within history.

The first is Gramsci's concept of 'cultural hegemony', but modified in two significant respects. First, 'culture' would be used in a totalizing sense which specifically embraces the mythic, the ritualistic, the symbolic, the corporeal, the behavioural, the semiotic rather than the traditionally narrow connotations of 'ideology' conceived in terms of doctrine and verbalized false consciousness.[7] Second, 'hegemony' would denote the dominance of a worldview whose primary function is not to mystify and legitimize the 'vested' interests of political elites pulling strings from behind the scenes, but rather to endow historical events with an intelligible narrative and shape that impart (authentic) meaning to the process of life and death for the mass of the population.[8]

The second concept that acquires considerable heuristic potential in the light of the new history is admittedly derived from the arcane realm of continental post-structuralism, namely what Deleuze and Guattari call 'territorialization'.[9] This refers to the way all radical social change involves replacing the existing semiotic system by another, a colonization of semantic space. For this to work the new elite cannot simply impose their values *en bloc* on the population from above through a campaign of crude propaganda. Rather the change takes place transversally or (to use their choice organic but non-hierarchical metaphor) 'rhizomically' through a subtle process of decoding and recoding the fabric of reality. The precondition to Hitler's seizure of power, for example, was the success of the Nazi campaign in infiltrating the social space of the Weimar Republic, even before the Depression unleashed by the Wall Street Crash, with its own alternative cosmology symbolized in the Swastika, the party uniform, and the 'Hitler greeting'. What it did 'was to energize a whole series of connections between the individual and the mass, through the intermediaries of the different segments of the social machine (the party, the army, the family)' (Brown 2000). People became supporters of Nazism, because at a molecular or cellular level of society it 'decoded existing social arrangements' and then recoded their desires and identities in terms of its own worldview, promising 'new forms of expression'.

> With Nazism, the swastika enters the workplace and the family, creating a kind of continuity. Mythology becomes the basis for colossal public spectacles, where the audience is united in their common experience. The elements are then put to work to gather together and forge what resembles an aesthetic constituency between the constituent parts of the territory. (Brown 2000)

The concept 'semiotic territorialization' adds a new dimension to orthodox historical explanations of how the Third Reich came into being. For example, it complements Ian Kershaw's brilliant account of the charismatic energies at work in Hitler's dramatic rise to power (1998). It also opens up new theoretical vistas to attempts to explain how any regime or civilization, ancient or modern, establishes or maintains its 'cultural hegemony'.

The gradual 'territorialization' of orthodox historiography by an anthropological approach to social realities is already well under way. To stay with our examples, the success of Lynn Hunt's *Politics, Culture, and Class in the French Revolution* helped popularize Ozouf's approach to the French Revolution in Anglophone academia, and in the wake of structuralism's achievement in widening the connotations of 'text' and 'reading' and establishing the way all culture is 'constructed', a whole literature has come into being on the role of spectacle, ritual, and the body in history. Meanwhile the last decade has seen a spate of works on the cultural, aesthetic, spectacular aspects of fascism, principally in Italy, but in other countries too, to a point where the neglect of 'fascist culture' by an earlier generation of scholars who did not recognize the seminal importance of Mosse's work now looks almost culpable. Another sign of the times was the 1996 'Art and Power' exhibition held in London, Barcelona and Berlin, whose catalogue presented the cultural dimension of the regimes of Franco, Mussolini, Hitler, and Stalin in terms that approximated closer to the definition of totalitarianism offered by Gentile than the ones that prevailed practically unchallenged (except by a film such as Stanley Kubrick's *Dr Strangelove*) as long as Russia was seen by the West as the 'evil Empire'.

If all these examples seem narrowly Eurocentric then perhaps a more eloquent testimony to the transformation occurring in historiography is provided by Christopher Taylor's, *Sacrifice as Terror: the Rwandan Genocide of 1994* (1999). His book convincingly argues that the atrocities committed by Hutus on the hundreds of thousands of Tutsi cannot be understood unless the historian focuses with unblinking eyes on the acts perpetrated on the bodies of the victims. These were acts in which the physical and the metaphysical converge, since they were 'enracinated in Rwandan ways of bodily experience and bodily predispositions lurking beneath the level of verbalization and rational calculation' (1999: 145). Thanks to this approach Taylor is able to reveal the crucial role played in the motivation of the perpetrators by the complex cosmological and mythical configurations of race, identity, the sacred and the impure which gave meaning to their acts. The violence was thus an essentially ritual, symbolic one rooted in a historically shaped fantasy world enacted on living human flesh:

> Rwandans lashed out against a perceived internal other that threatened in their imaginations both their personal integrity and the cosmic order of the state. It was overwhelmingly Tutsi who were the sacrificial victims in what in many respects was a massive ritual of purification, a ritual intended to purge the

nation of 'obstructing beings' as the threat of obstruction was imagined through a Rwandan ontology that situates the body politic in analogous relation to the individual human body. (Taylor 1999: 101)

As one reviewer points out, 'all these investigations into cultural symbols complement rather than replace historical and political analysis' (Stone 2001: 78–80). Thanks to the sophisticated 'anthropological perspective' that he applies, Taylor's account of genocide goes beyond those that seek to explain it:

> through notions of ideology (especially of the racist variety), psychology, political theory (especially that which deals with state development, moderniza- tion or globalization theory) or ethnic or territorial warfare. The scholarly discourse on genocide is lifted away from the highfalutin theories of impersonal forces and historical trends, and abandoned to the sublunary region of real people with real, overflowing passions doing terrifyingly real things to each other. (Stone 2001: 78–80)

If an African genocide seems a long way from the world of clothing and fashion, then one thing that might make the connection less opaque is Sarah Maza's chapter 'The Theatre of Punishment' in *From the Royal to the Republican Body. Incorporating the Political in Seventeenth and Eighteenth Century France* (1998). It is informed by an awareness of the chilling logic underlying public torture and ceremonial executions under the *ancien régime* analysed in Foucault's *Surveiller et Punir*. True to the cosmological, magical even, assumptions about kingship, power, and the person of the monarch which prevailed at the time, the body of the condemned became the locus for the ritual affirmation and obliteration of the crime. For the criminal was deemed to have offended 'not his or her fellow subjects, but the divinely ordained society and polity incarnated in the monarch' (1998: 193). Once again what seems like gratuitous pathological violence discloses a profound anthropological and psycho- logical rationale.

Maza's essay sits perfectly comfortably alongside chapters which demonstrate the extraordinarily rich symbolic universe whose axis was the physical body of the king, and reveal the degree to which the performing arts, especially ballet and social dance, became in the symbolic hothouse of Versailles 'technologies of power'. These essays and their bibliographical underpinning demonstrate the existence of an entire subdiscipline of history concerned with the body as the microcosm of historical realities and the cosmological speculations woven around them. The last essay is by Lynn Hunt and explores 'Freedom of dress in revolutionary France'. It contains the following assertion: 'questions of dress more broadly conceived went to the heart of the revolution in both its democratic and totalitarian aspects'. Only a few decades ago it would have smacked of interdisciplinary cross dressing or worse for a history professor to formulate such a proposition. Yet properly 'unpacked' in the context of the anthropological and semiotic revolution which historiography is undergoing it is by no means an absurd or aberrant contention.

The essays in Wendy Parkins's book are thus significant not just for the intrinsic fascination of their contents, but because they contribute to correcting a deeply ingrained bias in favour of the written document and observable socio-political phenomena and against the dimension of the symbolic and the semiotic that has distorted historiography for decades. (It is ironic that the Enlightenment's legacy was a sensitivity to what can be grasped by the intellect (the light of reason) and an insensitivity to what can seen in physical light.) The term 'phenomenon', one of the discipline's most used (and, as far as student essays are concerned, misspelled) terms, originally referred to the material realm of appearance, so it is more than appropriate if the visual is making a come back.

Treated 'anthropologically', a cultural history which takes seriously the realm where the aesthetic impinges on the political is far from being a mere (and typically feminine) complement or fashion accessory to 'real' (masculine) history. Nor are the clothes that the actors of history wear just decorative embellishment, for they often unconsciously invest their acts with significance and help vest their interests: imagine Hitler addressing a Nuremberg rally in a boiler suit. Or Armani leisure wear. In the modern age of high reflexivity it is designers who are increasingly involved in realizing the designs of the powerful on the weak, in perpetuating cultural and political processes that simultaneously aestheticize and anaesthetize.

A mature, semiotically informed, perspective sees the body as a material entity inscribed and pierced by the forces of collective mythopoeia to a point where clothes become the interface between the physical and the metaphysical. As Hunt suggests and these essays demonstrate, what people wear to conceal and expose their persons can take the historian to the core of complex social and political processes of stability and change, conformism and challenge to the status quo. Seen historically, dress is simultaneously cosmetic and functional, superstructure and base, surface and fundament, appearance and reality, private and public, ornament and the 'real thing'. Like the formidable hybrid between bra and breast plate, undergarment and body armour, both conic and iconic, which Madonna sported in one of her earlier incarnations as Post-modern

Woman. Or that wonder of male sartorial display *de rigueur* for the well-dressed man in fifteenth-century Europe: the codpiece.

Notes

1. Published in English as *Festivals and the French Revolution* (Chicago: Chicago, University Press, 1988).
2. Notably E. Gentile (1996); see also Falasca-Zamponi (1997), Linehan (2000), Griffin (2002).
3. See Stites (1989), Britt (1995), Golomstock (1990).
4. For example I. Boyd Whyte, 'Berlin, 1 May 1936', in Britt (1995).
5. For example Corbin (1986), whose forward opens 'Today's history comes deodorized.'
6. See for example Fenn (1997), Griffin (1999).
7. See also Mosse's reflections on 'culture' in the introduction to *The Fascist Revolution* where he sees it as 'dealing with life seen as a whole – a totality' (1999: xi).
8. For an elaboration of this theme see Griffin (2001).
9. The concept of 'territorialization' was explored in Deleuze and Guattari (1984 and 1988).

Bibliography

Unpublished Sources and Archives

ACF – AS (Archivio Centrale dello Stato – Agenzia Stefani) Italy.

ACF – PNF (Archivio Centrale dello Stato – Partito Nazionale Fascista, Direttorio [Uff. Stralcio]) Italy.

Annual Report of the Northern Protector of Aboriginals for 1899, (1900) Queensland Votes and Proceedings, 5.

Annual Report of the Northern Protector of Aboriginals for 1902, (1903) Queensland Parliamentary Papers, 2.

Annual Report of the Northern Protector of Aboriginals for 1903, (1904) Queensland Parliamentary Papers, 2.

Annual Report of the Chief Protector of Aboriginals for 1911, (1912) Queensland Parliamentary Papers, 3.

Archives parlementaires de 1787 à 1860 (1787–99), dir. I. Maridal, E. Laurent, first series.

Arch. Parl Francaise, (–2000).

B-P (Baden-Powell) Collection, Boy Scouts of America [BSA] – Murray, Kentucky.

Baden-Powell, O. (1930), Notebook on Dominions and Colonies, November 1930, Guide Association, London.

Barailhon, J.-F. (1795), *Projet sur le costume à donner à chacun des deux conseils législatifs, et à tous les fonctionnaires publics de la République française, présenté à la Convention nationale* (13 fructidor an III [30 August]).

BNF – HC (Bibliothèque Nationale de France, Departement des arts graphiques, Hennin Collection, Paris.

'Catholic Share in the Girl Guide', *The Catholic Woman's Outlook,* 2 (April 1925), religious policy folder, Guide Association, London.

Country history box – Malta, Guide Association, London.

Country history box – St Helena, Guide Association, London.

Country history box – St Lucia, Guide Association, London.

De Beaumont, M. (1920), 'Log of a Lilywhite Cadet', description of Commissioners' Conference, 4–11 October 1920, at Swanwick, Guide Association, London.

Description des ouvrages de peinture, sculpture, architecture et gravure exposés au Sallon du Louvre, par les artistes composans la Commune générale des Arts, le 10 Août 1793, l'An 2e de la République Française, une et indivisible, Paris, [n.d.]).

Devocelle, J.-M. (1988), 'Costume politique et politique du costume: approches théoriques et idéologiques du costume pendant la Révolution', *Mémoire de maîtrise*, Université de Paris I, 2 vols.

Girl Guide Association of Trinidad and Tobago (1974), *Diamond Jubilee 1914–1974* (souvenir magazine).

GSUSA (Girl Scouts of the US) Archive.

The History and Organization of World Scouting (1938), London: Boy Scouts Association, 2, TC/183, SA-London.

Hoover, Mrs H. (1926), 'The Girl Guide International Conference', TS, 14 May 1926, WAGGGS, International Council folder.

India-History Box, Guides Association, London.

Mazumdar, L., Interview, India Office Library MSS.Eur.T.46.

Lund, R. T. (1971), 'History of World Scout Bureau', TS 1-3, TC/86, SA-London.

Marion, K. (n. d.), MS autobiography, Suffragette Fellowship Collection, Museum of London.

Mitchell Collection, Museum of London.

O'Neill, M. (1980), *Musée des beaux-arts d'Orléans. Catalogue critique: Les Peintures de l'Ecole française des XVIIe et XVIIIe siècles,* thèse de doctorat de troisième cycle, Paris-Sorbonne, 2 vols.

L'Ordre de la marche de la fête qui aura lieu décadi prochain 10 nivose, l'an 2e de la République une et indivisible, en mémoire des armées françaises, et notamment à l'occasion de la prise de Toulon, Bibliothèque Historique de la Ville de Paris, 10530.

Polnoe sobranie zakonov, vol. 4, no. 1887.

Report of G. Walton's 1936 South Africa Tour; TC/10, Tours, Scout Association, London.

SA (Scout Association), London, *Annual Report,* 1930.

'Scouting and Religion', TS Adult Training Notebook, 1920s, 203, 212–14; TC/124, Scout Association, London.

Stephenson, S. J. (n. d.), *No Other Way,* Suffragette Fellowship, Museum of London.

Storrow, H. (1920), 'Girl Guiding from the Point of View of a Girl Scout', Girl Guide Box, Girl Scouts of the USA, New York City.

[Street, J.] (1960), Transcript of Interviews with Suffragettes, recorded at the White House, Albany Street, London NW1, March 1960, Suffragette Fellowship Collection, Museum of London.

'Verbatim Report of East London Conference on the Churches and the Boy Scout Movement', held 22 November 1930 at People's Palace, Mile End Road, 19–21; TC/229, SA-London.

Whitney, S. (1994), 'The Politics of Youth: Communists and Catholics in Interwar France', PhD dissertation, Rutgers University.

Yeoman, I. V. (1905–14), Scrapbooks of Newspaper Cuttings 1905–14, 15 vols, Pankhurst Collection, Murdoch University Library.

Published Sources

Alberdi, J. B. (1886), *Obras completas,* 8 vols, Buenos Aires: La Tribuna Nacional.

Albert, M. (1989), 'La Bestia y el Angel: imágenes de las mujeres en la novela falangista de la Guerra Civil', in Instituto de la Mujer, *Las mujeres y la Guerra Civil Falangista.*

—— (ed.) (1998), *Vencer no es convencer: Literatura e ideología del fascismo español,* Frankfurt and Madrid: Vervuert Verlag & Iberoamericana.

Alcalde, C. (1996), *Mujeres en el Franquismo: Exiliadas, nacionalistas y opositoras,* Barcelona: Flor del Viento.

Alegre, S. (1996), 'The Blue Division in Russia, 1941–1944: the filmic recycling of fascism as anticommunism in Franco's Spain', *Historical Journal of Film, Radio and Television,* 16: 349–64.

Allman, J. (1994), 'Making Mothers: Missionaries, Medical Officers and Women's Work in Colonial Asante, 1924–1945', *History Workshop,* 38: 23–47.

L'Ami du roi, des français, de l'ordre, et sur-tout de la vérité, par les continuateurs de Fréron, sous la direction de M. Montjoye (1791).

Anderson, B. (1991), *Imagined Communities: Reflections on the Origin and Spread of Nationalism,* London: Verso.

Andress, D. (2000), *Massacre at the Champ de Mars. Popular Dissent and Political Culture in the French Revolution,* London: The Royal Historical Society / Boydell Press.

Andrews, R. M. (1985), 'Social Structures, Political Elites and Ideology in Revolutionary Paris, 1792–1794: A Critical Evaluation of Albert Soboul's *Les Sans-culottes parisiens en l'an II*', *Journal of Social History,* 19: 71–112.

Aróstegui, J. (ed.) (1988), *Historia y memoria de la Guerra Civil: encuentro in Castilla y León,* 3 vols, Valladolid: Junta de Castilla y León.

Atkinson, D. (1992), *Suffragettes in the Purple, White and Green: London 1906–14*, London: Museum of London.

—— (1996), *The Suffragettes in Pictures,* Stroud: Sutton Publishing.

Le Babillard, journal du Palais royal et des Thuileries (1791).

Baden-Powell, R. (1942), *Scouting for Boys*, London: C. Arthur Pearson.

Balbás, C., Cabezali, E., Calleja, R., Cuevas, M., Chicote, Mª T., García-Nieto, Mª C., Lamuedra, E., (1988), 'La mujer en la guerra civil: el caso de Madrid', in J. Aróstegui (ed), *Historia y memoria de la Guerra Civil: Encuentro en Castilla y León,* 3 vols, Valladolid: Junta de Castilla y León.

Barnard, M. (1996), *Fashion as Communication*, London: Routledge.

Barthes, R. (1967), *The Fashion System*, New York: Hill and Wang.

Bauman, Z. (1999), *Culture as Praxis*, London: Sage.

Beckett, J. (1988), 'Aboriginality, Citizenship and National State', *Social Analysis*, 24 (Dec.): 3–18.

Belsey, C. and Belsey, A. (1990), 'Icons of Divinity: Portraits of Elizabeth I', in L. Gent and N. Llewellyn (eds), *Renaissance Bodies: The Human Figure in English Culture 1540–1660*, London: Reaktion.

Benewick, R. and Donald S. (1999), *The State of China Atlas*, New York: Penguin Books.

Benjamin, W. (1968), 'The Work of Art in the Age of Mechanical Reproduction', in *Illuminations*, New York: Schocken Books.

Berlant, L. (1997), *The Queen of America Goes to Washington City: Essays on Sex and Citizenship*, Durham NC: Duke University Press.

Bernstein, L. (1995), *Sonia's Daughters: Prostitutes and Their Regulation in Imperial Russia,* Berkeley: University of California Press.

Besas, P. (1985), *Behind the Spanish Lens: Spanish Cinema under Fascism and Democracy,* Denver, Colorado: Arden Press.

Bezobrazov, V. P. (ed), (1884), *Otchet o vserossiiskoi khudozhestvenno-promyslennoi vystavki 1882 goda v Moskve*, St Petersburg: Tipografiia v. Bezobrazova i Komp.

Billington-Greig, T. (1987), *The Militant Suffragette Movement*, [1911] reprinted in C. McPhee and A. FitzGerald (eds), *The Non-Violent Militant: Selected Writings of Teresa Billington-Greig*, London: Routledge & Kegan Paul.

Bindman, D. (1989), *In the Shadow of the Guillotine. Britain and the French Revolution,* London: British Museum.

Bonnet, J.-C. et al. (eds) (1994), *Le Nouveau Paris*, Paris: Mercure de France.

Bordes, P. (1985), *Le 'Serment du Jeu de paume' de Jacques-Louis David*, Paris: Editions de la Réunion des Musées Nationaux.

Borgese, A. (1937), *Goliath: The March of Fascism*, New York: Viking.

Borras, T. (1965), *Seis mil mujeres*, Madrid: Editorial Nacional.

La Bouche de fer (1791).

Bowlby, R. (1985), *Just Looking: Consumer Culture in Dreiser, Gissing and Zola*, New York: Methuen.

Brower, D. R. (1975), *Training the Nihilists: Education and Radicalism in Tsarist Russia*, Ithaca: Cornell University Press.

Brownfoot, J. (1990), 'Sisters under the skin: imperialism and the emancipation of women in Malaya, c. 1891–1941', in J. A. Mangan (ed), *Making Imperial Mentalities*, Manchester: Manchester University Press.

Browning, O. (ed) (1885), *The Despatches of Earl Gower, English Ambassador at Paris from June 1790 to August 1792*, Cambridge: Cambridge University Press.

Britt, D. (1995), *Art and Power, Europe under the Dictators 1930–45*, London: Hayward Gallery.

Budd, M. A. (1997), *The Sculpture Machine: Physical Culture and Body Politics in the Age of Empire*, New York: New York University Press.

Butler, J. (1990), *Gender Trouble: Feminism and the Subversion of Identity*, New York: Routledge.

—— (1993), *Bodies That Matter: On the Discursive Limits of Sex*, New York: Routledge.

—— (1996), 'Gender as Performance', in P. Osborne (ed), *A Critical Sense: Interviews with Intellectuals*, London: Routledge.

La Camelia, Buenos Aires: Imprenta Republicana, 1852.

'Campamentos femeninos' (1941), *Consigna* (Revista Pedagógica de la Sección Femenina de FET y de las JONS), 5, April.

Cannadine, D. (1983), 'The Context, Performance and Meaning of Ritual: The British Monarchy and the Invention of Tradition, c. 1820–1977', in E. Hobsbawm and T. Ranger (eds), *The Invention of Tradition*, Cambridge: Cambridge University Press.

Caron, P. (1910–64), *Paris pendant la Terreur. Rapports des agents secrets du Ministre de l'Intérieur*, 7 vols, Paris: Didier.

Carr, R. (intro) (1986), *Images of the Spanish Civil War*, London & Sydney: George Allen & Unwin.

Chan, A. H. (2000), 'Fashioning Change: nationalism, colonialism, and modernity in Hong Kong', *Postcolonial Studies*, 3 (3): 293–309.

Chaney, D. (1993), *Fictions of Collective Life: Public Drama in Late Modern Culture*, London: Routledge.

Chaudonneret, M.-C. (1988), 'Le mythe de la Révolution', in P. Bordes and R. Michel (eds), *Aux Armes et aux arts! Les arts de la Révolution 1789–1799*, Paris: Adam Biro.

Chen, X. (1999), 'Growing Up with Posters in the Maoist Era', in H. Evans and S. Donald (eds), *Picturing Power in the People's Republic of China: Posters of the Cultural Revolution*, Lanham: Rowman & Littlefield.

Chueca, R. (1983), *El fascismo en los comienzos del régimen de Franco: un estudio sobre FET-JONS*, Madrid: Centro de Investigaciones Sociológicos.

Cobb, R. (1970), *The Police and the People. French Popular Protest 1789–1820*, Oxford: Oxford University Press.

Comaroff, J. (1996), 'The Empire of Old Clothes: Fashioning the Colonial Subject', in D. Howes (ed), *Cross-Cultural Consumption: Global Markets Local Realities*, New York: Routledge.

Condart, L. (1995), *La Gazette de Paris. Un journal royaliste pendant la Révolution française (1789–1792)*, Paris: L'Harmattan.

Cook, S. (1999), 'Creating Wealth and Welfare: Entrepreneurship and the Developmental State in Rural China', *IDS Bulletin*, 30 (4): 60–70.

Corbin, A. (1986), *The Foul and the Fragrant: Odour and the Social Imagination*, Oxford: Berg.

El Corsario. Periódico Semanal, Compilador, Universal, Montevideo: Imprenta de la Caridad, 1840.

Craik, J. (1994), *The Face of Fashion. Cultural Studies in Fashion*, New York: Routledge.

—— (1996), 'Ethnic Clothes and a Cultural Policy Tool', *Culture and Policy*, 7 (2): 155–60.

Crispolti, E. (1987), *Il futurismo e la moda: Balla e gli altri*, Venice: Marsilio.

Croll, R. (1937), *Wide Horizons. Wanderings in Central Australia*, Sydney: Angus & Robertson.

Currie, E. (2000), 'Prescribing Fashion: Dress, Politics and Gender in Sixteenth-Century Italian Conduct Literature', *Fashion Theory* 4 (2): 157–78.

Dangerfield, G. (1961), *The Strange Death of Liberal England*, New York: Capricorn Books.

Davin, A. (1996), *Growing Up Poor: Home, School and Street in London, 1870–1914*, London: Rivers Oram Press.

Davis, F. (1992), *Fashion, Culture, and Identity*, Chicago: University of Chicago Press.

Day, D. (1998), *Australian Identities*, Melbourne: Australian Scholarly Publishing.

De Baecque, A. (1988), 'La figure du jacobin dans l'imagerie politique (1795–1799): naissance d'une obsession', *Sources: travaux historiques*, 14: 61–70.

—— (1993), *Le Corps de l'histoire. Métaphores et politique (1770–1800)*, Paris: Calmann-Lévy.

De Begnac, Y. (1950), *Palazzo Venezia: Storia di un regime*, Rome: La Rocca.

De Bonald, Vicomte (1908), *François Chabot, membre de la Convention (1756–1794)*, Paris: Emile-Paul.

Décade philosophique.

De Certeau, M. (1984), *The Practice of Everyday Life*, trans. S. Rendall, Berkeley: University of California Press.

Deleuze, G. and Guattari, F. (1984), *Anti-Oedipus: Capitalism and Schizophrenia*, London: Athlone Press.

—— (1988), *A Thousand Plateaus: Capitalism and Schizophrenia*, London: Athlone Press.

De Felice, R. (1981), *Mussolini il duce, II*, Turin: Einaudi.

De Grazia, V. (1989), 'Mass Culture and Sovereignty: The American Challenge to European Cinemas, 1920–1960', *Journal of Modern History*, 61: 53–87.

—— (1992), *How Fascism Ruled Women: Italy, 1922–1945*, Berkeley: University of California Press.

—— (1996), 'Nationalizing Women: The Competition between Fascist and Commercial Cultural Models in Mussolini's Italy', in V. de Grazia with E. Furlough (eds), *The Sex of Things*.

—— and Furlough, E. (1996), *The Sex of Things: Gender and Consumption in Historical Perspective*, Berkeley: University of California Press.

De la Mora, C. (1977), *Doble esplendor*, Barcelona: Crítica.

Del Noce, A. (1990), *Giovanni Gentile: Per una interpretazione filosofica della storia contemporanea*, Bologna: Il Mulino.

De Villette, C. (1792), *Lettres choisies de C.V. sur les principaux événemens de la Révolution*, Paris: n. p.

Devocelle, J.-M. (1991), 'Costume et Citoyenneté', *Révolution française*, actes des 113 et 114e Congrès nationaux des sociétés savantes (Strasbourg 1988–Paris 1989), Paris: Editions du Comité des Travaux Historiques et Scientifiques.

Dewdney, A. (1994), *Racism, Representation and Photography*, Sydney: Inner City Education Centre.

Dictionnaire des usages socio-politiques (1770–1815), (1985–88), 3 vols, Paris: Klincksieck.

Doklad Vysochaishe uchrezhdennoi Kommissiia dlia izsledovaniia poloz-heniia sel'skogo khoziastva i sel'skoi proizvoditel'nosti v Rossii (1873), St. Petersburg: Tipografiia tovarishchestva obshchestvennaia pol'za.

Donald, J. (1999), *Imagining the Modern City,* Minneapolis: University of Minnesota Press.

Donald, S. (1999), 'Children as Political Messengers: Art, Childhood and Continuity', in H. Evans and S. Donald (eds), *Picturing Power in the People's Republic of China: Posters of the Cultural Revolution,* Lanham: Rowman & Littlefield.

Dowd, D. (1948), *Pageant Master of the Republic: Jacques-Louis David and the Revolution,* Lincoln, University of Nebraska Press.

Dutton, M. (1998), *Streetlife China,* Cambridge: Cambridge University Press.

Eagleton, T. (1984), *The Function of Criticism: From* The Spectator *to Poststructuralism,* London: Verso.

Eckert, C. (1990), 'The Carole Lombard in Macy's Window', in J. Gaines and C. Herzog (eds), *Fabrications: Costume and the Female Body,* New York and London: Routledge.

'18 de julio', *Medina* (Semanario de la Sección Femenina*)* 19 July 1942.

Ellwood, S. (1987), *Spanish Fascism in the Franco Era,* London: Macmillan.

—— (1990), 'Falange Española and the Creation of the Francoist "New State"', *European History Quarterly,* 20: 2019–25.

Enders, V. L. (1999), 'Problematic Portraits: The Ambiguous Historical Role of the Sección Femenina', in P. B. Radcliff and V. L. Enders (eds), *Constructing Spanish Womanhood: Female Identity in Modern Spain,* New York: SUNY Press.

Enloe, C. (2000), *Maneuvers: The International Politics of Militarizing Women's Lives,* Berkeley: University of California Press.

Entwistle, J. (2000a), 'Fashion and the Fleshy Body: Dress as Embodied Practice', *Fashion Theory* 4 (3): 323–48.

—— (2000b), *The Fashioned Body: Fashion, Dress and Modern Social Theory,* Cambridge: Polity Press.

Evans, R. (1971), 'Queensland's First Aboriginal Reserve. Part 2. The Failure of Reform', *Queensland Heritage,* 2 (5): 3–15.

Evans, R. (1997), *In Defence of History,* London: Granta Books.

—— Saunders, K. and Cronin, K. (1993), *Race Relations in Colonial Queensland; A History of Exclusion, Exploitation and Extermination,* St Lucia: University of Queensland Press.

Falasca Zamponi, S. (1997), *Fascist Spectacle: The Aesthetics of Power in Mussolini's Italy,* Berkeley: University of California Press.

'La falda pantalon', *Medina,* 19 July 1942.

Farmborough, F. (1991), 'A Shining Light', in J. Fyrth with S. Alexander (eds), *Women's Voices from the Spanish Civil War,* London: Lawrence & Wishart.

Farquhar, M. A. (1999), *Children's Literature in China: from Lu Xun to Mao Zedong,* London: Edward Arnold.

Felski, R. (1989), *Beyond Feminist Aesthetics,* Cambridge: Harvard University Press.

—— (1995) *The Gender of Modernity,* Cambridge: Harvard University Press.

Fenn, R. (1997), *The End of Time: Ritual, Religion, and the Forging of the Soul,* London: SPCK.

Ferro, M. (1991), *Nicholas II: The Last of the Tsars,* trans. B. Pearce, New York: Oxford University Press.

Finnane, A. (1996), 'What should Chinese women wear? A national problem', *Modern China,* 22 (2): 99–131.

Fontecha, A., Gibaja, J. C. and F. Bernalte, (1988) 'La vida en retaguardia durante la guerra civil en zona franquista: Coca – Segovia – (1936–1939)', in J. Aróstegui (ed), *Historia y Memoria de la Guerra Civil,* vol. 2.

Fontenay, Abbe de (Louis Abel de Bonafous) (1791), *Journal général de France.*

Foster, R. (1989), 'Feasts of the Full Moon. The Distribution of Rations to Aborigines in South Australia: 1836–1861', *Aboriginal History,* 13 (1–2): 63–78.

Foucault, M. (1977), 'History of Systems of Thought', in D. F. Bouchard (ed) *Language, Counter-Memory, Practice: Selected Essays and Interviews,* trans. D. F. Bouchard and S. Simon, Ithaca: Cornell University Press.

—— (1987) 'The Ethic of Care for the Self as a Practice of Freedom. An Interview with Michel Foucault on January 20, 1984', in J. Bernauer and D. Rasmussen (eds), *The Final Foucault,* Cambridge, Mass.: MIT Press.

Fraser, N. (1989), *Unruly Practices: Power, Discourse and Gender in Contemporary Social Theory,* Cambridge: Polity Press.

—— (1992), 'Rethinking the Public Sphere: A Contribution to the Critique of Actually Existing Democracy', in C. Calhoun (ed) *Habermas and the Public Sphere,* Cambridge: MIT Press.

Fraser, R. (1979), *Blood of Spain: The Experience of Civil War 1936–1939,* London: Allen Lane.

Fulford, R. (1957), *Votes for Women,* London: Faber & Faber.

Fyrth, J. with Alexander, S. (eds) (1991), *Women's Voices from the Spanish Civil War*, Madrid: Taurus.

GA (Girl Guides Association) (1919), *Annual Report*, London: Girl Guides Association.

Gallego Méndez, M. T. (1983), *Mujer, Falange y Franquismo*, Madrid: Taurus.

Gan, E. (1996) 'The Ideal', in *Russian Women's Shorter Fiction: An Anthology, 1835–1860*, trans. J. Andrew, Oxford: Clarendon Press.

García i García, M. (1981), Catalogue of the Exhibition *La guerra civil española*, Madrid: Ministerio de Cultura.

García González, R. (1989), 'El taller del soldado en Valladolid (marzo 1937–diciembre 1938)', in Instituto de la Mujer, *Las mujeres y la Guerra Civil Española: III jornadas de estudios monográficos. Salamanca, octubre 1989*, Madrid: Ministerio de Cultura.

Garrioch, D. (1986), *Neighbourhood and Community in Paris 1740–1790*, Cambridge: Cambridge University Press.

Gatens, M. (1996), *Imaginary Bodies: Ethics, Power and Corporeality*, London and New York: Routledge.

Geffroy, A. (1985), 'Sans-culotte(s) (novembre 1790–juin 1792)', in A. Geffroy, J. Guilhaumou, S. Moreno, *Dictionnaire des usages socio-politiques (1770–1815)*, Paris: Klincksieck.

—— (1988), 'Désignation, dénégation: la légende des *sans-culottes* (1780–1980)', in C. Croisille, J. Ehrard, M.-C. Chemin (eds), *La Légende de la Révolution*, Actes du colloque international de Clermont-Ferrand (June 1986), Clermont-Ferrand: Université Blaise Pascal.

Gentile, E. (1996), *The Sacralization of the State in Italian Fascism*, Cambridge: Harvard University Press.

—— (2000), 'The Sacralisation of Politics: Definitions, Interpretations and Reflections on the Question of Secular Religion and Totalitarianism', *Totalitarian Movements and Political Religions*, 1 (1): 18–55.

Gentile, G. (1912), *L'atto del pensare come atto puro*, Florence: Sansoni.

—— (1913), *Riforma della dialettica hegeliana*, Florence: Sansoni.

—— (1916), *Teoria generale dello Spirito come atto puro*, Bari: Laterza.

—— (1917), *Sistema di logica come teoria del conoscere*, Pisa: Soperri.

Genty, M. (1987a), *L'Apprentissage de la citoyenneté. Paris 1789–1795*, Paris: Messidor/Editions sociales.

—— (1987b), *Paris 1789–1795: l'apprentissage du citoyenneté*, Paris: Messidor/Editions sociales.

Glinka, V. M. (1988), *Russkii voennyi kostium, XVIII-nachala XX veka*, Leningrad: Khudozhnik RSFSR.

Gloin, A. (1974), *Like Measles, It's Catching!*, Toronto: Girl Guides of Canada.

Gogol, N. (1960), 'The Overcoat', *The Diary of a Madman and Other Stories*, trans. A. McAndrew, New York: Signet Classics.

Golomstock, I. (1990), *Totalitarian Art*, London: Collins Harvill.

Gorbunova, M. K. (comp) (1882), *Sbornik statisticheskikh svedenii po Moskovskoi gubernii: Otdel khoziaistvennoi statistiki*, vol. 7, *vyp.* 4, Moscow: Tipografiia S. V. Gur'ianova.

Gorsas, A. (1791–2), *Courrier des LXXXIII Départements*.

Graham, H. (1995), 'Gender and the State: Women in the 1940s', in H. Graham and J. Labanyi (eds), *Spanish Cultural Studies*.

Graham, H. and Labanyi, J. (eds) (1995), *Spanish Cultural Studies: An Introduction. The Struggle for Modernity,* Oxford: Oxford University Press.

Gravelli, A. (*c.*1940), *Vademecum dello stile fascista*, Rome: Nuova Europa.

Grayzel, S. (1997), '"The Outward and Visible Sign of Her Patriotism": Women, Uniforms, and National Service During the First World War', *Twentieth Century British History*, 8 (2): 145–64.

Greenberg, J. (1990), 'Towards a History of Women's Periodicals in Latin America: A Working Bibliography', *Women, Culture and Politics in Latin America*, Berkeley: University of California Press.

Greenblatt, S. (1980), *Renaissance Self-Fashioning: From More to Shakespeare,* Chicago: University of Chicago Press.

Griffin, R. (1999), 'Party Time: Nazism as a Temporal Revolution', *History Today* 49 (4): 43–50.

—— (2001), 'Notes towards the definition of fascist culture: The prospects for synergy between Marxist and liberal heuristics', *Renaissance and Modern Studies*, 42 (forthcoming).

—— (2002), 'The Primacy of Culture: The Current Growth (or Manufacture) of Consensus within Fascist Studies', *Journal of Contemporary History*, 37 (1) (forthcoming).

El Grito de los Pueblos, Montevideo: 1831.

Gruber, A. (1972), *Les Grandes Fêtes et leurs décors à l'époque de Louis XVI,* Paris and Geneva: Droz.

Habermas, J. (1989), *The Structural Transformation of the Public Sphere: An Inquiry into a Category of Bourgeois Society,* trans. T. Burger with F. Lawrence, Cambridge: Polity Press.

—— (1992) 'Further Reflections on the Public Sphere', in C. Calhoun (ed), *Habermas and the Public Sphere*, Cambridge: MIT Press: 421–61.

Hamilton, C. (1920), *William: An Englishman,* New York: Frederick A. Stokes.

—— (1935) *Life Errant,* London: J. M. Dent & Sons.

Harris, J. (1981), 'The Red Cap of Liberty: A Study of Dress Worn by French Revolutionary Partisans 1789–94', *Eighteenth-Century Studies* 14: 283–312.

Heim, J.-F., Béraud, C. and Heim, P. (1989), *Les Salons de peinture de la Révolution française (1789–1799),* Paris: C.A.C. Edition.

Higonnet, A. and Albinson, C. (1997) 'Clothing the Child's Body', *Fashion Theory: The Journal of Dress, Body and Culture,* 1 (2): 119–44.

Higonnet, P. (1988), 'Sans-culottes', in F. Furet and M. Ozouf (eds), *Dictionnaire critique de la Révolution française,* Paris: Flammarion.

Hillman, E. (1999), 'Dressed to Kill? The Paradox of Women in Military Uniforms', in M. Fainsod Katzenstein and J. Reppy (eds), *Beyond Zero Tolerance: Discrimination in Military Culture,* New York: Rowman & Littlefield.

Hirsch, E. (1997), 'Voices from the Black Box: Folk Song, Boy Scouts and the Construction of Folk Nationalist Hegemony in Hungary, 1930–1944', *Antipode,* 29 (2): 197–215.

Holland, N. (1992), 'Fashioning Cuba', in A. Parker, M. Russo, D. Sommer and P. Yeager (eds), *Nationalisms and Sexualities,* London and New York: Routledge.

Holton, S. S. (1990), 'In Sorrowful Wrath: Suffrage Militancy and the Romantic Feminism of Emmeline Pankhurst', in H. L. Smith (ed), *British Feminism in the Twentieth Century,* Aldershot: Edward Elgar.

Hooper, B. (2000), 'Globalisation and Resistance in post-Mao China: the Case of Foreign Consumer Products', *Asian Studies Review,* 24 (4): 439–70.

Horn, D. (1994), *Social Bodies: Science, Reproduction, and Italian Modernity,* Princeton: Princeton University Press.

Hou, H. (1996), 'Beyond the Cynical: China Avant-garde in the 1990s', *Art AsiaPacific,* 3 (1): 42–51.

Hould, C. (1988), 'La Propagande d'état par l'estampe devant la Terreur', in M. Vovelle (ed), *Les Images de la Révolution française,* Paris: Publications de la Sorbonne.

Hudson, W. (1998), 'Citizenship and Multiple Identities', *Southern Review,* 31 (1): 54–63.

Huet, M.-H. (1982), *Rehearsing the French Revolution: The Staging of Marat's Death 1793–1979,* Berkeley: University of California Press.

Hughes, L. (1998), *Russia in the Age of Peter the Great,* New Haven: Yale University Press.

Hunt, L. (1984), *Politics, Culture and Class in the French Revolution,* Berkeley: University of California Press.

—— (1998), 'Freedom of Dress in Revolutionary France', in S. Melzer and K. Norberg (eds), *From the Royal to the Republican Body,* Berkeley: University of California Press.

El Iniciador, Montevideo: Imprenta Oriental, 1838–1839.

Instituto de la Mujer (1989), *Las mujeres y la Guerra Civil Española: III jornadas de estudios monográficos. Salamanca, octubre 1989,* Madrid: Ministerio de la Cultura.

Jameson, F. (1981), *The Political Unconscious. Narrative as a Socially Symbolic Act,* Ithaca, New York: Cornell University Press.

Jato, D. (1953), *La rebelión de los estudiantes (Apuntes para una historia del alegre SEU),* Madrid: CIES.

Jay, M. (1993), *Downcast Eyes: The Denigration of Vision in Twentieth-Century French Thought,* Berkeley: University of California Press.

Jones, C. and Spang, R. (1999), 'Sans-culottes, sans café, sans tabac: shifting realms of necessity and luxury in eighteenth-century France', in M. Berg and Helen C. (eds), *Consumers and Luxury. Consumer Culture in Europe 1650–1850,* Manchester: Manchester University Press.

Jones, J. (1996), 'Conquettes and Grisettes: Women Buying and Selling in Ancien Regime Paris', in V. de Grazia and E. Furlough (eds), *The Sex of Things.*

Jorgensen-Earp, C. (1997), *'The Transfiguring Sword': The Just War of the Women's Social and Political Union,* Tuscaloosa: University of Alabama Press.

Joseph, M. (1999), *Nomadic Identities: The Performance of Citizenship,* Minneapolis: University of Minnesota Press.

Jourdan, A. (1995), 'L'allégorie révolutionnaire, de la Liberté à République', *Dix-huitième siècle,* no. 27.

Journal des débats (1792).

Journal des sans-culottes (1792).

Jouve, M. (1978), 'L'image du sans-culotte dans la caricature politique anglaise. Création d'un stéréotype pictural', *Gazette des beaux-arts,* November: 187–96.

'Juquemos a ser amas de casa' (1947), *Bazar* (Revista de la SF de FET y de las JONS para las Juventudes), January and April–May.

Kahane, R. (1997), *The Origins of Postmodern Youth: Informal Youth Movements in a Comparative Perspective,* Berlin and New York: Walter de Gruyter.

Kaplan, J. H. and Stowell, S. (1994), *Theatre and Fashion: Oscar Wilde to the Suffragettes,* Cambridge: Cambridge University Press.

Kates, G. (1985), *The Cercle social, the Girondins, and the French Revolution*, Princeton: Princeton University Press.

Kenney, A. (1924), *Memories of a Militant*, London: Edward Arnold.

Kerr, R. (1932), *The Story of the Girl Guides*, London: Girl Guides Association.

—— (1936), *The Story of A Million Girls*, London: Girl Guides Association.

Kershaw, I. (1998), *Hitler*, vol.1, London: Penguin.

Kertzer, D. I. (1988), *Ritual, Politics and Power*, New Haven: Yale University Press.

Kidd, R. (1998), 'Deficits of the Past or Deceits of the Present? Defining Aboriginal Disadvantage', *Southern Review*, 31 (1): 11–17.

Klinger, C. (1995), 'The Concepts of the Sublime and the Beautiful in Kant and Lyotard', *Constellations*, 2 (2): 207–23.

Koon, T. (1985), *Believe, Obey, Fight: Political Socialization of Youth in Fascist Italy, 1922–1943*, Chapel Hill: University of North Carolina Press.

'Kostium russkii i obshcheevropeiskii', (1856), *Moda*, 14, 15 July: 114.

Kuchta, D. (1996), 'The Making of the Self-Made Man: Class, Clothing, and English Masculinity, 1688–1832', in V. de Grazia and E. Furlough (eds), *The Sex of Things*.

Lacroix, S. (1909), *Actes de la Commune de Paris pendant la Révolution*, Second Series, vol. 7, Paris: Cerf and Noblet.

La Marle, H, (1989), *Philippe Egalité, Grand Maître de la Révolution. Le rôle politique du premier sérénissime frère du Grand Orient de France*, Paris: Nouvelles Editions Satines.

Landes, J. (1988), *Women and the Public Sphere in the Age of the French Revolution*, Ithaca: Cornell University Press.

—— (1995), 'The Public and the Private Sphere: A Feminist Reconsideration', in J. Meehan (ed), *Feminists Read Habermas: Gendering the Subject of Feminism*, New York: Routledge.

Langlois, C. (1988), *La Caricature contre-révolutionnaire*, Paris: CNRS.

Lannon, F. (1991), 'Women and Images of Woman in the Spanish Civil War', *Transactions of the Royal Historical Society*, Sixth Series, 1: 213–28.

—— (1999), 'Los cuerpos de las mujeres y el cuerpo político católico: autoridades e identidades en conflicto en España durante las décadas de 1920 y 1930', *Historia Social*, 35: 65–80.

Laqueur, W. (1962), *Young Germany: A History of the German Youth Movement*, New York: Basic Books.

Leith, J. (1990), 'Images of *Sans-culottes*', in C. Hould and J. Leith (eds), *Iconographie et image de la Révolution française*, Actes du colloque tenu dans le cadre du 59e congrès de l'Association canadienne française pour l'avancement des sciences (15–16 May 1989), Montreal: 130–59.

Lilley, R. (2000) 'The Hong Kong Handover', *Communal plural,* 8. (2): 161–80.

Linehan, T. (2000), *British Fascism 1918–39: Parties, Ideology and Culture,* Manchester: Manchester University Press.

Lipovetsky, G. (1994), *The Empire of Fashion: Dressing Modern Democracy,* trans. C. Porter, Princeton: Princeton University Press.

London, J. (1996), 'Competing Together in Fascist Europe: Sport in Early Francoism', in G. Berghaus, *Fascism and Theatre: Comparative Studies on the Aesthetics and Politics of Performance in Europe, 1925– 1945,* Providence and Oxford: Berghahn.

Lytton, C. (1914), *Prisons and Prisoners: Some Personal Experiences,* London: William Heinemann.

McClintock, A. (1995), *Imperial Leather: Race, Gender and Sexuality in the Colonial Contest,* New York and London: Routledge.

McCracken, G. (1988), *Culture and Consumption: New Approaches to the Symbolic Character of Consumer Goods and Activities,* Bloomington: Indiana University Press.

MacDonald, R. H. (1994), *The Language of Empire: Myths and Metaphors of Popular Imperialism, 1880–1918,* Manchester: Manchester University Press.

Mackenzie, M. (1975), *Shoulder to Shoulder,* Harmondsworth: Penguin.

McVeigh, B. (1997), 'Wearing Ideology: How Uniforms Discipline Minds and Bodies in Japan', *Fashion Theory: The Journal of Dress, Body and Culture,* 1 (2): 189–215.

Marín, J. B. (1941), 'Por qué mueren los niños de España', *Medina,* 3 April.

La Mariposa. Periódico semanal de Literatura, Teatro, Modas, Noticias, Crónica Interior y Variedades, Montevideo: 1851–2.

Mármol, J. (1979), *Amalia,* 2 vols, Buenos Aires: Centro Editor de América Latina.

Martin, R. (1992), 'T-Shirt Coda', *Textile and Text,* 14 (3): 27–9.

Masiello, F. (1989), 'Angeles en el hogar argentino: el debate femenino sobre la vida doméstica, la educación y la literatura en el siglo XIX', *Anuario del IEHS,* 4: 265–91.

—— (1992), *Between Civilization and Barbarism: Women, Nation and Literary Culture in Modern Argentina,* Lincoln and London: University of Nebraska Press.

Maxwell, A. (1999), *Colonial Photography and Exhibitions. Representations of the Native and the Making of European Identities,* London: Leicester University Press.

Maynard, M. (1994), *Fashioned from Penury. Dress as Cultural Practice in Colonial Australia,* Cambridge: Cambridge University Press.

Maza, S. (1998), 'The Theatre of Punishment', in S. Melzer and K. Norberg (eds), *From the Royal to the Republican Body,* Berkeley: University of California Press.

Meadows, M. and Van Vuuren, K. (1998), 'Seeking an Audience: Indigenous People, the Media and Cultural Resource Management', *Southern Review,* 31 (1): 96–107.

Melman, B. (ed.) (1998), *Borderlines: Genders and Identities in War and Peace, 1870–1930,* New York and London: Routledge.

Milliot, V. (1995), *Les Cris de Paris, ou le peuple travesti. Les représentations des petits métiers parisiens (XVIe–XVIIIe) siècles,* Paris: Publications de la Sorbonne.

Mirzoeff, N. (1995), *Bodyscape: Art, Modernity and the Ideal Figure,* London and New York: Routledge.

Missori, M. (1986), *Gerarchie e Statuti del PNF: Gran Consiglio, Direttorio Nazionale, Federazioni Provinciali: Quadri e Biografie,* Rome: Bonacci.

Mitchell, H. (1977), *The Hard Way Up,* London: Virago.

Mladejovska, M. (1938), 'The Guide and Religion', *Council Fire,* 8 (3): 38–9.

La Moda, Buenos Aires: Imprenta de la Libertad, 1837–8.

Moniteur, (1792).

Monnier, R. (1981), *Le Faubourg Saint-Antoine (1789–1815),* Paris: Société des Etudes Robespierristes.

Mosse G. L. (1975), *The Nationalization of the Masses,* New York: Howard Fertig.

—— (1978), *Nazism: A Historical and Comparative Analysis,* New Brunswick: Transaction.

—— (1985), *Nationalism and Sexuality: Middle-Class Morality and Sexual Norms in Modern Europe,* Madison: University of Wisconsin Press.

—— (1996), *The Image of Man: The Creation of Modern Masculinity,* New York and Oxford: Oxford University Press.

—— (1999), *The Fascist Revolution: Toward a General Theory of Fascism,* New York: Howard Fertig.

Mouffe, C. (1992), Citizenship and Political Identity', *October,* 61: 28–32.

Muller, C. A. (2000), 'Du "peuple égaré" au "peuple enfant": le discours politique à l'épreuve de la révolte populaire en 1793', *Revue d'histoire moderne et contemporaine*, 47 (1): 93–112.

[Murray, J. and Brailsford, H. N.] (1911), *The Treatment of the Women's Deputation by the Metropolitan Police*, London: The Woman's Press.

Mussolini, B. (1934–39), *Scritti e discorsi*, 12 vols., Milan: Hoepli.

—— (1951–63), *Opera Omnia*, 36 vols, Florence: La Fenice.

Myers, J. (1995), *Orden y virtud. El discurso republicano en el régimen rosista*, Buenos Aires: Universidad Nacional de Quilmes.

Nadotti, M. (1999), 'The Denim Defense', *Ms.* June/July: 18–19.

Nash, M. (1991), 'Pronatalism and Motherhood in Franco's Spain', in G. Bock and P. Thane (eds), *Maternity and Gender Politics: Women and the Rise of the European Welfare States, 1880s–1950s*, London and New York: Routledge.

—— (1999), 'Un/Contested Identities: Motherhood, Sex Reform and the Modernization of Gender Identity in Early Twentieth-Century Spain', in P. B. Radcliff and V. L. Enders, *Constructing Spanish Womanhood: Female Identity in Modern Spain*, New York: SUNY Press.

Naudin, M. (1997), 'La réaction culturelle en l'an III: la représentation du Jacobin et du sans-culotte dans l'imaginaire de leurs adversaires', in M. Vovelle (ed), *Le tournant de l'an III. Réaction et Terreur blanche dans la France révolutionnaire*, Paris: Comité des Travaux Historiques et Scientifiques.

Neuberger, J. (1993), *Hooliganism: Crime, Culture, and Power in St. Petersburg, 1900–1914*, Berkeley: University of California Press.

Ometev, B. and Stuart, J. (1990), *St Petersburg: Portrait of an Imperial City*, O. Suslova and L. Ukhtomskaya (eds), New York: The Vendome Press.

Opisanie pervoi publichnoi vystavki rossiiskoi manufakturnykh izdelii v Sankt-Peterburge 1829 goda (1829), St. Petersburg: Tipografiia Ekspeditsii zagotovleniia Gosudarstvennykh bumag.

Oría, J. A. (1938), 'Prólogo', *La Moda*. Facsimile edition, Buenos Aires: Guillermo Kraft.

Otero, L. (1999), *La Sección Femenina*, Madrid: EDAF.

Ozouf, M. (1976), *La fete revolutionnaire 1789–1799*, Paris: Gallimard.

—— (1977), 'Le Simulacre et la fête', in J. Ehrard and P. Viallaneix (eds), *Les Fêtes de la Révolution*, Paris: Clermont Ferrand.

Pankhurst, E. (1979), *My Own Story* [1914] [As Told to Rheta Childe Dorr], London: Virago.

Pankhurst, E. S. (1931), *The Suffragette Movement: An Intimate Account of Persons and Ideals*, London: Longmans, Green & Co.

Parkins, W. (2000), 'Protesting Like a Girl: Embodiment, Dissent and Feminist Agency', *Feminist Theory* 1 (1): 59–78.

'Para estar en casa' (1937), *Mujer,* June.

Pastor, Mª I. (1984), *La educación femenina en la postguerra (1939–1945): El caso de Mallorca*, Madrid: Ministerio de Cultura.

Pateman, C. (1988), *The Sexual Contract*, Cambridge: Polity Press.

Patriote françois (1791).

Patton, C. and Caserio, R. L. (2000), 'Introduction: Citizenship 2000', *Cultural Studies,* 14.1: 1–14.

Payne, S. G. (1961), *Falange: A History of Spanish Fascism*, Stanford: Stanford University Press.

—— (1999), *Fascism in Spain 1923–1977*, Madison: University of Wisconsin Press.

'Peinado y maquillaje', (1937), *Mujer,* June.

Peiss, K. (1996), 'Making Up, Making Over: Cosmetics, Consumer Culture and Women's Identity', in V. de Grazia with E. Furlough (eds), *The Sex of Things.*

Pellegrin, N. (1989a), *Modes et Révolution*, Paris: Musée du Costume et de la Mode.

—— (1989b), *Les Vêtements de la Liberté. Abécédaire des pratiques vestimentaires françaises de 1780 à 1800,* Paris: Alinea.

Pemartín, J. (1941), *Teoría de la Falange,* Madrid: Editorial Nacional.

Pericoli, U. (1983), *Le divise del Duce*, Milan: Rizzoli.

Perrot, P. (1994), *Fashioning the Bourgeoisie: A History of Clothing in the Nineteenth Century*, trans. Richard Bienvenu, Princeton: Princeton University Press.

Perry, E. I. (1993a), 'From Achievement to Happiness: Girl Scouting in Middle Tennessee, 1910s–1960s', *Journal of Women's History,* 5 (2): 75–94.

—— (1993b), '"The Very Best Influence": Josephine Holloway and Girl Scouting in Nashville's African-American Community', *Tennessee Historical Quarterly* 52 (2): 73–85.

Peters, J. D. (1993), Distrust of Representation: Habermas on the Public Sphere', *Media, Culture and Society,* 15: 541–71.

Pethick Lawrence, E. (1909), 'The purple, white and green', in *The Women's Exhibition 1909 Programme*, London: WSPU.

—— (1938), *My Part in a Changing World,* London: Victor Gollancz.

Peukert, D. (1987), *Inside Nazi Germany: Conformism, Opposition and Racism in Everyday Life*, trans. R. Deveson, New Haven: Yale University Press.

Pfeiffer, L. B. (1912), 'The Uprising of June 20, 1792', *University Studies* [University of Nebraska, Lincoln], 12 (3): 1–147 / 197–343 (the volume has double pagination).

Phillips, R. (1997), *Mapping Men and Empire: A Geography of Adventure,* London and New York: Routledge.

Poovey, M. (1988), *Uneven Developments: The Ideological Work of Gender in Mid-Victorian England,* Chicago: University of Chicago Press.

Preston, P. (1999), *¡Comrades! Portraits from the Spanish Civil War,* London: HarperCollins.

Primo de Rivera, J. A. (1972), *José Antonio Primo de Rivera: Selected Writings,* ed. H. Thomas, London: Jonathan Cape.

Primo de Rivera, P. (1983), *Recuerdos de una vida,* Madrid: Ediciones Dyrsa.

Proctor, T. (1998), '(Uni)Forming Youth: Girl Guides and Boy Scouts in Britain, 1908–1939', *History Workshop Journal,* 45: 103–34.

—— (2000), '"A Separate Path": Scouting and Guiding in Interwar South Africa', *Comparative Studies in Society and History,* 42 (3): 605–31.

Proust, J. (1973), 'L'Image du peuple au travail dans les planches de l'*Encyclopédie*', *Images du Peuple au dix-huitième siècle,* Colloque d'Aix-en-Provence, 25 and 26 October 1969, Centre Aixois d'Etudes et de Recherches sur le dix-huitième siècle, Paris: Armand Colin.

Quicherat, J. (1879), *Histoire du costume français depuis les temps les plus reculés jusqu'à la fin du XVIIIe siècle,* Paris: Hachette.

Raeburn, A. (1973), *The Militant Suffragettes,* London: Michael Joseph.

Reimer, E. F. (1929), *Matching Mountains with the Boy Scout Uniform,* New York: E. P. Dutton & Co.

Reinhard, M. (1971), *Nouvelle Histoire de Paris. La Révolution 1789–1799,* Paris: Hachette.

Rempel, G. (1989), *Hitler's Children: The Hitler Youth and the SS,* Chapel Hill: Univeristy of North Carolina Press.

Repaci, A. (1972), *La Marcia su Roma,* Milan: Rizzoli.

Le Réviseur universel et impartial et bulletin de Madame de Beaumont (1792), n. 44, 11 April.

Reynolds, H. (1990), *With the White People,* Ringwood, Victoria: Penguin.

Rhondda, Viscountess [Haig, M.] (1933), *This Was My World,* London: Macmillan.

Richards, M. (1998), *A Time of Silence: Civil War and the Culture of Repression in Franco's Spain, 1936–1945,* Cambridge: Cambridge University Press.

Richardson, M. (1953), *Laugh a Defiance,* London: George Weidenfeld & Nicolson.

Riasanovsky, N. V. (1959), *Nicholas I and Official Nationality in Russia, 1825–1855,* Berkeley: University of California Press.

Ribeiro, A. (1988), *Fashion in the French Revolution,* London: Batsford.

—— (1995), *The Art of Dress. Fashion in England and France 1750–1820,* New Haven and London: Yale University Press.

Roberts, C. (ed) (1997), *Evolution and Revolution: Chinese Dress 1700s–1990s,* Sydney: Powerhouse Museum.

Roberts, M. L. (1993), 'Samson and Delilah Revisited: The Politics of Women's Fashion in 1920s France', *American Historical Review,* 98: 657–84.

—— (1994), *Civilisation without Sexes: Reconstructing Gender in Postwar France, 1917–1927,* Chicago and London: University of Chicago Press.

Roche, D. (1981), *Le peuple de Paris: essai sur la culture populaire au XVIIIe siècle,* Paris: Aubier Montaigne.

—— (1989), *La Culture des apparences. Une histoire du vêtement (XVIIe–XVIIIe siècles),* Paris: Fayard.

—— (1994), *The Culture of Clothing: Dress and Fashion in the Ancien Regime,* trans. J. Birrell, New York: Cambridge University Press.

Rodgers, E. (ed) (1999), *Encyclopaedia of Contemporary Spanish Culture,* London: Routledge.

Roosevelt, P. (1995), *Life on the Russian Country Estate: A Social and Cultural History,* New Haven: Yale University Press.

Rose, R. B. (1983), *The Making of the Sans-culottes. Democratic Ideas and Institutions in Paris, 1789–1792,* Manchester: Manchester University Press.

Ross, A. (1986), *John Philip, 1775–1851: Mission, Race and Politics in South Africa,* Aberdeen: Aberdeen University Press.

Rousseau, J.-J. (1968), *Politics and the Arts: Letter to M. D'Alembert on the Theatre,* [1758] trans. A. Bloom, Ithaca: Cornell University Press.

Rowse, T. (1990), 'Aboriginal as Historical Actors: Evidence and Inference', in S. Janson and S. Macintyre (eds), *Through White Eyes,* Sydney: Allen & Unwin.

—— (1996), 'Rationing the Inexplicable', in S. R. Morton and D. J. Mulvaney (eds), *Exploring Central Australia. Society, the Environment and the 1894 Horn Expedition,* Chipping Norton, NSW: Beatty & Son.

—— (1998), *White Flour, White Power. From Rations to Citizenship in Central Australia,* Cambridge: Cambridge University Press.

Rudé, G. (1959), *The Crowd in the French Revolution,* Oxford: Oxford University Press.

Salvatorelli, L. and Mira, G. (1952), *Storia del fascismo: L'Italia dal 1919 al 1945*, Rome: Edizioni di Novissima.

Sargeson, S. (1999), *Reworking China's Proletariat*, Houndmills: Macmillan.

Schein, L. (1994), 'The Consumption of Colour and the Politics of White Skin in Post-Mao China', *Social Text*, 41: 141–65.

Schmidt, W. A. (1867–1871), *Tableaux de la Révolution française, publiés sur les papiers inédits du département et de la police secrète de Paris*, 3 vols, Leipzig: Veit.

'Scouting and Peace', (1929), *Times,* 3 August.

'Scouts and Guides', (1929), *Berrow's Worcester Journal*, 23 March.

'Scouts of the World',(1929), *Times,* 1 August.

Sección Femenina de Falange Española Tradicionalista y de las JONS (n.d.), *Anuario de 1940,* n.p.

—— (1943), *Formación Familiar y Social,* Madrid: n.p.

Sección Femenina Tradicionalista y de las JONS (n. d.), *Formación Política: Lecciones para las Flechas*, Madrid: n.p.

Seldes, G. (1935), *Sawdust Caesar: The Untold History of Mussolini and Fascism*, New York: Harper.

Seventy-five Years of Scouting: A History of the Scout Movement in Words and Pictures (1982), London: Scout Association.

Sewell Jr, W. (1986), 'Visions of Labour: illustrations of the mechanical arts before, in, and after Diderot's *Encyclopédie*', in S. Kaplan and C. J. Knoepp (eds), *Work in France: Representation, Meaning, Organization, and Practice,* Ithaca and London: Cornell University Press.

Shaw, B. (1992), *When the Dust Come in Between. Aboriginal Viewpoints in the East Kimberly Prior to 1982*, Canberra: Aboriginal Studies Press.

Shepelev, L. E. (1991), *Tituly, mundiry, ordena v Rossiiskoi imperii*, Leningrad: Nauka.

Shephard, E. C. (1981), 'The Society Tale and the Innovative Argument in Russian Prose Fiction of the 1830s', *Russian Literature*, X: 111–62.

Shipov, P. (1901), *Russkaia voennaia odezhda*, St. Petersburg: Tipolitografiia N. Evstifeeva.

Shumway, N. (1991), *The Invention of Argentina*, Berkeley and Los Angeles: University of California Press.

Siegfried, S. (1995), *The Art of Louis-Léopold Boilly. Modern Life in Napoleonic France*, New Haven and London: Yale University Press.

Sinha, M. (1995), *Colonial Masculinity : the 'Manly Englishman' and the 'Effeminate Bengali' in the Late Nineteenth Century*, Manchester and New York : Manchester University Press.

Smith, B. G. (1989), *Changing Lives: Women in European History since 1700*, Lexington and Toronto: D. C. Heath & Co.

Smithson, M. (1992), 'A Misunderstood Gift: The Annual Issue of Blankets to Aborigines in NSW 1826–1848', *Push*, 30: 73–108.

Smyth, E. (1933), *Female Pipings in Eden*, Edinburgh: Peter Davies.

Soboul, A. (1958), *Les Sans-culottes parisiens en l'An II. Mouvement populaire et gouvernement révolutionnaire 2 juin 1793–9 thermidor an II*, Paris: Clavreuil.

'Sombreros', (1941), *Medina* 17 April.

Sonenscher, M. (1987), *The Hatters of Eighteenth-Century France*, Cambridge: Cambridge University Press.

—— (1989), *Work, Wages: Natural Law, Politics, and the Eighteenth-century French Trades*, Cambridge: Cambridge University Press.

—— (1991), 'Artisans, sans-culottes, and the French Revolution', in A. Forrest and P. Jones (eds), *Reshaping France: Town, Country, and Region during the French Revolution*, Manchester: Manchester University Press.

Sparks, H. (1997), 'Dissident Citizenship: Democratic Theory, Political Courage, and Activist Women', *Hypatia*, 12 (4): 74–110.

Stachura, P. (1975), *Nazi Youth in the Weimar Republic*, Santa Barbara and Oxford: Clio.

—— (1981), *The German Youth Movement, 1900–1945: An Interpretive and Documentary History*, London: Macmillan.

Stallybrass, P. and White, A. (1986), *The Politics and Poetics of Transgression*, London: Methuen.

Starns, P. (1998), 'Fighting Militarism: British Nursing during the Second World War', in R. Cooter, M. Harrison, and S. Sturdy (eds), *War, Medicine and Modernity*, Stroud: Sutton.

Steele, V. (1985), *Fashion and Eroticism: Ideals of Feminine Beauty from the Victorian Era to the Jazz Age*, Oxford: Oxford University Press.

—— (1998), *Paris Fashion: A Cultural History*, Oxford and New York: Berg.

Sternhell, Z. with Sznajder, M. and Asheri, M. (1994), *The Birth of Fascist Ideology: From Cultural Rebellion to Political Revolution*, Princeton: Princeton University Press.

Stites, R. (1978), *The Women's Liberation Movement in Russia: Feminism, Nihilism, and Bolshevism, 1860–1930*, Princeton: Princeton University Press.

—— (1989), *Revolutionary Dreams*, Oxford: Oxford University Press.

Stoler, A. L. (1989), 'Rethinking Colonial Categories: European Communities and the Boundaries of Rule', *Comparative Studies in Society and History*, 31 (1): 134–61.

Stone, D. (2001), 'The body, gender and genocide', *Patterns of Prejudice*, 35 (3): 78–80.

Suárez Fernández, L. (1993), *Crónica de la Sección Femenina y su tiempo*, Madrid: Asociación Nueva Andadura.

Tagliabue, J. (1999), 'Where Jeans are a Rape Defense', *New York Times* February 14: 2.

Taylor, C. (1999), *Sacrifice as Terror: The Rwandan Genocide of 1994*, Oxford: Oxford University Press.

Thane, P. (1988), 'The British Imperial State and the Construction of National Identities, in B. Melman (ed), *Borderlines: Genders and Identities in War and Peace, 1870–1930*, New York and London: Routledge.

Thirty Years of Guiding in New Zealand, 1923–1953, (1953), Auckland: Girl Guides Association of New Zealand.

Thomas, G. (1990), *The Novels of the Spanish Civil War*, Cambridge: Cambridge University Press.

Thomas, N. (1991), *Entangled Objects. Exchange, Material Culture and Colonialism in the Pacific*, Cambridge MA: Harvard University Press.

Thompson, V. M. (1990), *1910 . . . and Then A Brief History of the Girl Guides Association*, London: Girl Guides Association, 1990.

Thomson, J. (ed) (1989), *Reaching Back. Queensland Aboriginal People Recall Early Days at Yarrabah Mission*, Canberra: Aboriginal Studies Press.

Tickner, L. (1988), *The Spectacle of Women: Imagery of the Suffrage Campaign 1907–14*, London: Chatto & Windus.

Tidrick, K. (1990), *Empire and the English Character*, London: I.B. Taurus & Co., Ltd.

Tourneux, M. (1890–1913), *Bibliographie de l'histoire de Paris pendant la Révolution française*, 5 vols, Paris: Imprimerie nouvelle.

Tuetey, A. (1890–1914), *Répertoire général des sources manuscrites de l'histoire de Paris pendant la Révolution française*, 11 vols, Paris.

Turner, G. (1994), *Making it National: Nationalism and Australian Popular Culture*, St Leonards NSW: Allen & Unwin.

Tussaud, M. (1838), *Madame Tussaud's Memoirs and Reminiscences of France, Forming an Abridged History of the French Revolution*, London: Saunders & Otley.

Vacaciones', *Medina*, 10 July 1941.

Vasilich, G. (1912), 'Ulitsy i liudi sovremennoi Moskvy', *Moskva v ee proshlom i nastoiashchem*, XII: 3–16.

Vernon, J. (1994), 'Who's afraid of the "linguistic turn"? The politics of social history and its discontents', *Social History*, 19: 81–97.

Villaverde, C. (1995), *Cecilia Valdés. Novela de Costumbres Cubanas*, Mexico City: Editorial Porrúa.

Votes for Women, London, 1906–14.

The WAGGGS (1938), London: WAGGGS.

WAGGGS Information (1938), London: WAGGGS.

Walicki, A. (1989), *The Slavophile Controversy: History of a Conservative Utopia in Nineteenth-Century Russian Thought*, trans. H. Andrews-Ruscieka, Notre Dame: University of Notre Dame Press.

Warner, M. (1992), 'The Mass Public and the Mass Subject', in C. Calhoun (ed) *Habermas and the Public Sphere*, Cambridge, MA: MIT Press.

Watson, L. (1988), 'The Commonwealth Games in Brisbane 1982. Analysis of Aboriginal Protests', *Social Alternatives*, 7 (1): 37–43.

Weaver, K. (1992), *Bushels of Rubles: Soviet Youth in Transition*, Westport, CT and London: Praeger.

Weeks, T. R. (1996), *Nation and State in Late Imperial Russia: Nationalism and Russification on the Western Frontier, 1863–1914*, DeKalb: Northern Illinois University Press.

Weigel, S. (1985), 'Double Focus: On the History of Women's Writing', trans H. Anderson, in G. Ecker, *Feminist Aesthetics*, Boston: Beacon Press.

Weinberg, F. (1977), *El salón literario de 1837*, Buenos Aires: Hachette.

Weintraub, J. and Kumar K. (eds) (1997), *Public and Private in Thought and Practice: Perspectives on a Grand Dichotomy*, Chicago: University of Chicago Press.

[Weston, S.] (1793), *Letters from Paris during the Summer of 1792*, London: Debrett.

White, M. and Hunt, A. (2000), 'Citizenship: Care of the Self, Character and Personality', *Citizenship Studies*, 4 (2): 93–116.

Wilson, E. (1985), *Adorned in Dreams: Fashion and Modernity*, London: Virago.

Wilson, J. S. (1959), *Scouting Round the World*, London: Blandford Press.

Wintermute, A. (ed) (1989), *1789: French Art during the Revolution*, New York: Colnaghi.

Woolf, V. (1992), *Three Guineas*, [1938] Oxford: Oxford University Press.

Wortman, R. S. (1995), *Scenarios of Power: Myth and Ceremony in Russian Monarchy*, vol. 1, Princeton: Princeton University Press.

Wrigley, R. (1993), *The Origins of French Art Criticism: From the Ancien Régime to the Restoration,* Oxford: Oxford University Press.

—— (1996), 'From Ancien Régime Fall Guy to Revolutionary Hero: Changing Interpretations of Dorvigny's *Les battus qui paient l'amende* in Later Eighteenth-Century France', *British Journal of Eighteenth-Century Studies,* 19 (2): 124–54.

—— (1997), 'Transformations of a Revolutionary Emblem: The Liberty Cap in the French Revolution', *French History* 11 (2): 131–69.

Yates, R. L. (n. d.), *Infection. A Warning to Anti-Suffragists and Anti-Militants,* Suffragette Fellowship Collection, Museum of London.

Yeatman, A. (2001), 'Feminism and Citizenship', in N. Stevenson (ed), *Culture and Citizenship,* London: Sage.

Young, A. (1988), '"Wild Women": The Censure of the Suffragette Movement', *International Journal of the Sociology of Law,* 16: 279–93.

Young, I. M. (1987), 'Impartiality and the Civic Public: Some Implications of Feminist Critiques of Moral and Political Theory', in S. Benhabib and D. Cornell (eds), *Feminism as Critique: Essays on the Politics of Gender in Late-Capitalist Societies,* Cambridge: Polity.

Yuval-Davis, N. and Werbner, P. (eds) (1999), *Women, Citizenship and Difference,* London: Zed Books.

Zelnik, R. E. (ed) (1986), *A Radical Worker in Tsarist Russia: The Autobiography of Semen Ivanovich Kanatchikov,* Stanford: Stanford University Press.

Websites and Virtual Papers

Brown, S. (2000), 'Poster, placard, property', paper presented to 'Fascism and Aesthetics' seminar, University of Nottingham, http://devpsy.lboro.ac.uk/psygroup/sb/fascism

http://gsinfo.eachnet.com/s/news/news2000_0529_child.htm

http://edu.qz.fj.cn/law/form17.htm

http://sports.sina.com.cn/global/200006/0245750.shtml

http://www.jledu.com.cn/zjjw/jyxxyzx/11/expt13.htm

http://www.srft.com/odb/gggs/liuyi.html

http://www.genius99.com/magazine/xueqianjiaoyu/200005/10.htm

http://www.yihuapccity.com/yihuachild2000/index.htm

http://202.102.230.12/music/mp3/61/1.htm

http://www.cz.js.cn/xxkj/xxw/index.htm

http://web4.peopledaily.com.cn/item/ldhd/lipeng/1999/chxhd/hd0530.html

Index

Index

Index

Index

Index

and sport, 183
and consumption, 180–2
Sergent, Antoine-Francois, 30
Sharp, Evelyn, 110
Shaw, Bruce, 198
shopping
    and women, 98
Shumway, Nicholas, 79, 85
Slavophiles, 54, 69
Smith, Olivia, 102
Smyth, Ethel, 103
Soboul, Albert, 19
Sorel, Georges, 217
Sparks, Holloway, 100
Stalin, Joseph, 182, 223
Starace, Achille, 151, 159
Stasov, Vladimir, 55
Steele, Valerie, 80
Stephenson, Jessie, 106, 108
Stoler, Ann, 130
Storrow, Helen, 133
structuralism, 221, 223
suffragette movement, 12, 97–121 *passim*
    tactics of, 99
    deployment of fashion, 99
suffragette spectacles, 107
suffragette subject
    as consumer, 103
    as fashionable, 102–3
    as political agent, 107
    as soldier, 118–20
    stereotypes, 107, 110
swastika, 222

T-shirts, 200
    as communicative, 201
    as political protest, 202
Taylor, Christopher, 223–4
'territorialization', 222, 223
Terry, María Luisa, 180
Thibaudeau, Antoine, 31
Third Reich, 218, 219, 222
Thomas, Harold, 200
Thomas, Nicholas, 193
Tickner, Lisa, 101, 103
Tolstoy, Leo, 55
totalitarianism, 220
Turner, Graeme, 202, 203
Turner, Victor, 221

Uncita, Carina, 180
uniforms, 131, 162, 168, 172–3, 176
    and fascist identity, 168
    and gender, 13
    and masculinity, 13
    and Republicans (Spain), 168
    and women,
        in Spain 173, 176, 179
    and youth, 127, 129, 131
        in Spain, 169, 172
    Boy Scouts, 126–7, 132
        hats, 139
        regional variations 139–40, 141
    French Revolutionary, 9, 25–6
    Girl Guides, 132, 135
        in British Commonwealth, 135
        regional variations, 139, 141
    nurses, 177
    Russian civil, 51
    Russian military, 12, 52, 65
    school, 206–7
    sewing, 173
    see also black shirt, blue shirt
Unitarians, 72, 80, 84–5
    colours (light blue and green), 72

van Vuuren, Kitty, 203
Vasilich, G., 60
Villaverde, Cirol, 74
Vincent, Mary, 4, 13–14
Vittorio Emanuele III, 145, 146, 148
Voltaire
    pantheonization of, 22–5
Votes for Women, 102, 103, 106

Walcott, L. C., 136
Warner, Michael, 105
Watson, Michael, 203
Weber, Max, 217
Weigel, Sigrid, 91
Werbner, Pnina, 9
West, Mae, 181
Westernizers, 54
westernization
    in Russia, 50, 51, 53–4
White, Melanie, 11
Whitlam government, 189
Wilson, 'Belge', 138–9
Wilson, Elizabeth, 152